april 15, 2001
Gift from

ALSO BY HOLLY GARRISON

Comfort Food
The Thanksgiving Cookbook

The Periyali Cookbook

Holly Garrison

WITH

Nicola Kotsoni

AND

Steve Tzolis

ILLUSTRATED BY

Kathleen M. Skelly

VILLARD BOOKS

NEW YORK 1992

The Periyali Cookbook

NEW CLASSIC
GREEK COOKING

Library of Congress Cataloging-in-Publication Data
Garrison, Holly.
The Periyali cookbook: new classic Greek cooking / Holly Garrison with Nicola Kotsoni
and Steve Tzolis.—1st ed.
p.   cm.
Includes index.
ISBN 0-679-40385-X
1. Cookery, Greek.   2. Periyali (Restaurant)   I. Kotsoni, Nicola.   II. Tzolis,
Steve.   III. Title.
TX723.5.G8G37   1992
641.59495—dc20   92-53647

Manufactured in the United States of America
9   8   7   6   5   4   3   2
FIRST EDITION

To Charles Bowman,
with thanks from Nicola and Steve, for his incomparable
and consistent interpretation and presentation of fine Greek cooking,
and for playing such a large part in making sure that dining at Periyali
is always an immensely pleasurable experience;
and from Holly, for his generosity in sharing
his enviable culinary expertise,
but mostly for his seemingly endless patience and help
in seeing the recipes through to publication

Acknowledgments

Writing this cookbook can be compared to operating a successful restaurant. Every step of the way it's been a team effort. From the moment we got the book under way until its completion, each and every member of the staff at Periyali has remained interested, enthusiastic, and helpful, for which we want to thank them.

Also, many thanks to:

Madeleine Morel, our agent, whose brainchild this book was. And Emily Bestler, our editor, for the insightful contributions and objectivity she brought to the project.

Irene and Victor Gouras, for sharing their exceptional recipes and techniques for traditional Greek home cooking.

Nicola's mother, Angelica Kotsoni, for generously providing so many of the recipes that she has been cooking for her family for nearly fifty years, and Vicky Vitsou, Nicola's sister, who painstakingly transcribed them.

Steve's sister, Eleteria Stroueas, who not only gave us some of her best recipes, but showed us how to make them, too.

Nicholas (Nick) Gouras, for all of his help, especially in compiling the wine chapter.

Stephanie Curtis, for her precise and expert recipe testing, as well as for her evaluation and words about Greek wine.

Gale Steves, for her description of Easter in Greece.

Arlene Wanderman, president of Foodcom, Inc., and United States representative for the International Olive Oil Council, for allowing us to tap into her extensive knowledge of Mediterranean food, particularly her specialty, olive oil.

The Greek National Tourist Association, for providing so much general information about Greece and the Greek cuisine.

And to many of the purveyors of Greek wine and food, who are listed in the Sources section.

Finally, Mike and Steve Vavilis, for introducing one of the authors to *patsas, bougatsa,* and other glories of Greek cooking.

Contents

Introduction

$\mathcal{P}$erhaps it's because of their long and illustrious history that the Greeks feel so little need to rush into the future—or to rush anywhere, for that matter. They refuse to live by the clock—or by any rigid schedule—and have an enviable ability to savor the moment.

Culinary matters hold an important place in the minds and hearts of Greeks. Food is rarely eaten on the run. The Greeks take food seriously, and it is considered rude to interrupt a meal for anything other than a dire emergency. The most humble laborer will routinely take the time to lay out a midday meal brought from home in a willow basket. There, on a checkered napkin, perhaps neatly arranged over a flat rock, is fare such as a delicately fried fish; a hunk of grainy bread; chunks of cucumber, tomato, and peppers; a wedge of cheese; and a few olives. All of this may be accompanied by a few pleasurable swallows of local barrel wine. Whether at home, in jolly *tavernas,* or more formal restaurants, called *estiatoria,* Greeks apparently like nothing better than lingering around the dinner table until all hours with seemingly little regard for the following day.

Although an undeniable predilection for Italian cooking exists in western Greece, and a definite bias toward Middle Eastern food in the east, the long-held hypothesis that the native cuisine of Greece was liberally taken from the Venetians, the Turks, and other ethnic groups is an absurd one, since the beginnings of *all* Western cuisines can be traced directly to Greece. When cooking and civilized dining were at their zenith in Greece, the Romans were slurping gruel, and the nomadic Turks were warming and tenderizing chunks of meat between their saddles and their horses before tearing it apart to eat raw.

The truth is that the Greeks taught everyone else how to cook and eat. Early writings by Greek scholars (most notably Athenaeus, who wrote *The Philosophy of Dining* in A.D. 200) leave little doubt that Greece's glorious contributions to civilization also included a rich and exotic cuisine. Culinary schools flourished in ancient Athens and the chefs they turned out commanded the respect of their affluent employers who paid them generous and high salaries.

Off and on for centuries, the Greeks struggled under the domination of one invader or another, and preserving their culinary heritage was usually low on the list of priorities, when just eating —anything—was often the first consideration.

Although modern Greek food may lack a certain polish when compared to some of its sister cuisines in the Mediterranean basin, it may well be that the very simple character of Greek home cooking is what makes it so appealing. It is spicy without being hot, immensely satisfying without being rich. Lately there has been a concerted effort to return to the indigenous food and wine for which Greece was once famous. Certainly, from a health and nutrition viewpoint, this is food that one can feel good about eating, especially now that Mediterranean foods and preparation techniques have been recognized as some of the best in the world. For example, the benefits of olive oil, the common denominator in almost all Greek recipes, has recently been well documented, and a strong reliance on fresh fish, vegetables, and fruit makes this a generally praiseworthy diet.

To eat as the Greeks do, it's as important to establish the right mood and pace as it is to prepare the meal with care and the best ingredients available. Most Greeks don't sit down for dinner until as late as ten or eleven o'clock, although most Americans would probably faint from hunger by then. Even at that hour, plenty of time is allowed for *aperitifs* and conversation, which are accompanied by an assortment of little appetizers (*orektika*), often followed by Greek salad. A hearty wine is poured with the main course, and a platter of fresh fruit finishes the meal. Later, after more conversation, Greek coffee may be served with brandy or liqueur, along with Greek pastry or other sweets.

About the Recipes in This Book

One has only to spend a short time in a frenetic restaurant kitchen to understand why it's so difficult, and sometimes nearly impossible, to duplicate restaurant recipes precisely at home. Chefs, who are as naturally endowed with talent as any other artist, have also been trained to view ingredients, proportions, and preparation techniques differently than the home cook.

The only so-called "secrets" to a top chef's ability to turn out glorious plates of faultless food night after night are the skills acquired after years of training and the enthusiasm and willingness to spend whatever time it takes to do it. A tablespoon or two of sauce, which often makes the difference between good and great food, is more than likely the end result of a stock that took all day to simmer and reduce, a quite ordinary restaurant practice that most busy home cooks would understandably be just as anxious to skip. Restaurant cooking equipment—stovetops, ovens, and broilers that put out more intense heat—makes a difference, too. Even cooking vessels—immense and more than twice as heavy as those sold for home use—can significantly alter results, as well.

The recipes from Periyali in this book (denoted by a seagull above the recipe name) were developed and tested with the identical ingredients and most of the techniques that chef Charles Bowman uses every day to make the same dishes for the restaurant. Now and then small changes had to be made in order to facilitate preparation in the home kitchen, so that a particular dish would compare as closely as possible to the food that Periyali's patrons enjoy daily.

It is the authors' hope that *The Periyali Cookbook* is as happily received as the restaurant, and that the book will fulfill its main purpose of perpetuating and preserving a cuisine that came much too close to being lost to the ages.

Kali oreksi! (Good appetite!)

NICOLA, STEVE, AND HOLLY
NEW YORK, MAY 1992

The Story of Periyali

$\mathcal{N}$icola Kotsoni was trained as a classical ballet dancer and choreographer. Steve Tzolis was an Olympic bicycler turned successful real estate entrepreneur. Both have roots in Greece, and when Nicola came to New York in 1976 to pursue her dance career, they became friends.

Nicola, who had fond memories of a friend's elegant and lively wine bar in London, had made up her mind to open a restaurant someday. Steve considered the business demanding and thankless. Nevertheless, the friendship became a partnership when the two created the first of what was to eventually become a trio of some of New York's most popular restaurants, no small accomplishment in a town where restaurants come and go faster than fiddlehead ferns.

The story of Periyali began in 1983 after Nicola and Steve opened Il Cantinori, a Tuscan-style restaurant in the heart of Greenwich Village. Every night, friends and customers would pester the pair to name a place in New York City where a great Greek meal could be had. There were none, at least none with the kind of food that both Steve and Nicola were accustomed to eating in Greece. And so the idea for Periyali was born.

The partners admit that at first they had a hard time imagining a demand for an upscale Greek restaurant in Manhattan. And the timing was less than perfect, too, since they were already committed to opening Aureole, which has since become their third restaurant.

But friends who owned potential restaurant space on the ground floor of a brownstone in the Flatiron District of Manhattan were anxious to rent it reasonably. Still far from convinced, Nicola and Steve agreed to look. They took the space.

The idea was to create a friendly, comfortable atmosphere where home-style Greek food, most of it rarely served outside the islands and provinces of Greece, would be refined and lightened just enough to appeal to the urbane taste of New York diners.

The name Periyali, which has no exact English translation, is a romantic Greek word for *seashore* or *coastline*. It was chosen for the restaurant because so much of the food that would be served there originated in the Greek islands.

Both Nicola and Steve share a passion and an admiration for fine Greek food. It seemed to them that the only way to re-create the foods of their homeland was to find a Greek home cook who would be willing to come to New York and work with an American chef. They found the perfect cook—two perfect cooks, in fact—more easily than they had anticipated.

A friend of theirs mentioned that his parents had a restaurant on a Greek island that was simply an extension of their home, where they served Greek family food to the island's many visitors each summer. Nicola and Steve asked Irene and Victor Gouras for their help, and the couple came to New York soon after they closed their restaurant for the season. They agreed to work as consultants the following winter developing a menu and recipes for the soon-to-be Periyali.

As good luck would have it, super-chef Charles Palmer had a couple of spare weeks to lend a capable hand while waiting for the kitchen at Aureole to be completed. Palmer, in turn, recruited Charles Bowman, his talented, former sous chef at the River Café —the famous Brooklyn restaurant-on-a-barge just across the river from the spires of Manhattan—as the executive chef for Periyali.

Everyone's efforts finally came together in the original menu: an eclectic mixture of dishes that are rarely served outside of Greek homes; some combinations of Greek foods that few Greek cooks would ever think of putting together; and naturally, some of the more traditional things, done in "the Periyali way"—that is, for the most part, a lot less oily and a little less spicy.

When stepping into Periyali, what surprises one most is a sudden sense of entering another country. A couple of bold flower arrangements—Nicola's weekly ritual—first catch the eye, then a sturdy old table, on which is displayed a generous selection of seasonal fruits and sugar-coated and honey-dipped desserts, and more flowers, along with (in case you have any doubt about being in a Greek restaurant) an impressive jar of quince spoon sweets, the symbol of Greek hospitality.

Further back, another table is crowded with an array of *orektika* and *mezedes*, those tempting Greek appetizers from which many knowledgeable diners will choose to make a whole meal.

The walls are Greek-island white plaster that somehow manage to look permanently bathed in late-afternoon sunlight. Dark wooden beams cross the ceiling, and the white cotton tenting draped between them makes many diners think of Greek sailboats. On the walls are photographs of people and places on the island of Patmos plainly framed in the same dark wood as the beams and the wide-board floor. Other skillfully arranged decorations are an old hand plow, a grape press, and assorted urns, jars, and pieces of archaic and unusual cooking utensils that were collected from just about everywhere in Greece.

When Nicola and Steve are pinned down to name some of the reasons for Periyali's popularity, they say it's because they want the people who come into the restaurant to feel at home. And then they want those people, when they leave, to be well fed and happy.

HOLLY GARRISON

The Periyali Cookbook

Basic Recipes, Ingredients, and Techniques

One of the fundamental differences between restaurant and home cooking is the array of ingredients that the chef has at his or her command. When the chef requires a cup of stock, it's as close as a big saucepot on the back of the Garland stove. In fact, for anything that's needed, from six cups of chopped onions to intricate pastry handling, there are always many pairs of expert hands to be called into action.

The recipes and preparation techniques that follow are called for more than once in the recipes throughout this book. In the case of broths and stocks, substitutes and less time-consuming methods are discussed, but *not* taking shortcuts is often the very thing that sets restaurant recipes above the same recipes prepared at home. Broths and stocks are easy to make. They just take time. But they can be frozen in small containers and thawed quickly in the microwave or over low heat when needed.

Lamb or Beef Brown Stock

YIELD: ABOUT 6 CUPS

3 pounds lamb or beef bones, cut into
  2- or 3-inch pieces
2 large onions, unpeeled and
  quartered
2 large celery ribs, cut into 1-inch
  pieces
2 large carrots, cut into 1-inch pieces

3 or 4 garlic cloves, unpeeled
1 cup water
3 tablespoons tomato paste
1 cup parsley sprigs and stems
2 large bay leaves
1 teaspoon black peppercorns

Preheat the oven to 400°F. Place the bones in a heavy roasting pan. Roast for 30 to 40 minutes, turning occasionally until lightly browned. Add the onions, celery, carrots, and garlic, stirring until well mixed. Continue to roast, mixing and turning occasionally, until the bones and vegetables are richly browned, about 45 to 50 minutes. (Be careful not to allow anything to burn or the finished stock will be bitter.)

Spoon the bones and vegetables into a large, heavy soup pot. Add the water to the roasting pan. Place the pan over medium heat and stir up all the juices and brown bits. Pour over the bones and vegetables. Add the tomato paste, parsley sprigs and stems, bay leaves, and peppercorns, and enough water to cover by a couple of inches. Bring to a boil. Reduce the heat and simmer, uncovered, for 4 hours, adding a cup of hot water every 30 minutes or so to replace the liquid that boils away. (The idea here is to extract as much flavor as possible from the bones and vegetables.) Remove from the heat and set aside to cool.

With a slotted spoon, lift the bones and most of the vegetables from the stock and discard. Strain the stock through a colander lined with a double thickness of cheesecloth into a large bowl. Chill until any fat rises to the surface and congeals; lift off and discard. Ladle the stock into containers with tight-fitting lids. The stock can

4
The Periyali Cookbook

be refrigerated for several days. Freeze for longer storage, up to 6 months. If freezing, allow about ½ inch of headspace for expansion in each container.

Chicken Broth

YIELD: ABOUT 10 CUPS

5 pounds chicken backs, necks, and wings

3 large celery ribs, coarsely chopped (2 cups)

1 large onion, coarsely chopped (1 cup)

1 medium-size carrot, coarsely chopped (½ cup)

2 or 3 garlic cloves, coarsely chopped

2 tablespoons dried thyme leaves, crumbled

1 teaspoon black peppercorns

2 bay leaves

1 tablespoon salt

5 quarts water

Rinse the chicken parts and place them in a large soup pot. Add the celery, onion, carrot, garlic, thyme, peppercorns, bay leaves, salt, and water. Bring to a boil, skimming off the foam with a large spoon as it rises to the surface. Reduce the heat to a quick simmer. Cover and simmer for about 1½ hours. Uncover and continue to simmer slowly for about 1 hour, or until the liquid has reduced to about half of what it was originally. Set the broth aside to cool. Skim the fat from the surface, then strain the broth through a colander lined with a double thickness of cheesecloth into a large bowl. Ladle the broth into containers with tight-fitting lids. The broth can be refrigerated for several days. Freeze for longer storage, up to 6 months. If freezing, allow about ½ inch of headspace for expansion in each container.

Freshening Canned Chicken or Beef Broth

❧❧❧❧❧

YIELD: 7 TO 8 CUPS

Canned chicken or beef broth can be substituted for broth made from scratch and can be improved considerably by simmering briefly with fresh vegetables and seasonings.

---

4 cans (13¾ to 14½ ounces) clear salted or unsalted chicken or beef broth

3 large celery ribs with leaves, coarsely chopped (2 cups)

1 large unpeeled onion, coarsely chopped (1 cup)

2 medium-size carrots, coarsely chopped (1 cup)

2 large garlic cloves, coarsely chopped

2 cups water

2 or 3 parsley sprigs

1 bay leaf

½ teaspoon dried thyme leaves, crumbled

6 black peppercorns

Combine all of the ingredients in a large saucepan and bring to a boil. Reduce the heat and simmer, tightly covered, for about 30 minutes. Strain the broth into a large bowl through a colander lined with a double thickness of cheesecloth. If not using immediately, cool the broth and then pour it into 1- or 2-cup containers with tight-fitting lids. The broth can be refrigerated for several days. Freeze for longer storage, up to 6 months. If freezing, allow about ½ inch of headspace for expansion in each container.

Fish Broth

YIELD: 5 TO 5½ CUPS

*B*ottled clam juice is sometimes used as a substitute for fish broth, but we don't recommend it. However, if you must, use a mixture of half clam juice and half water. Frozen fish stock concentrates, available in specialty food stores would be a better choice.

---

2 tablespoons regular (not extra-virgin) olive oil

4 medium-size celery ribs, coarsely chopped (1½ cups)

1 medium-size onion, coarsely chopped (½ cup)

1 medium-size carrot, coarsely chopped (½ cup)

3 or 4 large garlic cloves, coarsely chopped

2 teaspoons dried tarragon leaves, crumbled

6 black peppercorns

2 bay leaves

1 teaspoon salt

1 can (6 ounces) tomato paste

2 quarts water

2 pounds fish heads and bones

Heat the olive oil in a large soup pot or Dutch oven. When it is hot, add the celery, onion, and carrot and cook over medium-high heat, stirring frequently, until slightly softened. Stir in the garlic, tarragon, peppercorns, bay leaves, salt, and tomato paste. Add the water and bring to a boil over high heat. Lower the heat and simmer, partially covered, for 20 minutes. Stir in the fish heads and bones and continue to simmer, tightly covered, stirring occasionally, for about 40 minutes. When the broth has cooled, strain it into a large bowl through a colander lined with a couple of thicknesses of cheesecloth, pressing down hard on the solids with the back of a spoon to extract as much of the liquid as possible. Discard the fish bones and vegetables. If not using immediately, cool the broth and then pour it into 1- or 2-cup containers with tight-fitting lids. The broth can be refrigerated for several days. Freeze for longer storage, up to 6 months. If freezing, allow about ½ inch of head-space for expansion in each container.

Clarified Melted Butter

The point of clarifying butter is to remove the milky solids, which will burn when subjected to high heat. Both salted and unsalted butter can be clarified.

Place the butter in a small, heavy saucepan and melt it over low heat. Remove from the heat and set aside until the solids settle to the bottom of the pan. Spoon off the foam and then carefully pour off the clear fat (which is clarified butter) and discard the residue. If not using immediately, refrigerate the butter (it will solidify and must be remelted) until needed. It will keep for several weeks in the refrigerator, and for about 6 months if it is frozen.

Giant White Beans

YIELD: ABOUT 7 CUPS

1 pound (about 3 cups) giant white beans (see page 291)　　　　　*2 teaspoons salt*

Spread the beans out on a work surface and sort through them, removing any foreign matter and picking out any beans that are broken, shriveled, or discolored. Place the beans in a large bowl and cover with water. At this point, a few will undoubtedly float to the surface. This indicates that, for one reason or other and none of them good, an air pocket has formed inside. Skim off these beans, as well as any bean skins that may float to the surface, and discard them. Drain the beans into a colander and rinse under running water. Return the beans to the bowl and cover generously with fresh water, remembering that they will more than double in size when they are rehydrated. Set aside for at least 4 hours.

Drain the beans and place in a large heavy saucepan or Dutch oven. Cover by about an inch with cold water. Bring to a boil over high heat and boil for 10 minutes, skimming off the foam with a large spoon as it rises to the surface. (Although the foam would eventually disappear, it might later leave a gritty film on the cooked beans.) Reduce the heat so that the beans simmer slowly. Cover and simmer for 1 to 1½ hours, stirring gently every now and then, until the beans are tender, but not falling apart; add the salt during the last 30 minutes of cooking time. Drain in a colander and use as the recipe directs.

Homemade Yogurt

For the recipes in this book, we used a good, thick sheep's-milk yogurt, which is not always easy to find (see page 303). Rather than using a watery "diet" yogurt, making your own yogurt is a better alternative. It won't taste like sheep's-milk yogurt, of course, but it will be thick and rich-flavored, two very important elements in Greek cooking.

2 cups whole or part-skim milk
3 tablespoons dry milk

2 tablespoons whole-milk yogurt

Rinse a 2-quart saucepan with water. (This will help prevent the milk from sticking to the bottom and side of the pan.) Add the milk to the saucepan and stir in the dry milk. Set over medium-low heat and cook just until the milk begins to boil, or until a thermometer inserted in the milk registers about 215°F. Remove from the heat and set aside until the temperature drops to 115°F. Meanwhile, fill a 2-cup, wide-mouth insulated container (such as a thermos) with hot water and set aside. Stir the yogurt into the milk, being careful not to dislodge any of the brown crust that may have formed on the bottom of the pan. Pour the hot water out of the insulated container. Pour the milk mixture into the container, cover tightly, and set aside in a warm place, undisturbed, just until the yogurt sets, about 8 to 10 hours. Uncover the yogurt and refrigerate, undisturbed, until cold and thick. Cover tightly and keep refrigerated until ready to use. The yogurt will keep well for a couple of weeks.

Thickened Yogurt

Thickening (or draining) yogurt gives it more body and prevents it from "weeping" when it is combined with other foods.

Lay out a 16-inch square of double-thickness cheesecloth on a work surface. Place up to 2 cups of plain, whole-milk yogurt (preferably sheep's-milk) in the center of the cheesecloth. Bring up the corners of the cheesecloth and tie them onto the handle of a wooden spoon. Suspend the spoon over a deep bowl, making sure that the bottom of the cheesecloth bag is a couple of inches above the bottom of the bowl. Place in the refrigerator to drain for 8 to 10 hours or overnight. Scrape the drained and thickened yogurt off the cheesecloth into a bowl. Cover and refrigerate for several days until ready to use.

HOLLY GARRISON

How to Work with Phyllo

Phyllo is easy to work with as long as it is kept moist, since these extraordinarily thin leaves of pastry dough dry out and crumble very quickly when they are exposed to the air. The moment the *phyllo* is removed from the box and unfolded, it must be covered completely, first with a piece of plastic wrap or waxed paper, and then with a damp towel. (If the damp towel is placed directly on the *phyllo,* the pastry leaves may stick together.)

Virtually every recipe calling for *phyllo* also calls for it to be brushed first with melted, clarified butter to keep it from disintegrating, but, even more important, to keep the leaves separate so that they will bake up into flaky layers.

Fillings for *phyllo* should not be excessively moist, which may make the dough soggy.

STEP 1. Thaw unopened frozen *phyllo* in the refrigerator for about 8 hours or overnight, and then bring it to room temperature (this takes about 2 hours) before removing from the box. *Phyllo* that is stored in the refrigerator should also be brought to room temperature before using.

STEP 2. Remove the *phyllo* from the box, cut open the sealed bag containing the sheets, and carefully unroll the sheets onto a smooth, *dry* surface.

STEP 3. Immediately cover the *phyllo* with a piece of waxed paper or plastic wrap, and then with a damp towel.

STEP 4. Keep the *phyllo* covered as you work with it. Do not leave it uncovered for more than a minute or so.

STEP 5. To prevent the particularly fragile edges from cracking, brush them with butter first, then work from the center out, brushing any wrinkles toward the outside.

NOTE: We have used Apollo brand ultra-thin *phyllo* dough in testing the recipes that appear in this book. There are 27 to 30 sheets of *phyllo* in a 1-pound box, each measuring about 12 by 17 inches.

Generally, ½ cup (1 stick) of melted butter is needed to brush sheets of *phyllo*.

Spinach-and-Feta-Cheese Filling

YIELD: ABOUT 4 CUPS

*T*his is a fabulous filling, and once you've worked with it, you will undoubtedly find countless uses for it besides the ones given in this book.

½ cup plus 1 tablespoon extra-virgin
  olive oil
1 medium-size onion, shredded
  (½ cup)
1 medium-size leek, chopped (white
  part only)
2 packages (10 ounces each) frozen
  chopped spinach, thawed and
  drained and squeezed between palms
  of hands to remove most of the
  liquid

2 tablespoons chopped fresh dill
1 teaspoon salt
¼ teaspoon white pepper
2 eggs
¾ cup crumbled feta cheese
½ pint regular (small-curd) cottage
  cheese
1 tablespoon grated Parmesan cheese
1 tablespoon dry bread crumbs

Heat 1 tablespoon of the olive oil in a large skillet. When it is hot, add the onion and leek and cook over medium heat, stirring frequently, until lightly browned. Stir in the spinach and the remaining ½ cup olive oil. Continue to cook, stirring, until the mixture stops steaming. Stir in the dill, salt, and pepper until well blended. Turn the mixture into a large bowl and refrigerate until cooled. When ready to proceed, stir in the eggs, cheeses, and bread crumbs until very well blended.

How to Work with Grape Leaves

Whether they are packed in brine or fresh, grape leaves need some preliminary preparation before they are used.

Carefully remove the brined grape leaves from the jar or can. (They are packed in rolls resembling fat cigars.) Spread either brined or fresh grape leaves in a single layer in a large, shallow pan. Add enough boiling water to cover the leaves generously and set aside to soak and soften until the water is cool.

Rinse the leaves with cool water and blot dry with paper towels. Snip the woody stem from the bottom center of each leaf. Lay each leaf flat, vein side up, on a work surface, overlapping the bottom of the leaf slightly where the stem has been removed.

Place the filling about ½ inch up from the bottom and fold as directed in the recipe. The leaves should not be too tightly packed, since almost all fillings expand, at least a little, as they cook.

The Meze: A Feast of Small Appetizers

To most Americans, who otherwise haven't the foggiest idea what Greeks eat, the omnipresent appetizers that play such a vital role in this venerable cuisine may be the most familiar and the best part of the whole Hellenic food show.

The *meze* ("the appetizer") can be merely a snack or a lot more substantial. It is offered and eaten at all times of the day, frequently to accompany an *ouzo* or a glass of wine, but it is primarily the time-honored segue into the main course, and what is not consumed before the main dish arrives remains on the table to be eaten along with the meal as side dishes—also technically absent from the Greek menu.

In the center of the dining room at Periyali, a pivotal location is given over to a large and rustic table, crowded with platters and bowls of an ever-changing variety of *mezedes* (plural), or *orektika,* as appetizers are also known. This is the *meze* table, and it is a veritable Greek institution. On it is an artful display of tempting tidbits, dips, and salads, the best of which, in Greece, are more likely to be served at home or in drinking establishments, called *ouzeries,* rather than in *tavernas* and other restaurants.

Despite a well-known passion for *ouzo* and *retsina* wine, the Greeks actually aren't very big drinkers. And when they do indulge, you can be sure that every round of drinks will be accompanied by a round of *mezedes.* The Greeks have always adhered to the wisdom of not drinking on an empty stomach. Not so long

ago, a large variety of *mezedes* was handed out free to patrons of *ouzo* bars and cafés, but nowadays, if you want anything much more than a few slices of cucumber and a tiny piece of *feta,* you must buy them.

The *meze* table, with its varied and often seasonally dictated offerings, is a fundamental part of Greek culture and hospitality. When you enter a Greek home, no matter how bare the larder, some small sustenance will be forced upon you to accompany your wine.

Periyali patrons who occasionally choose to make selections from the *meze* table and order from the left-hand side of the menu can literally cover the table with a satiating assortment of these intriguing little specialties and skip the main course entirely.

Mezedes, American-Style

Nibbling on *mezedes* is a form of eating that can work itself nicely into American styles of informal entertaining. This is the perfect food for a buffet or any sort of less-than-formal dining. If you want to set a *meze* table to accompany drinks, or in place of the first course, the selection certainly needn't be as vast as Periyali's, but it should be varied, with a well-planned balance and contrast of tastes and textures that are spicy and bland, soft and chewy, smooth and coarse, and a sizzling hot appetizer or two to offset the cool salads and dips.

The whole point of a *meze* table is to offer many little dishes, which at first might seem like a formidable undertaking for today's otherwise busy party-givers. But because so many of the Greek appetizers can be wholly or partially prepared ahead of time, serving an impressive variety is actually rather easy.

Do as the Greeks do, and keep the main course down to one spectacular dish, for instance a big casserole of *pastitsio* or *moussaka* that is served a little later on, accompanied by a Greek salad and more of the *meze.*

There seems to be an endless number of Greek appetizers, and it would require a volume three times as large as this one even to begin to record all of them. But as you become familiar with the

a 1-pound box, each measuring about 12 by 17 inches.

Generally, ½ cup (1 stick) of melted butter is needed to brush sheets of *phyllo*.

Spinach-and-Feta-Cheese Filling

YIELD: ABOUT 4 CUPS

*T*his is a fabulous filling, and once you've worked with it, you will undoubtedly find countless uses for it besides the ones given in this book.

½ cup plus 1 tablespoon extra-virgin olive oil

1 medium-size onion, shredded (½ cup)

1 medium-size leek, chopped (white part only)

2 packages (10 ounces each) frozen chopped spinach, thawed and drained and squeezed between palms of hands to remove most of the liquid

2 tablespoons chopped fresh dill

1 teaspoon salt

¼ teaspoon white pepper

2 eggs

¾ cup crumbled feta *cheese*

½ pint regular (small-curd) cottage cheese

1 tablespoon grated Parmesan cheese

1 tablespoon dry bread crumbs

Heat 1 tablespoon of the olive oil in a large skillet. When it is hot, add the onion and leek and cook over medium heat, stirring frequently, until lightly browned. Stir in the spinach and the remaining ½ cup olive oil. Continue to cook, stirring, until the mixture stops steaming. Stir in the dill, salt, and pepper until well blended. Turn the mixture into a large bowl and refrigerate until cooled. When ready to proceed, stir in the eggs, cheeses, and bread crumbs until very well blended.

How to Work with Grape Leaves

Whether they are packed in brine or fresh, grape leaves need some preliminary preparation before they are used.

Carefully remove the brined grape leaves from the jar or can. (They are packed in rolls resembling fat cigars.) Spread either brined or fresh grape leaves in a single layer in a large, shallow pan. Add enough boiling water to cover the leaves generously and set aside to soak and soften until the water is cool.

Rinse the leaves with cool water and blot dry with paper towels. Snip the woody stem from the bottom center of each leaf. Lay each leaf flat, vein side up, on a work surface, overlapping the bottom of the leaf slightly where the stem has been removed.

Place the filling about ½ inch up from the bottom and fold as directed in the recipe. The leaves should not be too tightly packed, since almost all fillings expand, at least a little, as they cook.

wide range and well-defined parameters of the *meze,* you will undoubtedly be inspired to create some of your own very good ones with ingredients you happen to have on hand.

Marinated Olives

YIELD: ABOUT 2¼ CUPS

Olives are *always* present on the *meze* table. The big bowls of fleshy green and black olives that are set on the bar at Periyali disappear almost as quickly as they can be replenished. Regional olives are the quintessential Greek snack food, and are often combined with a chewy loaf of bread and a slab of *feta* cheese for a light and surprisingly satisfying meal.

Greek olives are so naturally luscious that there is really no need to embellish them. Some varieties have already been dressed with olive oil after curing, but, if not, a brief liaison with a little fruity olive oil before serving will keep them shiny and add a delicate flavor and aroma. If you want to add a little more oomph to your olives by marinating them, keep it simple and subtle. The idea is to enhance the olive's delicate flavor, not to overwhelm it.

For more about olives, see page 294.

---

1 pound (about 2¼ cups) large
  black or green Greek olives, or a
  mixture of both
1 large garlic clove, thinly sliced
¼ cup extra-virgin olive oil
1 tablespoon lemon juice

¼ teaspoon dried oregano leaves,
  crumbled
¼ teaspoon dried thyme leaves,
  crumbled
Sprigs of fresh oregano or thyme, for
  garnish

Blot the olives dry on paper towels. (If the olives have not already been slit, a small cut can be made in each one to help absorb the flavor of the marinade.) Toss the olives in a medium-size bowl with the garlic. In a small bowl, beat the olive oil, lemon juice, oregano, and thyme. Stir into the garlic and olives until well blended. Transfer to a container with a tight-fitting lid. Cover and set aside at room temperature for several days, or up to several weeks, turning the container occasionally to redistribute the olives and marinade. There's no need to refrigerate the olives, since the oil will keep them fresh. Serve the olives in a bowl with a few fresh sprigs of oregano or thyme tucked here and there. As the olives are removed from the marinade, more olives can be added to it. This may be done several times, adding a little more olive oil, as necessary, before starting over with a new marinade.

A Trio of Dips from Patmian House

Three traditional Greek dips hint at enticing and more substantial offerings to come, and are one of the popular ways to begin lunch and dinner at Periyali. Fish Roe Dip, Roasted Eggplant Salad, and Cucumber and Yogurt Salad are served together on a plate, with glossy Kalamata olives, a small serving of lightly dressed Mixed Salad Greens, and small ovals of Seasoned Toasted Bread. The dips are part of the collection of recipes originally developed for Periyali by Irene and Victor Gouras, who serve the same savory trio at their summer restaurant on the Greek island of Patmos.

Plenty of chewy, crusty bread and sweet butter is also on the table, the latter being something of an American requirement. According to Irene, if you were dining with a Greek family in their home, you would more likely be offered a large bowl of bread cubes to use for dipping, and a bottle of pale green olive oil in place of the butter.

Fish Roe Dip
TARAMOSALATA

One restaurant reviewer described Periyali's version of *taramosalata* as so light that it seemed more like a vapor than a puree. This seasoned mixture of salted mullet or cod roe (*tarama*), bread, and olive oil was originally concocted to serve during the meatless Lenten season. Now it is commonly served with drinks in Greek *ouzeries,* and certainly no table of appetizers could be considered complete without it. Charles makes the *taramosalata* a day ahead of serving so that the flavors have a chance to get acquainted, but it should be eaten within a day or two after that, since the fish roe tends to become too potent if held for much longer.

8 ounces (about 8 slices) firm
  homemade-style white bread
1 tablespoon chopped red onion
1 small garlic clove, chopped
1/4 cup tarama (see page 302)
2 tablespoons lemon juice

1 tablespoon white-wine vinegar
1/4 cup extra-virgin olive oil
1/4 cup vegetable oil
1/4 teaspoon sugar
Salmon or golden whitefish caviar, or
  a few Kalamata olives, for garnish

Trim the crusts from the bread and spread the slices out on a tray to dry for about 24 hours.

In the container of a food processor, place the onion, garlic, *tarama,* lemon juice, and vinegar. Blend or process until as smooth as possible, scraping down the side of the container several times. With the processor running, gradually add a mixture of both oils through the feed tube. The oil must be added slowly enough so that it forms an emulsion.

Fill a large bowl with cool water. Drop the dried bread into the water, one slice at a time. When it is soaked, squeeze out as much water as possible and drop it into the processor feed tube. When all the bread has been added, add the sugar and process until smooth. Taste and add a little more vinegar and lemon juice, if necessary. The finished consistency should be something like softly whipped cream, just firm enough to mound slightly when dropped from a spoon. Keep in mind that the dip will tighten up as it chills, so if it seems heavy at this point, gradually beat in a little water. Scrape into a serving bowl. Cover tightly and chill for several hours before serving. Garnish servings with a few grains of caviar or an olive.

NOTE: If *tarama* isn't available, or if it's too assertive for your taste, Charles suggests substituting golden whitefish caviar (*not black*, which would give the mixture a muddy appearance), which has a milder flavor, is a little less salty, and can be found easily in specialty food stores. In any event, he says, use caviar, either salmon or golden whitefish, for the garnish, since *tarama* is much too strong-tasting to eat by itself.

Roasted Eggplant Salad
MELITZANOSALATA

Although it's referred to as a salad (as are many Greek dips), *melitzanosalata* is almost always a rough puree. At Periyali, the charcoal-grilled, smoky-flavored eggplant is finely chopped, which, as well as giving the dip a more interesting texture, is also more typical of Greek home cooking.

---

2 medium-size eggplants (about 1¼ pounds each)
2 tablespoons white-wine vinegar
1 to 2 tablespoons lemon juice
1 tablespoon extra-virgin olive oil
1 tablespoon vegetable oil
2 tablespoons shredded red onion

1 large garlic clove, put through a garlic press
½ teaspoon sugar
¼ teaspoon salt
⅛ teaspoon pepper
Chopped flat-leaf parsley, for garnish

Select long, slim eggplants, which will roast more evenly than those that are more bulbous. Puncture each eggplant several times on all sides with the tip of a knife to prevent them from exploding while they grill and to allow the smoky flavor of the charcoal fire to be absorbed into the flesh. Place the whole eggplants on a grill 3 or 4 inches above medium-hot coals. Grill, turning occasionally, for about 30 minutes, or until the eggplants are charred all over and are very soft and just starting to collapse. Remove to a platter. When cool enough to handle, cut off the stems and strip away the charred skin. Place the eggplants in a colander set over a deep bowl. Cover with plastic wrap and allow to drain for about 24 hours in the refrigerator.

Place the drained eggplants on a work surface and cut in half lengthwise. Spread open the sections of the eggplant halves and remove the seeds, which tend to be bitter. They will pull away in strips, and it will be impossible to get them all, but do the best you can. Chop the eggplant very finely and place in a medium-size bowl.

Mix the vinegar, lemon juice, olive and vegetable oils, onion, garlic, sugar, salt, and pepper in a small bowl. Stir into the eggplant until thoroughly combined. Cover and chill for several hours to allow the flavors to blend. Serve at room temperature sprinkled with parsley.

NOTE: If it's more convenient, the eggplants can be oven-roasted. Pre-heat the oven broiler. Puncture the eggplants as instructed above and place directly on the oven rack 6 to 8 inches below the source of the heat. Roast, turning occasionally, until the eggplants are charred all over, and are very soft and starting to collapse.

Cucumber and Yogurt Salad
TZATZIKI

YIELD: ABOUT 3 CUPS; 6 TO 8 APPETIZER SERVINGS

Cucumbers turn up often in the *meze,* probably because they're a cool contrast for often-spicy companions. In Greece, this salad is particularly good in the spring and early summer when young, fine-textured cucumbers are at their peak. Although *tzatziki* is al-ways served as an appetizer in Greece, Americans would find it equally delicious eaten along with the main course, especially roasted lamb, for which it has a special affinity.

1 English cucumber (see page 291)
 or 2 regular cucumbers (about
 1 pound)
1 teaspoon salt
2 cups Thickened Yogurt
 (see page 11)
¼ cup red-wine vinegar
1 tablespoon extra-virgin olive oil

1 or 2 garlic cloves, put through a
 garlic press
½ teaspoon sugar
⅛ teaspoon white pepper
½ cup sour cream
1 to 2 tablespoons minced fresh dill
Very thin slices of cucumber and
 sprigs of dill, for garnish

Peel the cucumber and cut it into ¼-inch cubes. Place the cubes in a colander. Sprinkle with the salt and toss to mix well. Place the colander over a bowl and cover with plastic wrap. Refrigerate for 8 to 10 hours or overnight to drain.

Pat the drained cucumber with paper towels to remove as much liquid as possible. Turn into a large bowl. Stir the yogurt into the cucumber, mixing gently until thoroughly blended. Stir in the vinegar, olive oil, garlic, sugar, and pepper. Blend in the sour cream, then the minced dill. Taste and add salt, if necessary. Refrigerate for an hour or two before serving to allow the flavors to mingle. Arrange 2 thin cucumber slices topped with a sprig of dill alongside each serving.

A Quicker Cucumber Salad Although this salad is not as thick and intensely flavored as the traditional version, this is a good method to use when time is limited. Follow the instructions given for the traditional *tzatziki*, but reduce the standing time for the cucumber to 30 minutes. Use 1½ cups whole milk yogurt instead of Thickened Yogurt, and place it in a large strainer that has been lined with a double thickness of paper towels or a coffee filter. Drain for 30 minutes. Mix with the remaining ingredients as directed above and serve immediately.

Beet Dip

YIELD: 1 CUP

*F*resh anything is almost always infinitely better than canned, but in this case, there's little discernible difference, and not having to cook beets from scratch can be a real time-saver. This is an especially pretty dip that can also be used as a dressing over shredded romaine or tender Boston lettuce, which, by the way, are two of the only lettuce varieties you're likely to find in Greece.

---

1 can (8¹/4 ounces) sliced or whole
  beets, drained, or 3 or 4 tiny fresh
  beets (about ¹/2 pound)
1 small red onion, coarsely chopped
  (¹/4 cup)

¹/2 cup Thickened Yogurt (see
  page 11)
¹/4 teaspoon salt

If using whole, canned beets, cut them into quarters. (If using fresh beets, cut off the greens, leaving about 1 inch of the stems on each. Rinse the beets and place in a large saucepan with enough lightly salted water to cover by about an inch. Bring to a boil. Cover and boil gently over medium heat for about 20 minutes, or until the beets are tender. Drain and trim off the roots and stems, then rub off the skins under cold running water. Cut the beets into quarters.) Place the beets and onion in the container of a food processor or blender and process until very finely chopped, but not quite pureed. Mix the yogurt with the salt in a small bowl. Scrape the beet mixture into the yogurt and blend thoroughly. Serve immediately, or cover and refrigerate until needed. The dip can be served chilled or at room temperature.

Seasoned Toasted Bread

YIELD: ABOUT 50 SLICES

The thin ovals of toasted bread that accompany the dips at Peri-yali are simple to make and keep well for a week or so when stored in a tightly covered container. Be sure to make the slices very thin, as otherwise the toast will be hard instead of crisp.

---

8 ounce-loaf French bread, about
  2¹/₂ inches in diameter
¹/₄ cup extra-virgin olive oil
1¹/₂ teaspoons dried oregano leaves,
  crumbled

1¹/₂ teaspoons dried thyme leaves,
  crumbled

Preheat the oven to 300°F. Cut the bread into ⅛-inch slices. (An electric knife does this very efficiently, so if you have one, use it.) In a large bowl, toss the bread slices while gradually adding the olive oil until each piece is moistened. Mix the oregano and thyme together on a piece of waxed paper. Gradually sprinkle the herbs over the bread, tossing until they are lightly and evenly coated. Spread the slices in a single layer on one or two baking sheets and bake for 10 to 15 minutes, watching closely, until pale golden.

Dried-Bean Cuisine

Dried beans and peas, known as *pulses,* are highly regarded in Greece, particularly during Lent, when they become a dietary necessity and make frequent appearances on the table as both appetizers and main dishes. Beans grow well in the thin topsoil that covers much of Greece, and the crops are so essential that the village priest is often called in to bless the seeds before they're sown.

As highly esteemed as protein- and fiber-rich dried beans are by the Greeks—and nowadays by health-conscious Americans, as well—most cooks view them as something of a nuisance, since from-scratch bean recipes always begin with directions to soak them for hours (four hours is actually long enough) before cooking can even begin.

When confronted with dried beans, before skipping on to the next recipe, remember that beans require absolutely *no* attention while they soak, and usually just minimal attention while they cook. Besides, you can employ this reliable quick-soak method: Rinse the beans in a colander, place in a large saucepan, and cover them generously with cold water. Bring to a boil and boil for one minute. Remove from the heat and set aside to soak for one hour. Drain and rinse and the beans are ready to go.

Irene and Victor's Giant White Beans with Garlic Sauce

GIGANDES SKORDALIA

YIELD: 7 CUPS; 8 TO 12 APPETIZER SERVINGS

Gigandes are very large white beans that are closely related to butter beans. At Periyali they are transformed into a sturdy, but surprisingly refined, appetizer after they have been dressed and marinated in mildly seasoned olive oil that does not detract at all from their subtle, buttery flavor and almost creamy texture. A generous spoonful of Periyali's delicate *skordalia* accompanies the beans, along with a small portion of lightly dressed Mixed Salad Greens.

---

1 recipe Giant White Beans (see page 9)
1/2 cup extra-virgin olive oil
1/2 teaspoon salt
1/4 teaspoon white pepper

1 tablespoon chopped flat-leaf parsley
Flat-leaf parsley sprigs, for garnish
Periyali's Almond Skordalia (see page 230)

Prepare the beans. Mix the olive oil, salt, pepper, and parsley in a small bowl. Pour over the warm beans and toss gently with a wooden spoon until well mixed. Cover and chill for several hours to allow the flavors to develop. Serve the beans at room temperature, garnished with parsley sprigs and accompanied by a small portion of Periyali Almond *Skordalia*.

Split Yellow Pea Puree

*E*veryone who tries this puree is surprised to find how healthful it is—that's how rich and good it tastes. Like most dips, this one keeps very well. Try it with a few olives, spread on crackers, or with bread, as a nourishing and satisfying snack when you're rushing around and don't have time to sit down and eat a proper meal.

1 cup dry yellow split peas
1 medium-size onion, chopped
  (1/2 cup)
1/4 cup regular (not extra-virgin)
  olive oil
1/4 cup plus about 1 tablespoon
  lemon juice
2 1/2 cups water
1 large garlic clove, put through a
  garlic press
1 small red onion, cut in half
  lengthwise through the stem and
  then into very thin lengthwise slivers,
  reserving some of the slivers for
  garnish

3 to 4 tablespoons extra-virgin
  olive oil
1/2 teaspoon salt
1/8 teaspoon freshly ground black
  pepper
Chopped flat-leaf parsley, for garnish

Sort through the peas and pick out any debris. Rinse with cold water and drain. Place the peas in a heavy, medium-size saucepan. Add the chopped onion, regular olive oil, 1/4 cup of the lemon juice, and water. Bring to a boil. Reduce the heat, cover and simmer very slowly for about 2 hours, stirring occasionally, until the mixture is very soft, almost a puree, and very thick. (After the first hour, watch carefully and add a little hot water from time to time to prevent the mixture from sticking to the bottom of the pan.) Remove from the heat and set aside, covered, to cool. When cool, process briefly in a food processor, or mash with a wooden spoon, until the peas are reasonably smooth. By hand, blend in the garlic, slivered onion, and extra-virgin olive oil. Stir in the salt and pepper. Cover and refrigerate for several hours or overnight to give the flavors time to develop. To serve, bring to room temperature. Taste and adjust the seasoning, adding a little more extra-virgin olive oil, salt, and pepper, if needed, and the remaining lemon juice to taste. Spoon onto a serving plate, swirling the mixture into an attractive pattern with the back of a spoon. Sprinkle with the reserved onion slivers. Drizzle with a little extra-virgin olive oil and a few drops of lemon juice if desired. Sprinkle with parsley and serve surrounded by Seasoned Toasted Bread.

HOLLY GARRISON

Tiny Eggplants in Tomato Sauce

YIELD: 8 APPETIZER SERVINGS

*M*idsummer is the best time to serve this simple and fresh-tasting appetizer, when tiny local eggplants, plump and shiny, make their appearance at the market or, if you're lucky, in your own garden. This must be eaten within a few hours after it's made; otherwise the dark juice from the cooked eggplant begins to seep into the tomato sauce and gives it a slightly bitter flavor.

---

2 or 3 large garlic cloves, cut into 16 thin slices

1 teaspoon salt

1/8 teaspoon freshly ground black pepper

8 tiny eggplants (about 3 or 4 inches in length)

2 to 3 tablespoons regular (not extra-virgin) olive oil

1 can (14 1/2 ounces) whole tomatoes, undrained and chopped (see Note)

1 tablespoon chopped flat-leaf parsley

Toss the garlic slices in the salt and pepper on a piece of waxed paper until well coated. Rinse the eggplants and trim away the leaves on the stem. Cut a deep slit in both sides of each eggplant and insert a slice of the seasoned garlic into each slit.

Heat the olive oil in a large, deep skillet or sauté pan. When it is hot, add the eggplant and cook over medium-high heat, turning frequently, until lightly browned. Stir the tomatoes and their liquid into the pan and bring to a boil. Reduce the heat, cover, and simmer over medium heat for 10 to 15 minutes, basting the eggplant occasionally until it is tender. Remove the eggplant to a serving platter. Raise the heat under the tomatoes and simmer, stirring, until slightly thickened. Season to taste with salt and pepper and spoon over the eggplant. Cool and serve at room temperature, sprinkled with parsley.

NOTE: The easiest way to chop canned tomatoes is to use clean kitchen scissors and cut them up in the can.

Black-eyed Pea Salad

YIELD: 4 SERVINGS

After a comparison taste test we decided that the canned-pea version of this popular Periyali salad could be a very handy shortcut.

1 can (about 15 ounces) black-eyed peas or 2 cups cooked black-eyed peas
1 small red onion, finely chopped (1/4 cup)
2 tablespoons chopped flat-leaf parsley

1/8 teaspoon salt
Pinch of white pepper
2 tablespoons extra-virgin olive oil
1 tablespoon red- or white-wine vinegar
Chopped flat-leaf parsley, for garnish

Drain the peas in a colander and rinse with cool water; drain thoroughly. (If using dried peas, prepare as the package directs.) Turn into a medium-size bowl and toss gently with the onion, parsley, salt, and pepper. Add the olive oil and vinegar and toss again until well blended. Set aside at room temperature for a couple of hours to allow time for the flavors to permeate the peas. Serve sprinkled with parsley.

Irene Gouras's Rice-Stuffed Grape Leaves

DOLMATHAKIA

*W*hen she serves these at her restaurant on Patmos, Irene takes the time to use tiny fresh grape leaves, filling each one with a miniscule amount of the rice stuffing, a tedious and time-consuming effort that her patrons appreciate. However, the stuffed leaves can be cooked a day or so ahead of time and rewarmed in a microwave oven, or served at room temperature. Irene serves the *dolmathakia* as part of the *meze* table. They can also be used to decorate a Greek salad, if you like.

If you happen to have access to a vineyard, it's worth begging a few fresh grape leaves from the vintner (make certain that the leaves have not been treated with toxic chemicals), if only to see how they compare with those that are packed in brine.

---

1 jar grape leaves in brine, or about 32 medium-size fresh grape leaves (see page 14)

1 medium-size onion, shredded (1/2 cup)

1 medium-size carrot, scraped and shredded (1/2 cup)

3 or 4 scallions, thinly sliced, including some of the green tops (1/4 cup)

1 tablespoon chopped fresh dill

1 tablespoon finely chopped fresh mint leaves

2 teaspoons chopped flat-leaf parsley

2 whole canned tomatoes, drained and the juice reserved

1/2 cup plus 2 tablespoons converted raw rice

1 teaspoon salt

1/4 teaspoon freshly ground black pepper

1/8 teaspoon sugar

1/4 cup extra-virgin olive oil

2 tablespoons reserved juice from canned tomatoes

2 cups Chicken Broth (see page 5)

1/4 cup lemon juice

Prepare the grape leaves as directed on page 14.

In a medium-size bowl, combine the onion, carrot, scallions, dill, mint, parsley, tomatoes, rice, salt, pepper, and sugar. Stir in the olive oil and tomato juice.

Place about 1 tablespoon of the rice mixture just below the center of each leaf. Fold the bottom of the leaf over the filling; fold the sides in over the filling, then roll the leaf into a small oblong package. Do not fold too tightly, since the rice will swell when it cooks.

Lay the stuffed leaves, folded side down, in the bottom of a heavy, medium-size saucepan, fitting them together neatly, but not too tightly. Mix the chicken broth and lemon juice and pour over the grape leaves, so that they are just covered, adding a little water, if necessary. Place a heavy plate, slightly smaller than the diameter of the saucepan, over the top of the grape leaves to keep them from moving around and unrolling during cooking. Cook at a slow simmer over medium-low heat for about 45 minutes, or until the rice is tender. If serving at room temperature, place the stuffed leaves in a container and drizzle with a little olive oil to prevent them from drying out.

To serve cool, garnish with lemon wedges and drizzle with a little extra-virgin olive oil. If served warm, these are excellent with Hot Lemon Sauce for Vegetables made with the cooking liquid left in the pan, or Thickened Yogurt for dipping.

Pickled Baby Octopus
(or Shrimp)

YIELD: ABOUT 8 APPETIZER SERVINGS

This is the *meze* of choice to accompany a glass of *ouzo*. Even without *ouzo* it is sensational. If you like, the octopus can be prettily arranged on tender lettuce leaves and served as a more formal first course. Large shrimp can be substituted for octopus if you're squeamish about the latter. Pickled octopus languishes in big glass jars all over Greece, but it takes courage to order it.

---

4 cups water

1 cup dry white wine

4 medium-size carrots, coarsely chopped (about 2 cups)

1 large onion, coarsely chopped (1 cup)

2 teaspoons salt

6 black peppercorns

2 bay leaves

2 pounds dressed baby octopus or large shrimp (see Note)

PICKLING JUICE

2 large garlic cloves, thinly sliced

¾ cup extra-virgin olive oil

¼ cup red-wine vinegar

½ teaspoon salt

¼ teaspoon dried oregano leaves, crumbled

¼ teaspoon dried thyme leaves, crumbled

6 black peppercorns

GARNISH

Flat-leaf parsley sprigs

Combine the water, wine, carrots, onion, salt, peppercorns, and bay leaves in a large, heavy saucepan. Bring to a boil over high heat and boil slowly, uncovered, for 15 minutes.

While the broth boils, cut the top part of the head off each octopus and discard it, leaving the tentacles attached to the lower part of the head. Cut off and discard the tips of the tentacles if they look thin and scraggly. Rinse the octopus in cool water, then lower it into the boiling broth, tentacles first. Lower the heat, then cover and simmer very gently for about 15 minutes. Test for tenderness with a kitchen fork or the tip of a knife, which should meet little resistance. If the octopus seems tough, continue to simmer 5 to 10 minutes longer. Remove from the heat and cool the octopus in the cooking broth. When the octopus has cooled, remove the purple skin from the tentacles, which tends to be bitter, by running your fingers down each tentacle several times. Rinse the octopus in the cooking broth. Cut the tentacles off close to the head and discard the head.

Place the tentacles in a medium-size bowl. Mix the pickling juice ingredients in a small bowl; pour over the octopus, stirring to combine. Cover tightly and refrigerate for at least 24 hours, or up to 3 or 4 days, stirring occasionally. When ready to serve, remove the tentacles from the marinade and place in a serving bowl. Garnish with sprigs of parsley tucked here and there.

NOTE: Baby octopuses, weighing about 8 ounces, are often available frozen and prepacked in 2-pound boxes. If these little octopuses are not available, larger ones can be substituted and the cooking time increased slightly, but rarely for more than 45 minutes. Cut the larger tentacles into pieces before pickling.

To substitute shrimp for the octopus, peel 2 pounds of large shrimp and stir them into the reduced broth. When the broth returns to a boil, cover and remove from heat. When the shrimp has cooled, drain and place in the pickling juice. Cover and chill for several hours, or up to 24 hours, before serving.

Pickled Vegetables

One of the high points of restaurant dining in Greece is waiting to find out just what appetizers, aside from the ever-present Greek salad, will appear within seconds after everyone's knees are tucked under the table, if the order is left to the waiter's discretion. Depending on the cook's mood and creativity, these can be very good, even inspired, as happened one Sunday afternoon at a *taverna* set beside a pebbly beach on the far side of Patmos. Perhaps it had to do with a red and blue fishing boat beached just in front, or long wispy clouds drifting across the deep-blue sky like chiffon scarves, but we all agreed that the bowl of pickled potatoes and zucchini we were served couldn't have been better.

---

*½ pound (about 8) small
  new potatoes
3 or 4 large garlic cloves, peeled and
  cut into thick slices
1 teaspoon salt
4 small zucchini (about
  4 ounces each)
6 large scallions, cut on the diagonal
  into 1-inch pieces, including some
  of the green tops*

*6 tablespoons lemon juice
3 tablespoons extra-virgin olive oil
½ teaspoon dried oregano leaves,
  crumbled
Freshly ground black pepper, to taste*

Peel the potatoes (if they are very new and fresh, you can actually rub the skins off with your fingers) and place them in a Dutch oven or other large, heavy saucepan with the garlic and salt. Add enough water to cover by about ½ inch. Bring to a boil over high heat. Reduce the heat and simmer, covered, until the potatoes are just starting to soften, about 5 minutes. Meanwhile, lightly scrub and trim the zucchini. Cut crosswise into quarters (or sixths or eighths if they are larger) so that the pieces are approximately the same size as the potatoes. Add the zucchini to the potatoes and continue to simmer, uncovered, until both vegetables are barely tender, about 5 minutes. Add the scallions and cook 1 minute longer. With a slotted spoon, transfer the vegetables, including the garlic, to a medium-size bowl. Measure out ½ cup of the cooking liquid to a small bowl, discarding the remainder. Add the lemon juice, olive oil, oregano, pepper, and a little more salt, if you think it's needed, to the reserved cooking liquid. Stir until well blended, then pour over the warm vegetables. Cool completely, uncovered, stirring occasionally until cool. Cover and refrigerate for about 12 hours or overnight, stirring occasionally, to give the flavors time to be absorbed into the vegetables. Serve chilled or at room temperature.

Roasted Peppers with Olive Oil and Vinegar

YIELD: 8 TO 12 APPETIZER SERVINGS

Large, fleshy peppers, fresh off the vine, are the best candidates for roasting. The Greeks seem wedded to green peppers, but red, yellow, or any other color bell pepper can be used. If you have the charcoal grill going, you might want to roast the peppers on that; otherwise the oven method is easy and reliable.

6 large bell peppers
Extra-virgin olive oil
Balsamic or red-wine vinegar

Salt and freshly ground black pepper,
* to taste*
Chopped flat-leaf parsley, for garnish

Preheat the oven broiler. Place the peppers on the rack in a broiling pan. Roast 4 to 6 inches below the source of heat for about 15 minutes, turning frequently until the skins are charred and blistered, but still firm enough to hold their shape. Remove from the oven and place the peppers in a paper bag, twisting the top closed. Set aside until the peppers are cool enough to handle. Using your fingers and a paring knife, peel off the skin, which will come away quite easily. Pull out the core and remove the seeds. Cut the peppers into wide strips and arrange them on a serving platter. Drizzle with olive oil and vinegar. Season lightly with salt and pepper and sprinkle with chopped parsley.

Fresh Yogurt Cheese with Olive Oil and Herbs

YIELD: ABOUT 1 CUP CHEESE; 8 CHEESE BALLS

It's surprisingly simple to make a good spreading cheese with an interesting, subtle flavor using homemade or purchased yogurt. The cheese has a fresh tangy taste, and its richness is determined by the amount of fat in the yogurt. If made from lower-fat yogurt, the cheese will be more tart, less creamy. The cheese can be lightly salted and used as is, or seasoned with herbs and garlic. Or form it into little balls and marinate them in herb-flavored olive oil. Other Mediterranean delicacies—sun-dried tomatoes, olives, or roasted peppers, for instance—can be added to the cheese as it marinates.

1 recipe for Homemade Yogurt (see page 10) or 2 cups whole-milk or part-skim yogurt
Salt, to taste
1/3 cup extra-virgin olive oil
1 teaspoon lemon juice
1 large garlic clove, thinly sliced
1 teaspoon dried oregano leaves
1 teaspoon dried thyme leaves

1/8 teaspoon freshly ground black pepper
Chopped or slivered sun-dried tomatoes (optional)
Pitted and sliced Kalamata olives (optional)
Roasted red pepper strips (optional; see page 37)

Lay out several layers of cheesecloth on a work surface. Spoon the yogurt into the center of the cheesecloth. Bring up the ends and tie them together to form a bag. Hang the bag over the handle of a spoon, then suspend the spoon over a deep bowl to catch the whey as it drains from the cheese. Set aside at room temperature for 12 to 24 hours, or until the mixture becomes a firm, creamy cheese. (The longer it hangs the firmer the cheese will be.) Remove the cheese from the cloth to a bowl and season to taste with salt. Refrigerate until very firm.

Cut the cheese into 8 equal pieces. Very gently roll the pieces between the palms of your hands to form balls. As they are formed, place the balls in a shallow bowl. Mix the olive oil, lemon juice, garlic, oregano, thyme, and pepper in a small bowl. Pour over the cheese. Sun-dried tomatoes, olives, or roasted red peppers can also be added, but in that case you may have to add a little more marinade. Cover and refrigerate for several hours or up to several days. Bring to room temperature and remove the garlic before serving. Serve as a spread with chunks of crusty bread or toast.

Herb Cheese Into the fresh salted cheese stir fresh or dried herbs, such as dill or oregano or mint, and parsley to taste, along with a little garlic, if you like. Form the cheese into a disk or pack into a crock. Cover and refrigerate for several hours, or up to several days.

Radishes with Scallions and Feta

❧ ❧ ❧ ❧

YIELD: 6 APPETIZER SERVINGS

Summer visitors to Greece rarely encounter a radish, since the growing season for them ends abruptly with the onset of heat and drought. But the Greeks adore them, and soon after the beginning of the autumn rains, radishes start popping up and return to the *meze* table. Often they are eaten just as they're pulled, with their tiny roots and tender leaves still attached. In any case, radish preparations are generally simple ones. In most parts of the United States we're fortunate to have huge, juicy radishes all summer long, the best time to serve this salad. The addition of scallions is our own innovation, since the use of "spring onions," as they are referred to in Greece, is rather limited there and it's not likely that they would be combined with radishes.

---

*2 cups thinly sliced radishes
(about 2 bunches)*
*1 cup thinly sliced scallions, including
some of the green tops
(10 to 12 scallions)*
*¼ cup chopped cilantro
(fresh coriander)*

*½ teaspoon dried oregano
leaves, crumbled*
2 tablespoons red-wine vinegar
¼ cup extra-virgin olive oil
½ cup crumbled feta *cheese*

Arrange the radishes and scallions in layers in a large bowl, sprinkling each layer with some of the coriander and oregano. Drizzle with a mixture of the vinegar and olive oil. Sprinkle with the *feta* cheese. Toss just before serving.

Beetroot Salad

PANTZARIA SALATA

YIELD: 6 APPETIZER SERVINGS

Although beetroots were extremely popular in ancient Greece, these days it's the tender, young beet greens that are prized, harvested before the root has had a chance to develop. When the beet itself is eaten, it's almost always sliced and served with onion rings and a simple vinegar or lemon and olive oil dressing. The contrast between the dark red beet slices and the white onion rings makes this an attractive addition to the *meze* table, and canned beets can be pressed into service if you're rushed, although sweet, fresh beets are infinitely better.

---

6 medium-size beets (about 2 pounds) or 2 cans (about 16 ounces each) sliced beets, drained
½ cup Olive Oil and Red-Wine Vinegar Dressing (see page 233), parsley omitted

2 small white onions, thinly sliced and the slices separated into rings (½ cup)
Chopped flat-leaf parsley, for garnish

Cut the greens from the beets, leaving about 1 inch of the stems on each. Rinse and scrub the beets and place them in a large saucepan with enough water to cover by a couple of inches. Bring to a boil. Cover and boil gently over medium heat for 30 to 40 minutes, or until the beets are tender; drain. Trim off the roots and stems, then rub off the skins under cold running water. Slice the beets thinly into a bowl. Add the dressing and toss until the slices are well coated. Just before serving, arrange the beet and onion rings on a large, shallow platter and sprinkle with parsley.

41

HOLLY GARRISON

Marinated Artichoke Bottoms

*L*eaving the stems attached to the quartered artichoke bottoms makes this a very attractive and unusual presentation. Arrange as they do at Periyali with the stems up on a large platter, surrounded with many paper-thin lemon slices.

---

4 large artichokes with long stems
1/4 cup plus 2 tablespoons extra-
   virgin olive oil
3 tablespoons balsamic vinegar
1 tablespoon lemon juice

1 tablespoon chopped flat-leaf parsley
1/4 teaspoon salt
1/8 teaspoon freshly ground pepper
Very thin lemon slices, for garnish

In a large saucepan, bring enough lightly salted water to a boil to cover the artichokes. Rinse the artichokes, but do not trim the leaves or remove the stems. Drop the artichokes into the boiling water. Cover and boil slowly for 35 to 45 minutes, or until tender; drain.

While the artichokes are cooking, mix the olive oil, vinegar, lemon juice, parsley, salt, and pepper in a medium-size bowl and set aside.

When the artichokes are cool enough to handle, strip off all of the leaves to expose the hairy, thistlelike choke attached to the bottom. Scrape the choke off the artichoke bottoms and discard. Cut each bottom into quarters, leaving a quarter of the stem attached to each one. Add the artichoke bottoms to the marinade and stir to coat. Cover lightly and set aside at room temperature for several hours, stirring occasionally. To serve, drain and arrange, stems up, on a large platter with the lemon slices.

Tomatoes (or Peppers) Stuffed with Rice

YEMISTES DOMATES LADERES ME RIZI

YIELD: 8 APPETIZER SERVINGS

Stuffed tomatoes and peppers are as traditional as stuffed grape leaves, but a whole lot easier and faster to do, since there's none of the precise folding and arranging. This is quite a handy recipe to have when the tomatoes start coming in faster than you can think of ways to eat them. Bell peppers, green, red, or yellow (green ones are more typically Greek, but yellow and red are prettier) may be used instead of, or in addition to, the tomatoes. However, the peppers will hold more filling, so figure on 4 to 6 small peppers for the amount of filling given below, and spoon 1 to 2 tablespoons of chicken broth over each pepper after it's filled.

---

8 firm medium-size tomatoes (about 6 ounces each)

1 small onion, shredded (¼ cup)

¼ cup shredded carrot

2 or 3 scallions, thinly sliced, including some of the green tops (2 tablespoons)

1 tablespoon finely chopped fresh mint leaves

1½ teaspoons chopped fresh dill

1 teaspoon chopped flat-leaf parsley

½ teaspoon salt

⅛ teaspoon freshly ground black pepper

¼ cup plus 2 tablespoons regular (not extra-virgin) olive oil

⅓ cup pine nuts

¼ cup plus 1 tablespoon converted raw rice

½ cup Chicken Broth (see page 5)

Extra-virgin olive oil

Cut the tops off the tomatoes, setting them aside to use as lids after the tomatoes are stuffed. Gently squeeze out the seeds. Hollow out the tomatoes with the tip of a spoon. Finely chop the pulp, reserving it and the juice.

In a medium-size bowl, combine the onion, carrot, scallions, mint, dill, parsley, salt, pepper, 2 tablespoons of the regular olive oil, and the reserved tomato flesh and juice. Stir in the pine nuts and rice until well combined.

Preheat the oven to 375°F. Spoon the filling into the tomatoes until they are about three-fourths full. (Don't overstuff; there must be room for expansion as the rice cooks.) Put the tops back on the tomatoes. Set the tomatoes in a shallow baking pan that is just large enough to hold them all comfortably. Pour the remaining ¼ cup regular olive oil and the chicken broth into the bottom of the pan. Bake for about 55 minutes, basting occasionally, until the rice is tender. (Peppers will require about 15 minutes more baking time.) Remove from the oven and set aside to cool. Set the tomatoes on a serving platter and drizzle with extra-virgin olive oil.

Tomato and Onion Salad

❧ ❧ ❧ ❧

YIELD: 6 SERVINGS

Time after time the Greeks demonstrate that the simplest of preparations are often the best. When not served as an appetizer, this salad is particularly good as a companion for *Souvlaki* or Nicola's Mother's Meatballs.

4 large, ripe tomatoes (about 2 pounds), cored and coarsely chopped	1 teaspoon dried oregano leaves, crumbled
1 large red onion, coarsely chopped (1 cup)	Extra-virgin olive oil
	Red-wine vinegar

In a large bowl, gently toss the tomatoes, onion, and oregano. Serve with olive oil and vinegar added to taste.

Tomatoes Stuffed with Orzo and Wild Mushrooms

YIELD: 4 SERVINGS

A splash of extra-virgin olive oil is what these tomatoes need when they're served cool as part of the *meze* table. Served warm (a brief stint in the microwave reheats them perfectly), they're also quite nice alongside grilled meat, seafood, or poultry.

---

4 medium-size, firm, ripe tomatoes
  (about 6 ounces each)
Sugar
Salt, to taste
Freshly ground black pepper, to taste
2 tablespoons regular (not extra-
  virgin) olive oil
2 tablespoons butter
1 cup coarsely chopped shiitake
  mushroom caps

1 small onion, finely chopped
  (¼ cup)
2 large garlic cloves, minced
½ cup orzo
2 cups Chicken Broth (see page 5)
2 tablespoons shredded graviera,
  kefalotiri, or Parmesan cheese
1 tablespoon chopped flat-leaf
  parsley, for garnish

Cut the tops off the tomatoes, remove the cores, and hollow out the insides, leaving about a ¼-inch shell. Lightly sprinkle the inside of each tomato with a few grains of sugar, salt, and pepper and set aside.

Heat 1 tablespoon of the olive oil and 1 tablespoon of the butter in a large skillet. When it is hot, add the mushrooms and cook over medium-high heat, stirring constantly, until soft. Remove with a slotted spoon and set aside. Add the remaining olive oil and butter to the skillet. Add the onion and cook over medium heat, stirring frequently, until softened. Add the garlic and cook, stirring, for 20 seconds longer. Stir in the orzo until each grain is well coated with the oil-and-butter mixture. Stir in 1 cup of the chicken broth and simmer slowly over medium-low heat until the liquid is absorbed. Continue to simmer slowly, gradually adding about ½ cup more of the broth until the orzo is about three-quarters cooked and still very firm to the tooth. Remove from the heat and stir in the reserved mushrooms, cheese, and parsley.

Preheat the oven to 400°F. Heat the remaining chicken broth (about ½ cup) to a boil. Spoon the orzo mixture into the prepared tomatoes, mounding the tops slightly. Arrange the tomatoes in a baking dish that is just large enough to hold them comfortably. Pour the hot chicken broth into the bottom of the baking dish. Cover the dish tightly with foil and bake for 20 minutes. Uncover and bake 10 minutes longer, basting a couple of times with the juices in the bottom of the dish. Serve warm or at room temperature, sprinkled with parsley.

Pickled Onion Rings

·e·e·e·e·

YIELD: 6 TO 8 APPETIZER SERVINGS

The Greeks are passionate about their onions—big ones, little ones, red ones, white ones, raw or cooked in almost everything. If you like the nip of raw onions, you'll enjoy these mellow, crunchy rings served just as they are on a plate of assorted appetizers, or to accompany plain grilled fish, meat, or poultry. The longer the onion rings marinate the less hot and more intensely flavored with the marinade they become.

2 large red onions (about 8 ounces each), cut into ¼-inch slices and the slices separated into rings
1½ cups boiling water
¾ cup red-wine vinegar

2 tablespoons sugar
1 tablespoon salt
⅛ teaspoon freshly ground black pepper
Chopped flat-leaf parsley, for garnish

Place the onion rings in a medium-size bowl. Combine the boiling water, vinegar, sugar, salt, and pepper in a small bowl. Pour over the onion rings. Cover and set aside at room temperature for 2 to 24 hours. Remove the onion rings with a slotted spoon to a platter. Sprinkle with parsley to serve.

An Assortment of Traditional Hot Appetizers

For diners who can't decide which of these popular hot appetizers to order, Periyali will gladly send out a handsome presentation of the zucchini fritters and both kinds of *phyllo* pies on a dinner-size plate, garnished with a few sprigs of lightly dressed Mixed Salad Greens and lemon wedges. The restaurant arranges these two-bite-size appetizers in pairs, with a small square of *feta* cheese accompanying the *tiropita,* and one or two fresh spinach leaves tucked under the *spanakopita.* The pies should be served sizzling hot, so plan ahead. (The fritters can be fried while the pies bake or reheat.)

Irene and Victor's Zucchini Fritters

KOLOKITHOKEFTES

YIELD: ABOUT 24 FRITTERS

*V*egetable fritters are encountered frequently in Greece. In most cases, they are merely pieces of vegetables, batter-dipped and fried, very tasty, but far from spectacular. On the other hand, the Gourases' version of zucchini fritters—tiny patties, formed with a thick, batterlike fusion of shredded zucchini, onion, grated cheese, mint, and other seasonings—are unique and quite unforgettable.

6 medium-size zucchini (about 3 pounds)	*2 teaspoons finely chopped fresh mint leaves*
1 small onion	*¼ cup all-purpose flour*
1 teaspoon salt	*¼ cup dry bread crumbs*
1 egg	*Granulated flour (see page 291)*
¼ cup grated kefalotiri *or Parmesan cheese*	*Regular (not extra-virgin) olive oil or vegetable oil, for frying*
¼ cup grated kasseri *or Parmesan cheese*	

Shred the zucchini and onion into a colander. Add the salt and toss together until well blended. Place the colander over a bowl. Cover with plastic wrap and allow to drain for 12 hours or overnight in the refrigerator.

Place the zucchini mixture in the center of a cotton kitchen towel and squeeze out as much of the remaining moisture as possible. Turn the mixture into a large bowl. Beat the egg in a small bowl with the cheeses and mint. Stir into the zucchini until well blended. Mix the all-purpose flour and bread crumbs on a sheet of waxed paper. Stir into the zucchini mixture, a tablespoon at a time, until the mixture holds together and can be formed into patties measur-

ing about 2 inches in diameter and ⅜ inch thick. (The fritters can be made ahead up to this point and chilled for several hours before frying.)

Just before frying, sprinkle the granulated flour on a sheet of waxed paper and lightly dredge the fritters. Pour enough oil into a large skillet to measure about ⅛ inch. When it ripples, add the fritters and fry until well browned on both sides, adjusting the heat as necessary, for 5 to 6 minutes total cooking time. The cooked fritters can be held in a 200°F oven while the remainder are being fried. Serve hot.

Cheese Pies and Spinach-and-Cheese Pies
TIROPITA AND SPANAKOPITA

Watching Edwin, the pastry chef at Periyali, turn out little spinach and cheese pies is a study in fluid and faultless motions that come with making hundreds of these delicious morsels every day. You may very well be all thumbs in your first attempts to fold sharp-edged triangles and neat rolls, but a little practice does make perfect, and even though your initial efforts may not be as geometrically precise as Edwin's, that won't affect the flavor.

Fortunately, the pies can be made and baked well ahead of serving time, and even frozen. If they are to be eaten within an hour or two, reheat in a 375°F oven for 10 minutes, or microwave on high for 30 seconds. The pies can also be baked ahead and refrigerated in a single layer, covered, until ready to serve. Allow to warm to room temperature before reheating. Or pack the baked pies carefully in a flat container with a tight-fitting lid and freeze them. Reheat the frozen pies on a baking sheet in a 375°F oven for about 15 minutes.

One more thought. If the amount of butter called for in these recipes disturbs you, Charles suggests an equal mix of Clarified Melted Butter and regular (not extra-virgin) olive oil, which will reduce the cholesterol and saturated fat considerably. The flip side of this technique is that the baked *phyllo* will not be as flaky and the exquisite buttery flavor not as pronounced.

Cheese Pies

TIROPITA

YIELD: 48 PIES; ABOUT 16 APPETIZER SERVINGS

1½ cups crumbled feta *cheese*
1 cup regular (small-curd) cottage
  cheese
2 tablespoons grated graviera *or*
  Parmesan cheese
¼ cup all-purpose flour
2 eggs

¼ teaspoon white pepper
1 package (1 pound) ultra-thin
  phyllo *dough, thawed according to*
  package directions
2 cups (4 sticks) Clarified Melted
  Butter (see page 8)

Before starting to make these pies, please read "How to Work with *Phyllo*" (see page 12).

Stir the cheeses and flour together in a medium-size bowl. Beat the eggs with the pepper in a small bowl. Add the eggs to the cheese mixture and stir hard until well blended.

Remove 24 sheets of *phyllo* from the package. (This is 4 more sheets than are needed; the extra 4 are insurance for a few that might tear.) Wrap the remaining sheets tightly in plastic wrap or foil, return to the package, and refrigerate or refreeze.

Lay the stack of 24 sheets of *phyllo,* the longest side facing you, on a large, flat work surface. Using a ruler and a pizza cutter or the tip of a sharp knife, cut the *phyllo* into 3 strips, each about

5½ inches wide. Take 12 of the strips and fold in half crosswise. Cut at the fold to make 24 pieces. Fold in half again and cut to make 48 rectangles. (These will be used as patches to reinforce the *phyllo* under the filling.)

Lay 2 strips of pastry on the work surface, short ends facing you. Brush both strips lightly and completely with butter, starting at the center and working out toward the edges. Place one of the rectangular patches, as shown, crosswise about an inch from the bottom and butter the patch. (Always remember to keep any pastry that you're not actually working with covered, as explained in "How to Work with *Phyllo*," so that it won't dry out.)

Working quickly with one strip at a time, place 1 rounded measuring teaspoonful of the filling in the center of the patch as shown. Fold the sides in over the filling; butter the folds. Starting at the

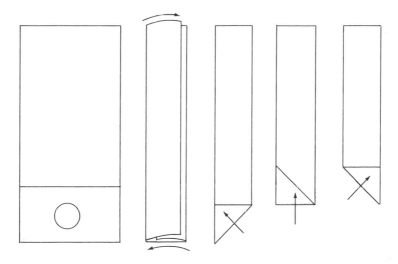

bottom, fold into a triangle shape as shown. Continue folding, making sure that with each fold the bottom edge is parallel with the alternate side edge. Lightly butter the finished triangle and place on an ungreased baking sheet. Continue until all of the cheese is used. You should have 48 triangles.

Bake in the top third of the oven for 10 minutes. Brush with butter again and continue to bake for 10 to 15 minutes, or until golden. Remove from the oven and serve immediately or cool on wire racks to be reheated later.

Spinach-and-Cheese Pies

YIELD: 48 ROLLS

1 recipe Spinach-and-Feta-Cheese
  Filling (see page 13)
1 package (1 pound) ultra-thin
  phyllo dough, thawed according to
  package directions

2 cups (4 sticks) Clarified Melted
  Butter (see page 8)

Preheat the oven to 400°F. Remove 24 sheets of *phyllo* from the package. (This is 4 more sheets than are actually needed; the extra 4 are insurance for a few that might tear.) Wrap the remaining sheets tightly in plastic wrap or foil, return to the package, and refrigerate or refreeze.

Lay the stack of 24 sheets of *phyllo,* the longest side facing you, on a large, flat work surface. Using a ruler and a pizza cutter or the tip of a sharp knife, cut the *phyllo* into 3 strips, each about 5½ inches wide. Take 12 of the strips and fold in half crosswise. Cut at the fold to make 24 pieces. Fold in half again and cut to make 48 rectangles. (These will be used as patches to reinforce the *phyllo* under the filling.)

Lay 2 strips of pastry on the work surface, short ends facing you. Brush both strips lightly and completely with butter, starting at the center and working out toward the edges. Place one of the rectangular patches, as shown, crosswise about an inch from the bottom and butter the patch. (Always remember to keep any pastry that you're not actually working with covered, as explained in "How to Work with *Phyllo,*" so that it won't dry out.)

Working quickly with one strip at a time, place 1 rounded measuring teaspoonful of the spinach-and-cheese filling in the center of the bottom of the patch. Fold the sides in over the filling; butter the folds. Roll into a cylinder shape as shown. Lightly butter the finished roll and place on an ungreased baking sheet seam side

Place the onion rings in a medium-size bowl. Combine the boiling water, vinegar, sugar, salt, and pepper in a small bowl. Pour over the onion rings. Cover and set aside at room temperature for 2 to 24 hours. Remove the onion rings with a slotted spoon to a platter. Sprinkle with parsley to serve.

An Assortment of Traditional Hot Appetizers

For diners who can't decide which of these popular hot appetizers to order, Periyali will gladly send out a handsome presentation of the zucchini fritters and both kinds of *phyllo* pies on a dinner-size plate, garnished with a few sprigs of lightly dressed Mixed Salad Greens and lemon wedges. The restaurant arranges these two-bite-size appetizers in pairs, with a small square of *feta* cheese accompanying the *tiropita,* and one or two fresh spinach leaves tucked under the *spanakopita.* The pies should be served sizzling hot, so plan ahead. (The fritters can be fried while the pies bake or reheat.)

Irene and Victor's Zucchini Fritters

KOLOKITHOKEFTES

❧❧❧❧

YIELD: ABOUT 24 FRITTERS

*V*egetable fritters are encountered frequently in Greece. In most cases, they are merely pieces of vegetables, batter-dipped and fried, very tasty, but far from spectacular. On the other hand, the Gourases' version of zucchini fritters—tiny patties, formed with a thick, batterlike fusion of shredded zucchini, onion, grated cheese, mint, and other seasonings—are unique and quite unforgettable.

---

6 medium-size zucchini (about 3 pounds)

1 small onion

1 teaspoon salt

1 egg

1/4 cup grated kefalotiri or Parmesan cheese

1/4 cup grated kasseri or Parmesan cheese

2 teaspoons finely chopped fresh mint leaves

1/4 cup all-purpose flour

1/4 cup dry bread crumbs

Granulated flour (see page 291)

Regular (not extra-virgin) olive oil or vegetable oil, for frying

---

Shred the zucchini and onion into a colander. Add the salt and toss together until well blended. Place the colander over a bowl. Cover with plastic wrap and allow to drain for 12 hours or overnight in the refrigerator.

Place the zucchini mixture in the center of a cotton kitchen towel and squeeze out as much of the remaining moisture as possible. Turn the mixture into a large bowl. Beat the egg in a small bowl with the cheeses and mint. Stir into the zucchini until well blended. Mix the all-purpose flour and bread crumbs on a sheet of waxed paper. Stir into the zucchini mixture, a tablespoon at a time, until the mixture holds together and can be formed into patties measur-

KATHLEEN H. SHELLY

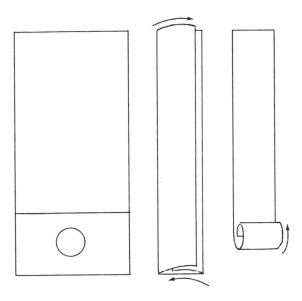

down. Continue until all of the filling is used. You should have 48 rolls.

Bake in the top third of the oven for 10 minutes. Brush with butter again and continue to bake for 10 to 15 minutes, or until golden. Remove from the oven and serve immediately or cool on wire racks to be reheated later.

Cheese Baked in Grape Leaves

YIELD: ABOUT 20 PIECES

Tart, briny grape leaves provide a good flavor and texture contrast for *manouri* cheese, which is rather rich and bland and becomes very soft and fluid when it's heated.

---

12 ounces manouri *or firm ricotta*
 (not the creamy, curd-style) cheese
20 grape leaves in brine

Extra-virgin olive oil
Lemon wedges, for garnish

Preheat the oven to 350°F. Trim off the rind, if any, and cut the cheese into cubes measuring ¾ to 1 inch.

Prepare the grape leaves as directed in "How to Work with Grape Leaves" (see page 14). Place a piece of cheese about ½ inch from the base of each leaf. Fold the bottom over the cheese, then fold in the sides and roll into a neat package. Place seam side down in a shallow baking dish that has been lightly greased or coated with nonstick vegetable spray. Repeat with the remaining cheese and grape leaves. Brush the tops of the packages with olive oil. Bake for 10 to 15 minutes until hot. Serve while still hot and melting with crusty bread and lots of freshly squeezed lemon juice.

Broiled Haloumi Cheese Seasoned with Lemon and Mint

The flavor and texture of this semi-soft, chalk-white goat's cheese from Cyprus is similar to mozzarella, although *haloumi* is more salty, and sometimes flavored with a hint of mint. *Haloumi* is usually served as a table cheese, although it's superb when grilled, fried, or broiled. The Cypriots traditionally serve chunks of *haloumi* with watermelon, a refreshing and different sort of combination to keep in mind.

1 pound haloumi *or salted
  mozzarella cheese*
3 tablespoons extra-virgin olive oil

2 tablespoons lemon juice
3 teaspoons minced fresh mint leaves

Preheat the oven broiler. Rub 6 gratin dishes with about 1 tablespoon of the olive oil and set aside. Cut the cheese into 6 equal slices. Place in the prepared dishes. Fill each cheese-filled dish with cold water, then, holding the cheese in the dish, pour off the water. Place the dishes on the oven rack about 6 inches below the source of heat. Broil for about 5 minutes, watching carefully, until golden brown and bubbly. Remove from the broiler and sprinkle each serving with 1 teaspoon olive oil, 1 teaspoon lemon juice, and ½ teaspoon mint. Serve immediately, accompanied by crusty bread.

Variation A variation as served in Cyprus: *Haloumi* can also be fried and served over crisp greens. To fry, cut the cheese into ½-inch slices. Heat ¼ inch of regular olive oil in a skillet. When it ripples, add the cheese and cook over medium-high heat for about 30 seconds on each side, or until golden. Place on a bed of greens and eat hot, drizzled with extra-virgin olive oil and lemon juice.

Saganaki

*T*his method of preparing cheese refers to the small, two-handled pan, shaped something like a gratin dish, in which it is usually cooked. Any hard cheese can be used for *saganaki*. Nicola likes hers made with *kasseri*. Steve prefers *graviera*. I like any cheese the cook cares to use, as long as it's served on a shady patio overlooking the sea. The secret to *saganaki* is to make sure the butter or olive oil is very hot and the cheese is very cold when the two meet. Frying time should be brief. Flaming the finished cheese with brandy is a nice little touch, but not done very often in Greece, except in restaurants to impress the tourists.

---

1 pound kasseri, graviera, *or*
  kefalotiri *cheese*
Cornstarch
1/2 cup (1 stick) Clarified Melted
  Butter (see page 8) or regular (not
  extra-virgin) olive oil, or a mixture
  of both, for frying

1/4 cup lemon juice
2 tablespoons brandy, heated just
  until lukewarm (optional)

Cut the cheese into four ½-inch slices. Rinse under cold water and shake to remove excess water. Sprinkle the cornstarch on a sheet of waxed paper. Dredge the cheese in the cornstarch until lightly coated. Place the cheese in the freezer for at least 30 minutes, or up to several hours, before frying. Remove from the freezer just before frying.

   Heat the clarified butter in a large nonstick skillet. When it is very hot, almost to the point of smoking, fry the cheese slices on both sides until lightly browned. Sprinkle each slice with 1 table-spoon lemon juice. Have the brandy warmed. Ignite it and pour over the cheese. Place the cheese on warm serving plates and serve immediately with a Greek Country Salad and bread.

Little Mashed-Potato Cakes from Pelion

An automobile trip around the J-shaped Pelion peninsula on the eastern coast of central Greece is a thrill-a-minute ride that's undoubtedly safer if the driver has seen the views before. The two-lane road—narrow at that—hairpins through mountains and tiny villages that cling precipitously to the steep slopes. But the drive does offer unparalleled views, often straight down into lush green valleys strewn with immense boulders, and occasional glimpses of the sea.

Although mountainous Pelion may be more notable for winter skiing and seaside retreats, it's also the place where these robust potato cakes originated. They are a blend of mashed potatoes, *tarama,* and enough bread crumbs to hold things together, the perfect concoction in which to use Nicola's Mother's Zakinthos-Style *Skordalia,* especially any that is left over.

FOR EACH CUP OF LEFTOVER SKORDALIA:
3 slices firm bread (1 ounce each)
1 tablespoon tarama *(see page 302)*
Granulated flour (see page 291),
 for dredging patties

Regular (not extra-virgin) olive oil or vegetable oil, for frying

---

Trim the crusts from the bread and discard. Tear the bread into tiny pieces and spread out on a piece of waxed paper. Set aside to dry for several hours.

Stir the *tarama* and dry bread into the refrigerator-cold *skordalia* until well blended. Form into small patties about 2 inches in diameter and ½ inch thick. (The patties can be made ahead up to this point and refrigerated for several hours before frying.)

Just before frying, sprinkle the flour on a sheet of waxed paper and lightly dredge the patties in it. Pour enough oil into a large skillet to measure about ⅛ inch. Set the skillet over medium-high heat. When the oil begins to ripple, arrange the cakes in the skillet and fry until crisp and golden brown on both sides. The patties tend to be fragile, so turn and handle them gently.

Fresh Sausage Grilled in Grape Leaves

YIELD: 8 APPETIZER SERVINGS

Although Greece is not thought of as a sausage-eating nation, in fact even the smallest town produces its own fresh and dried sausages, which are not quite the same as the sausages by the same names made in a town 15 miles away. The Greeks have never much bothered about standardization, and that means food varies a little or a lot, from region to region and even from one tiny hamlet to another.

Greek sausage is most often made from pork or beef, and sometimes from a combination of the two. Favorite seasonings include cumin and fennel seeds, onion, parsley, black pepper, and plenty of salt, and sometimes garlic, orange or lemon peel, and mint. When the sausage is shaped into cylinders, strung on a skewer, and cooked over an open fire, it becomes part of the large family of *souvlaki,* one of the world's great street foods and the specialty of tiny hole-in-the-wall restaurants found everywhere in Greece.

If you like, you can experiment with the seasonings and make a couple of variations to suit your own taste. We've also enjoyed this mixture when it has been rolled into marble-size balls and fried or baked to serve as a hot appetizer. Or fry larger cylinders of sausage and then simmer them for a little longer in tomato sauce to serve as a light, simple meal, accompanied by bread and a salad.

About 24 grape leaves
1 pound ground pork
1 small onion, minced (¼ cup)
1 tablespoon chopped flat-leaf parsley
1 teaspoon salt
1 teaspoon lightly crushed cumin seed

1 teaspoon lightly crushed fennel seed
½ teaspoon freshly ground
  black pepper
Extra-virgin olive oil
Lemon wedges

Prepare the grape leaves as directed in "How to Work with Grape Leaves" (see page 14) and set aside.

In a medium-size bowl, mix the pork, onion, parsley, salt, cumin, fennel, and pepper. Shape into 1½-inch balls and flatten slightly. Place a ball of sausage about ½ inch from the base of each leaf. Fold the bottom over the sausage, then fold in the sides and roll into a neat package. Brush each little bundle with olive oil and place folded side down on a plate to keep it from unwrapping.

Prepare a bed of medium-hot charcoal. Thread 3 wrapped meatballs on an 8-inch wooden skewer, spearing through the grape leaves in such a way as to hold them securely. Repeat with the remaining wrapped meatballs. Place the skewers on the grill about 4 inches above medium-hot coals. Cook, turning frequently, until the pork is well done, about 15 minutes. (Cut into a sausage to be sure). The unwrapped sausage can also be oven-broiled about 4 inches below the source of heat for about 15 minutes. Serve with plenty of lemon wedges.

Skewered Meat

SOUVLAKI

❧❧❧❧

YIELD: 8 APPETIZER SERVINGS

*L*ivadhia is a town in central Greece that's famous for its skewered lamb chunks and fat chickens roasted over a charcoal fire. Here dozens of little *souvlaki* places line the main street, and if no one has given you an opinion as to which ones are the best, you'll probably do just as well if you pick the one directly across the street from where you park the car. You can order these meat-strung skewers plain, or with pita bread that's been filled with cucumber and yogurt salad and chopped tomatoes and onions for a more substantial meal. The chicken comes to the table chopped into many pieces, with big wedges of lemon.

---

1 small onion, ¼ cup minced
¼ cup lemon juice or dry red wine
2 tablespoons regular (not
  extra-virgin) olive oil
½ teaspoon dried oregano
  leaves, crumbled

1 pound lean, boneless lamb or beef,
  cut into ½- to ¾-inch cubes
Salt and freshly ground black pepper,
  to taste

In a medium-size bowl, mix the onion, lemon juice, olive oil, and oregano. Add the meat and stir until well coated. Cover and refrigerate for several hours or overnight, stirring occasionally.

Prepare a bed of hot charcoal. Thread the meat tightly onto 6 six-inch skewers, dividing evenly. If oven broiling, cook about 6 inches below the source of heat for 3 to 5 minutes, or fairly close to medium-hot coals, turning frequently for 3 to 4 minutes. What you're aiming for is meat that's well browned on the outside, but still pink and juicy in the center. Season with salt and pepper and serve immediately.

Grilled Calamari

CALAMARIA TIS SCHARAS

If you have a reliable seafood merchant from whom you can obtain fresh, cleaned squid pouches, this simple appetizer goes together quickly and makes good use of the charcoal grill while you and your hungry guests are waiting impatiently for the hot coals to tame down.

---

12 small squid pouches
1/4 cup regular (not extra-virgin)
  olive oil
1/4 teaspoon dried oregano
  leaves, crumbled
2 tablespoons butter
2 tablespoons extra-virgin olive oil

2 large garlic cloves, minced
1/3 cup lemon juice
1/8 teaspoon freshly ground
  black pepper
Chopped flat-leaf parsley, for garnish

Rinse the squid pouches and pat dry on paper towels. With a pair of scissors, cut the squid down one side so that the pocketlike body can be spread flat. It will look like a little white sail. Place the squid in a large bowl and toss with regular olive oil and oregano until well coated. Set aside until ready to grill.

Prepare a bed of hot charcoal. Remove the squid from the marinade. Thread a 6-inch wooden skewer down each triangular side of the squid. (This will prevent them from curling up on the grill.) Just before grilling the squid, heat the butter and extra-virgin olive oil in a small saucepan over medium-low heat. Add the garlic and cook, stirring constantly, until the garlic is golden. Stir in the lemon juice and pepper and continue cooking until the mixture simmers. Remove from the heat and set on the edge of the grill to keep warm.

Lay the squid on the grill about 3 inches above very hot coals. Grill for 2 or 3 minutes, turning once, or just until the squid is opaque and appetizingly charred at the edges. Transfer the squid to a platter and remove the skewers. Drizzle with the hot butter sauce. Sprinkle with parsley and serve immediately with chunks of bread.

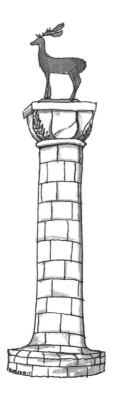

First-Course Salads and Main-Course Soups

The first thing to understand when eating Greek in Greece is that there are two courses at most— appetizers and main dishes; no dessert and no coffee—more often than not served in a rather haphazard fashion. The food comes when it's ready, or when the waiter is ready to bring it to you, just one of the charming Greek idiosyncrasies that drive foreign diners wild.

To be reasonably sure that the fried potatoes come with the grilled fish rather than with the check, order the potatoes and the fish at the same time, and don't order the fish until all of the appetizers are on the table. This method guarantees nothing, you understand, but at least there's half a chance of getting what you want when you want it.

The menu at Periyali, which reflects far less casual and more sequential eating patterns, lists appetizers and American-restaurant-style first courses together. Admittedly, some of the first courses at Periyali, although firmly rooted in home-style Greek cooking and perfectly wonderful when someone else is preparing them, may be a little much for the home cook to handle comfortably, so you may want to consider serving these as a main dish, or at least plan following courses that are reasonably simple to execute.

The Omnipresent Greek Salad

Almost without exception, it appears before every meal, usually a symphony of fresh vegetables sprinkled with pungent oregano and glistening with plenty of fragrant olive oil.

The Greek salad, famous the world over, is a very simple composite of sliced cucumber, tomato wedges, green pepper rings, chopped or slivered red onion, and little cubes of *feta* cheese, garnished with Kalamata or other juicy Greek olives and surrounded by fat lemon wedges. Sometimes the salad is served on shredded romaine lettuce, and often a few anchovy fillets are crisscrossed on top. Less often, stuffed grape leaves are added. The lemon wedges are squeezed over the salad at the table to taste. If the olive oil appears to have been added with a heavy hand, it's because the oil and juices from the lemon and vegetables left in the bottom of the dish serve a secondary purpose as a dip for chunks of bread speared with a fork. They also make a very palatable sauce when spooned over grilled fish or meat.

Greek Country Salad
CHORIATIKI

YIELD: 4 TO 6 SERVINGS

---

1 pound feta cheese

1½ English cucumbers (see page 291) or 3 regular cucumbers (about 1½ pounds)

2 medium-size ripe tomatoes, cut into wedges

1 medium-size red onion, thinly sliced and the slices separated into rings (½ cup)

1 cup Periyali's Salad Dressing (see page 66)

12 large romaine lettuce leaves (see Note)

8 anchovy fillets (optional)

16 Kalamata olives

12 green olives

Cut the *feta* cheese into small cubes and place them in a large bowl. Peel the cucumbers and slice them thinly. Add the cucumbers, tomato wedges, and onion rings to the cheese. Pour the dressing over the cheese mixture and toss gently until well mixed.

Arrange the lettuce leaves on a large platter. Spoon the cheese mixture over the lettuce. Lay the anchovies over the salad and garnish with the olives.

NOTE: The lettuce can be torn into bite-size pieces, if you prefer. In that case, you will need about 6 cups of torn lettuce.

Periyali's Mixed Salad Greens

The salad greens at Periyali can vary slightly from day to day depending on what's in season and impeccably fresh at the market. Charles prefers a combination of mild and peppery varieties, such as rocket (arugula), frisée (a light green, spidery endive), radicchio, and sometimes red-leaf lettuce. Lamb's lettuce (mâche) and watercress would also be delicious.

When choosing greens, always try to achieve a harmonious balance of colors, flavors, and textures. Rinse the greens in plenty of cold water. Drain thoroughly and wrap loosely in a cotton towel. Store in the crisper section of the refrigerator for no more than a couple of days. To serve, tear the greens into bite-size pieces, but not so small that they lose their shape and identity. Shortly before serving, toss with just enough dressing so that each leaf glistens.

For each cup of loosely packed greens you will need about 2 teaspoons of dressing.

Periyali's Salad Dressing

¼ cup Chicken Broth (see page 5)
1 tablespoon red-wine vinegar
1 teaspoon balsamic vinegar
1 tablespoon lemon juice
½ cup plus 2 tablespoons regular
   (not extra-virgin) olive oil
⅓ cup extra-virgin olive oil
¾ teaspoon minced fresh thyme or
   ⅛ teaspoon dried thyme
   leaves, crumbled

¾ teaspoon minced fresh oregano or
   ⅛ teaspoon dried oregano
   leaves, crumbled
½ teaspoon minced flat-leaf parsley
½ teaspoon minced chives
¾ teaspoon salt
Pinch white pepper

Bring the chicken broth to a boil in a small saucepan. Reduce the heat and simmer until reduced by half, to about 2 tablespoons. Remove from the heat and pour into a medium-size bowl; set aside until just warm. Stir in the vinegars and lemon juice. Begin adding a mixture of the oils, drop by drop at first and then in a thin, steady stream, beating constantly with a wire whisk until the mixture thickens. Beat in the herbs, salt, and pepper. Cover and store in the refrigerator. Bring to room temperature and beat lightly to remix before using.

Sautéed Wild Mushrooms Served over Mixed Greens

The Greeks have as vast and varied a selection of wild mushrooms as France, Italy, or any other European country. Even porcini mushrooms grow there—and probably truffles, too, if anyone ever bothered to look—but many Greeks are convinced that porcini are poisonous, so there's no point in trying to convince them otherwise.

As with *horta,* the wild field greens, it takes years of experience to know which of the hundreds of mushroom varieties growing prolifically in Greece during the fall and winter are edible and flavorful.

Unfortunately, the Greek repertoire of mushroom preparations is limited. Usually they are simply pickled, or floured and fried. Occasionally, whatever varieties have been collected are chopped and fried and served over wild greens, the humble origin of this elegant first-course salad.

1¼ pounds of a mixed variety of mushrooms (shiitake, crimini, white trumpet, chanterelle, golden oak, oyster, or whatever is available and looks fresh)
Regular (not extra-virgin) olive oil
Vegetable oil

1 small red onion, thinly sliced and the slices separated into rings
2 tablespoons red-wine vinegar
Salt and freshly ground black pepper, to taste
Periyali's Mixed Salad Greens, lightly dressed (see page 65)

Keep the different varieties of mushrooms separate as you work with them, since each variety requires a slightly different cooking time.

Rinse the mushrooms briefly in cool water and pat dry on paper towels, or wipe with damp paper towels. Gently twist off the shiitake stems and discard them. Trim away any parts of the mushrooms that look dry and unappetizing. Thinly slice each variety.

Heat about a tablespoon each of the olive oil and vegetable oil in a large skillet. When it is hot, add one of the mushroom varieties and cook over high heat, stirring and tossing just until lightly browned. Don't allow the mushrooms to cook down too much. In most cases 2 or 3 minutes total cooking time should do it. Turn the mushrooms into a large bowl. Repeat this procedure with the remaining mushrooms, placing them all together in the bowl after they are cooked.

Add a little more olive oil to the skillet, just enough to coat the bottom. When it is hot, add the onion rings and cook over medium-high heat, stirring almost constantly, until the rings are soft and brown, adjusting the heat as necessary. Remove the skillet from the heat and stir in the vinegar. Return the mushrooms to the pan and mix with the onion rings until well blended. Season to taste with salt and pepper.

To serve, divide the greens among 4 salad plates. Spoon the warm mushrooms over the greens and serve immediately.

Skewered Marinated Swordfish with Vegetables
XIFIAS SOUVLAKI

YIELD: 16 SKEWERS; 8 FIRST-COURSE SERVINGS

Both tuna and mako shark are very satisfactory substitutes for swordfish, since the dense, almost meatlike flesh of all three is not likely to fall apart when it's grilled. We think that swordfish and shark taste best when cooked until just done through, but tuna can be served on the rare side, if you like.

1 swordfish steak weighing about 1½
  pounds, cut into ¾-inch cubes
1 large red bell pepper, cored, seeded,
  and cut into ¾-inch squares
1 large green bell pepper, cored,
  seeded, and cut into ¾-inch squares
1 medium-size red onion, separated
  into layers and the layers cut
  into ¾-inch squares
1 medium-size zucchini, cut into
  ¼-inch slices and the slices cut
  into quarters

¼ cup lemon juice
Salt and freshly ground black pepper,
  to taste
1½ teaspoons minced fresh oregano
  or ½ teaspoon dried oregano leaves,
  crumbled
¾ cup extra-virgin olive oil
Eggplant and Semolina
  (see page 171)

Alternately thread the swordfish and vegetables onto sixteen 8-inch bamboo skewers, starting and ending with a piece of fish, and placing 3 pieces of each kind of vegetable between each piece of fish. Each skewer should contain 4 pieces of fish and 3 sets of the vegetable combinations. As they are finished, place the skewers in a large, shallow pan.

In a medium-size bowl, mix the lemon juice, salt, pepper, and oregano. Gradually beat in the olive oil until well blended. Generously brush this mixture onto all sides of the skewered fish and vegetables. Cover and refrigerate for at least 2 or 3 hours—12 hours is better.

Prepare a bed of hot charcoal, or preheat the oven broiler. Place the skewers on the grill about 3 inches above the coals, or 4 to 6 inches below the heat source, for about 5 minutes, turning to cook evenly, or until firm and just done through. Serve hot or at room temperature accompanied by a spoonful of Eggplant and Semolina.

Grilled Chicken and Fennel Brochettes

KOTOPOULO SOUVLAKI

YIELD: 8 FIRST-COURSE SERVINGS

*I*t's the dark meat of the thighs that makes these grilled chunks of chicken so moist and tender. If you want to, you can substitute breast meat for the thighs, but the grilling and baking time have to be reduced slightly, since white meat dries out and toughens quickly. Searing the brochettes over hot charcoal for flavor before oven-finishing them is a restaurant technique we explain at the end of this recipe. The brochettes can be finished over charcoal, if you like, although the intensity and irregularity of charcoal heat makes it difficult to cook the chicken evenly.

---

8 boneless chicken thighs
  (about 1½ pounds)
MARINADE
½ cup regular (not extra-virgin)
  olive oil
¼ cup extra-virgin olive oil
¼ cup lemon juice
3 tablespoons minced fresh oregano or
  1 tablespoon dried oregano leaves,
  crumbled
FENNEL
2 large fennel bulbs

3 cups water
1 tablespoon lemon juice
2 teaspoons salt
SAUCE
1 cup Chicken Broth (see page 5)
2 tablespoons extra-virgin olive oil
2 tablespoons lemon juice
1 teaspoon chopped flat-leaf parsley
1 teaspoon dried oregano leaves,
  crumbled
Eggplant and Semolina (see page
  171)

Remove the skin from the thighs and discard it. Cut each thigh into 4 equal pieces. In a medium-size bowl, mix the ingredients for the marinade. Toss the chicken pieces in the marinade until well coated. Cover and refrigerate for 4 to 24 hours—the longer the better—stirring occasionally.

Rinse the fennel; cut off the spindly ribs and about ½ inch from the root end. Separate the bulbs into layers. Cut the layers into 1¼-inch squares to make 24 pieces. Bring the water with the lemon juice and salt to a boil in a medium-size saucepan. Drop in the fennel and boil for 1 minute. Drain into a colander and rinse with cool water. Cover and refrigerate until ready to proceed.

To make the sauce, combine the chicken broth, olive oil, lemon juice, parsley, and oregano in a small saucepan. Bring to a boil and simmer until reduced by about half. Set aside until ready to proceed.

Alternately thread 4 pieces of chicken and 3 pieces of fennel onto an 8-inch wooden skewer, beginning and ending with the chicken. Season lightly with salt and pepper. Repeat with the remaining chicken and fennel pieces to make 8 brochettes.

RESTAURANT TECHNIQUE FOR CHARCOAL SEARING: Prepare a bed of hot charcoal. Place the skewers on the grill about 4 inches above the coals for about 5 minutes, turning to sear evenly. Remove from the grill and set aside until ready to finish in the oven, following the directions given below.

TECHNIQUE FOR OVEN SEARING: Preheat the oven broiler. Pat the chicken dry (it won't sear as nicely otherwise) on paper towels and arrange the skewers in the bottom of a broiling pan. Broil as close to the source of heat as possible for about 5 minutes, turning to sear all sides. (The brochettes can also be seared on an electric or stove-top grill, following the manufacturer's instructions.)

OVEN FINISHING: Preheat or reduce the oven temperature to 400°F and transfer the baking pan to a lower rack. (If the brochettes have been charcoal- or grill-seared, place the skewers in the bottom of a broiling pan.) Pour the sauce into the pan with the brochettes. Bake for about 20 minutes, turning occasionally, until the chicken is cooked through and the sauce is reduced slightly. Push the chicken and fennel off the skewers onto serving plates. Serve warm accompanied by a spoonful of Eggplant and Semolina.

Seared Quail with Spinach and Wild Mushrooms

ORTYKIA

YIELD: 6 FIRST-COURSE SERVINGS

*M*any of Periyali's patrons are so taken with this first course that they call to make sure it will be on the menu (it usually is) before they make reservations. This is a somewhat time-consuming preparation to serve as a first course, even if someone else bones the tiny birds for you, but it is not difficult. If you like, try it as a main course for four rather than a first course for six. In that case, serve two quails per person and add another half pound or so of mushrooms. The other ingredients remain the same. Using frozen spinach saves time, but as long as you're going to the trouble and expense of preparing a recipe of this caliber, why not take a little more trouble and use fresh spinach?

Speaking of money, the price of quail varies a lot. If purchased fresh from a specialty butcher, the wee birds are likely to cost nearly twice as much as they would if you can find them frozen in a Greek or Middle Eastern grocery store, where they're more ordinary fare and not considered such a delicacy.

---

6 quail, each weighing
  about 6 ounces
1 tablespoon minced fresh thyme
  leaves or 1 teaspoon dried
  thyme leaves, crumbled
1 tablespoon minced fresh oregano
  or 1 teaspoon dried oregano
  leaves, crumbled
2 scallions, finely chopped
  (2 tablespoons)
2 tablespoons chopped
  flat-leaf parsley

1/2 cup extra-virgin olive oil
2 pounds fresh spinach or 2 packages
  (10 ounces each) frozen
  whole-leaf spinach
1/4 cup plus 2 tablespoons regular
  (not extra-virgin) olive oil
Salt, to taste
Freshly ground black pepper, to taste
1/2 pound shiitake mushrooms
2 tablespoons butter
Crumbled feta cheese (optional)

Bone the quail, or ask the butcher to do it for you. To bone the birds yourself, cut the backbone away with poultry shears and lay the quail out flat, skin side down. With a small, sharp knife, carefully remove the breast and collar bones, rib cage, and the thigh bone in each leg. Cut off the wing tips. (The quail is so tiny that, if you'd rather, you can simply cut out the backbone, remove the wing tips, and flatten the bird as much as possible with the heel of your hand. However, when done this way the birds will be more difficult to eat and will not be quite as attractive.)

Place the quail in one layer in a shallow pan, skin side down. Sprinkle evenly with thyme, oregano, scallions, and parsley and drizzle with the extra-virgin olive oil. Cover and marinate in the refrigerator for several hours or overnight, turning occasionally.

Wash the spinach in several changes of cold water and cut away the tough stems. (If using frozen spinach, thaw and drain in a colander, pressing down with the back of a spoon to remove the excess liquid.) Heat 2 tablespoons of the regular olive oil in a large skillet. Add half of the spinach and cook over high heat, stirring constantly, until well cooked down. Remove from the skillet and set aside. Heat another 2 tablespoons of oil and repeat with the remaining spinach. (If using frozen spinach, it can be cooked all at once in 2 tablespoons of oil.) Return the reserved spinach to the skillet. Season lightly with salt and pepper and set aside.

Remove the stems from the mushrooms and discard. Rinse the caps and pat dry on paper towels. Cut the caps into ¼-inch slices. Heat the remaining 2 tablespoons of oil and the butter in the same skillet over high heat. When it is hot, add the mushrooms and cook over high heat, stirring almost constantly, until limp. Season lightly with salt and pepper and set aside.

Preheat the oven broiler. Remove the quail from the marinade and pat dry with paper towels. Arrange on the rack of a broiling pan skin side down. Season lightly with salt and pepper. (Place the pans containing the spinach and the mushrooms over very low heat to rewarm while searing the quail.) Broil the quail about 4 inches below the source of heat for 3 to 4 minutes on the first side and about 3 minutes on the second side, or until the birds feel firm when pressed with a finger. (If the quail are not boned, cooking time may be a minute or so longer.)

To serve, place the spinach on a serving platter or divide evenly among dinner plates. Place the quail on the spinach and divide the mushrooms evenly over each serving. Sprinkle very lightly with crumbled *feta* cheese, if desired.

Sautéed Sweetbreads Served over Warm Giant Beans

GLIKADAKIA

YIELD: 4 FIRST-COURSE SERVINGS; 2 MAIN-COURSE SERVINGS

The combination of supernal sweetbreads and very uncelestial dried beans may seem incongruous, but the results are delectable. Because there's a lot to do to complete this dish at the last moment, it's a good idea to keep the main course simple. You can also take the easy way out and serve this as a main dish for two. Or double all of the ingredients to serve four.

1 pound sweetbreads
1 tablespoon red-wine vinegar
1 tablespoon salt

WARM BEANS
1/2 cup Chicken Broth (see page 5)
1 tablespoon extra-virgin olive oil
1/4 teaspoon pressed garlic
Salt, to taste (depending on the saltiness of the broth)
Freshly ground black pepper, to taste
2 cups cooked Giant White Beans (see page 9)
2 teaspoons chopped flat-leaf parsley

FINISHING
Salt and freshly ground black pepper, to taste
Granulated flour (see page 291), for dredging sweetbreads
2 tablespoons regular (not extra-virgin) olive oil
1 tablespoon butter
1 tablespoon red-wine vinegar
3/4 cup Chicken Broth
2 teaspoons extra-virgin olive oil
2 teaspoons chopped flat-leaf parsley, for garnish

Rinse the sweetbreads, then cover them with cold water in a medium-size saucepan. Add the vinegar and salt. Bring to a simmer over medium-high heat. Adjust the heat so that the water barely moves for 15 minutes. Drain and immediately cover the sweetbreads with cold water, adding a few ice cubes so that they will cool quickly. When the sweetbreads have cooled, drain them and pull off any loose pieces of the thin membrane that covers them; also trim away any little chunks of white fat. Be careful when you do this, since the sweetbreads should not be pulled apart any more than necessary. Place the sweetbreads on a plate. Cover with plastic wrap and weight with something heavy, for instance another plate with a heavy can set on top. Refrigerate overnight or for up to 24 hours, during which time the sweetbreads will flatten and give up their excess liquid.

Shortly before serving time, prepare the beans. Place the broth, olive oil, garlic, salt, and pepper in a large skillet. Bring to a boil over high heat and stir in the cooked beans. Reduce the heat until the broth simmers. Continue to cook, stirring, until most of the liquid has been absorbed. Add the parsley and toss to mix. Set aside and keep warm while cooking the sweetbreads.

Pat the sweetbreads dry on paper towels and cut into ¼-inch slices. Sprinkle sparingly with salt and pepper and dredge lightly in flour. Heat the regular olive oil in a large skillet over high heat. When it is very hot, add the sweetbread slices. Add the butter and cook over medium-high heat, turning once, until the sweetbreads are golden brown. Remove the sweetbreads from the pan with a slotted spoon. Divide the warm beans among 4 plates. Arrange the sweetbread slices over the beans, dividing evenly. Swirl the vinegar into the hot skillet. Stir in the broth and extra-virgin olive oil. Cook over high heat, stirring frequently, until reduced to about ¼ cup. Pour over the sweetbread slices and sprinkle with parsley.

Sautéed Chicken Livers Served over Warm Lentils

SIKOTAKIA ME FAKES

YIELD: 6 FIRST-COURSE SERVINGS; 3 TO 4 MAIN-COURSE
SERVINGS

It's not absolutely necessary to soak the livers in milk, but Charles believes that this step helps to draw out any inherent bitterness in the livers and gives them a sweeter, more delicate flavor. If you should decide to serve this as a main course for four, you might want to add a few more livers.

LIVERS

1 pound large chicken livers

1 cup milk

Salt and freshly ground black pepper,
  to taste

1/4 cup granulated flour (see
  page 291)

1/4 cup regular (not extra-virgin)
  olive oil

Chopped flat-leaf parsley, for garnish

LENTILS

1 cup dry lentils

4 cups water

2 teaspoons salt

1/4 cup extra-virgin olive oil

3 tablespoons shredded onion

2 tablespoons shredded carrot

1 small garlic clove, minced

1/8 teaspoon freshly ground black
  pepper

Rinse the livers and trim away any little pieces of membrane and yellow fat that may cling to them. Cut the livers in half and place them in a medium-size bowl. Stir in the milk. Cover and refrigerate for several hours or overnight.

Pick through the lentils, removing any foreign matter. Place them in a medium-size saucepan and cover by about ½ inch with cold water. Bring to a boil over high heat. Reduce the heat and simmer for about 2 minutes. Drain the lentils into a strainer and rinse very well. Rinse the saucepan and return the lentils to it. Add the water and 1½ teaspoons of the salt. Bring to a boil over high heat. Reduce the heat and simmer for 10 to 12 minutes, or until just tender. (The lentils should still have a little "bite" left in them.) Drain and set aside.

Heat the extra-virgin olive oil in a large skillet over high heat. Add the onion, carrot, and garlic and cook over medium-high heat, stirring frequently, until softened. Add the lentils and the remaining ½ teaspoon salt and the pepper, stirring until well blended. Set aside while cooking the livers.

Remove the livers from the milk and pat dry on paper towels. Season lightly with salt and pepper. Sprinkle the flour on a piece of waxed paper. Roll the livers in the flour until lightly coated.

Heat the regular olive oil in a large skillet over high heat. When it is hot, add the livers and cook over medium-high heat for 1 or 2 minutes on each side, or until golden brown. Reduce the heat and continue cooking and turning until the livers are firm and just cooked through, about 3 minutes.

To serve, divide the lentils among 6 plates. Arrange the livers on top, dividing evenly. Drizzle a little extra-virgin olive oil over each serving and sprinkle with parsley.

Pan-Seared Scallops and Fennel

YIELD: 4 FIRST-COURSE SERVINGS

When this dish is served at Periyali, the scallops are seared for a few seconds on the grill, which gives them those appetizing grid marks and a decidedly distinctive flavor. But we question whether or not it's worth lighting the charcoal grill for such a small job, so we seared the scallops in a very hot skillet and it worked quite well. (You could also use an electric or stove-top grill.) We would also recommend this salad (which, as it happens, is as healthful as it is delicious) as the main course for lunch or a light supper.

1/4 cup extra-virgin olive oil
2 tablespoons lemon juice
1 teaspoon minced fresh thyme, or
   1/4 teaspoon dried thyme leaves,
   crumbled
6 very large sea scallops, cut into
   1/4-inch, horizontal slices
1/4 cup Chicken Broth (see page 5)
2 small fennel bulbs, trimmed and
   cut into thin vertical slices (about
   3 cups)

1 large ripe tomato, seeded and finely
   chopped (1 cup)
1 English cucumber (see page 291),
   cut in half lengthwise and the halves
   cut into very thin slices
1 tablespoon chopped fresh dill
Dill sprigs, for garnish

Mix 3 tablespoons of the olive oil with the lemon juice and thyme in a small bowl. Add the scallop slices and toss until well coated with the oil mixture. Cover and place in the refrigerator for up to 24 hours (the longer the better), stirring occasionally.

Place the chicken broth, the remaining tablespoon of oil, and the fennel in a large skillet. Bring to a simmer over medium-high heat. Reduce the heat and simmer gently until the fennel is crisp-tender. Remove the fennel with a slotted spoon to a large bowl with the tomato, cucumber, and chopped dill. Reduce the juices remaining in the skillet over high heat until they are syrupy. Remove from the heat and set aside to cool. Pour the cooled pan juices over the fennel and tomato mixture and toss gently until well blended. Divide the fennel mixture among 4 salad plates. Brush a little of the scallop marinade on the cooking surface of an electric or stove-top grill, or in the bottom of a large, nonstick skillet. Set the grill for high heat, or the stove-top grill or skillet over medium-high heat. When it is very hot, add the scallop slices and sear briefly on both sides. Arrange on the salads, dividing evenly, and serve immediately garnished with dill sprigs.

Baby Artichokes with Wild Mushrooms

YIELD: 4 FIRST-COURSE SERVINGS

*U*npretentious combinations of certain foods, such as this salad, are taken for granted by the Greeks and are served quite routinely. The presentations may not always be *haute,* but the ingredients are, more often than not, immaculately fresh and certainly innovative.

---

8 baby artichokes
Cut lemon, for rubbing artichokes
1 cup Olive Oil and Lemon Dressing
  (see page 233)
½ pound shiitake mushrooms
2 tablespoons regular (not extra-virgin) olive oil

1 garlic clove, put through a
  garlic press
Salt, to taste
Freshly ground black pepper, to taste
4 cups chopped romaine lettuce
Chopped flat-leaf parsley, for garnish

Rinse and drain the artichokes. Bend back the outer green leaves and snap them off at the base until you reach a point where the leaves are half green (at the top) and half yellow. Cut off the top cone of leaves at the point where the yellow color meets the green. Cut the stem even with the base, then cut in half and in quarters vertically. If there are any purple or pink leaves visible, cut them out. Rub the exposed areas of the artichoke with lemon juice.

In a large saucepan, bring enough salted water to a boil to cover the artichokes. When the water boils, drop in the artichokes. Reduce the heat, cover and simmer until tender, 8 to 10 minutes; drain. While the artichokes are still warm, marinate in the dressing for at least 30 minutes at room temperature.

Twist the mushroom stems to remove them from the caps and discard. Wipe the caps with damp paper towels and cut into ¼-inch strips. Heat the olive oil in a large skillet over high heat. When the oil ripples, add the mushroom strips and cook over high heat, stirring and tossing, until limp. Add the garlic and continue to cook, stirring constantly, for 30 seconds. Remove from the heat and season with the salt and pepper. To serve, divide the lettuce among 4 salad plates. Arrange the artichokes with the dressing and mushrooms over the lettuce, dividing evenly. Sprinkle with parsley and serve immediately.

Red Onions and Rocket

YIELD: 4 FIRST-COURSE SERVINGS

Glorious big bunches of peppery rocket (also known as arugula) and freshly pulled red onions, lying side by side on a stand at a city green market, inspired this marriage of two popular Greek ingredients. The composition of bright green rocket leaves and magenta onion slices, sprinkled with snowy *feta*, is as tasty as it is eye-appealing.

2 large red onions, cut into thin
  vertical slices (2 cups)
1/4 cup extra-virgin olive oil
2 tablespoons red-wine vinegar
1/4 teaspoon salt
1/8 teaspoon freshly ground black
  pepper

1/2 teaspoon minced fresh
  oregano leaves
1 bunch rocket (arugula), trimmed,
  rinsed, and drained
1/2 cup crumbled feta cheese
  (optional)

Scatter the onion slices on a large platter. In a small bowl, beat the olive oil, vinegar, salt, and pepper until well blended; pour over the onions. Set aside at room temperature for about 1 hour, occasionally turning the onions in the dressing. Just before serving, scatter the oregano and rocket leaves over the onions; mix briefly. Sprinkle the *feta* cheese over the salad, if desired, and serve immediately before the greens begin to wilt.

Watermelon with Red Onions and Mint

Watermelon is a favorite summertime refreshment in Greece, where it's often used as an ingredient rather than simply being sliced and served as is. At first bite, the combination of watermelon and onion is somewhat startling to Americans who are accustomed to adding nothing more to their watermelon than maybe a light dusting of salt.

---

1 seedless watermelon or piece of watermelon, weighing about 6 pounds

1 medium-size red onion cut into very thin vertical slivers (about 1/2 cup)

1/2 cup minced fresh mint leaves

1/4 cup plus 2 tablespoons regular (not extra-virgin) olive oil

3 tablespoons red-wine vinegar

1/4 teaspoon salt

1/4 teaspoon freshly ground black pepper

Rocket (arugula) leaves

Cut the watermelon into 1-inch slices. Trim away the rind and cut the flesh into 1-inch cubes. You should have about 8 cups. Place the cubes in a large bowl with the onion and mint and toss gently. (The recipe can be made ahead up to this point and chilled for an hour or two, but no longer, before serving.) Mix the olive oil, vinegar, salt, and pepper in a small bowl. Just before serving, pour over the watermelon mixture and toss gently. Serve over rocket leaves.

"Wondrous Curls"

These were the poetic words that the writer Athenaeus used long ago to describe octopus tentacles, a culinary delicacy dear to the heart of every Greek. So dear, in fact, that if Periyali were located in a Greek seaside village, most likely there would be a clothesline strung across the garden, draped with an octopus or two drying in the summer sun.

Not too long ago, when this eight-legged cephalopod was much more abundant in Greek waters, it was commonplace to see fishermen and their families beating octopus against a rock or a pier to tenderize it. Forty whacks has presumably always been the prescribed number, but many Greeks say that this merciless beating should go on for at least thirty minutes. Nowadays, mechanical tenderization has all but replaced this once-necessary custom, at least in the United States, where fresh and frozen octopus is sold ready to cook, meaning that it has been mechanically tenderized and the innards and ink sac have been cleaned out of the head. (If you should happen to come upon an octopus straight out of the deep, you're on your own, except that some experts say that beating isn't necessary for very small octopuses, and that freezing an octopus before it's cooked will have the same tenderizing effect.

Octopus in Red-Wine Marinade Grilled over Charcoal
OKTAPODI SCHARAS

YIELD: 4 APPETIZER SERVINGS

Grilled octopus is undoubtedly the most popular (and famous) first course at Periyali. This is a dish not often served in American

restaurants, and when it is, more often than not it's disappointingly tough and dry. Grilled octopus is daily fare at Periyali, where care is taken to make sure that every order comes to the table warm, tender, and juicy, with plenty of extra wine sauce to mop up with chunks of bread.

Eating octopus for the first time is a little like eating snails for the first time. But once they've mustered the courage to try it, most American diners, who initially find curly tentacles and suction cups more than a little off-putting, keep coming back for more.

---

2 ready-to-cook octopuses, weighing about 2 pounds each

4 medium-size carrots, chopped (2 cups)

3 small celery ribs, chopped (1 cup)

1 medium-size onion, chopped (½ cup)

2 bay leaves

1 tablespoon salt

½ teaspoon peppercorns

1 teaspoon dried thyme leaves, crumbled

1 teaspoon dried oregano leaves, crumbled

2½ cups dry red wine

4 cups water

MARINADE

2 tablespoons extra-virgin olive oil

2 tablespoons red-wine vinegar

2 tablespoons dry red wine

½ teaspoon dried thyme leaves, crumbled

½ teaspoon dried oregano leaves, crumbled

½ teaspoon salt

⅛ teaspoon freshly ground black pepper

SAUCE

1½ cups strained octopus cooking broth

⅓ cup extra-virgin olive oil

1 tablespoon lemon juice

1 teaspoon red-wine vinegar

3 tablespoons butter

1 teaspoon finely chopped flat-leaf parsley

GARNISH

Chopped flat-leaf parsley

Lemon wedges

Cut the top part of the head off the octopus and discard it. Rinse the lower part of the head with the attached tentacles in cool water. Place the octopus in a 5- or 6-quart Dutch oven or other large, heavy saucepan, tentacles first. Add the carrots, celery, onion, bay leaves, salt, peppercorns, thyme, oregano, wine, and water. Bring to a slow boil. Lower the heat, cover, and simmer very gently for 25 minutes. Test the octopus for tenderness with a kitchen fork, which should meet little resistance. If the octopus seems tough, continue to simmer for about 10 minutes, or until tender. Remove from the heat and cool the octopus in the cooking broth. Remove the octopus from the broth and cut the tentacles off close to the body, discarding the body. Strain off 1½ cups of the cooking broth to make the sauce later; cover and refrigerate. Reserve the remaining broth. Remove the purplish skin from the tentacles, which tends to be bitter, by rubbing and pushing it off, rinsing the tentacles occasionally in the cooking broth. The skin will come off rather easily, except around the suction cups, where it can be left on. As the tentacles are cleaned, rinse them in the broth, drain, and place them in a medium-size bowl. Add the marinade ingredients and stir to coat. Cover and refrigerate for at least 24 hours, although 2 or 3 days would not be too long, stirring occasionally.

Shortly before serving, make the sauce by combining the reserved cooking broth, olive oil, lemon juice, and vinegar in a medium-size saucepan. Cook over high heat, whisking frequently, until the sauce is reduced by about half. As the sauce begins to thicken, whisk constantly to help it thicken. Off the heat, whisk in the butter until melted; stir in the parsley.

Prepare a bed of medium-hot charcoal. Remove the tentacles from the marinade and blot dry on paper towels. Grill close to the coals, turning frequently, just until heated through, about 4 minutes total grilling time. The tentacles may also be oven-broiled. To serve, arrange 2 tentacles on each of 4 plates. Spoon the sauce over each serving, dividing evenly. Sprinkle with chopped parsley and serve with lemon wedges and plenty of crusty bread to soak up the sauce.

Crisp Calamari Served on Mixed Greens

CALAMARAKIA TIGANITA

YIELD: 4 FIRST-COURSE SERVINGS

*I*f you have a reliable source for seafood, where you can be sure that the cleaned squid is immaculately fresh, then this is a first course that comes together very rapidly, since there's nothing to do except cut the pouches into rings and fry them. At Periyali the warm rings and pretty little tentacles, which look like stars after they're fried, are arranged over mixed greens, but they're also wonderful when served plain with *skordalia* or *taramosalata* on the side for dipping. And should you decide to double or triple the recipe and serve this as a main course, we assure you no one will complain.

1½ pounds fresh squid, or 12 ounces of pouches and 4 ounces of tentacles, if using cleaned squid

Salt and ground white pepper, to taste

Granulated flour (see page 291)

Regular (not extra-virgin) olive oil or vegetable oil or a mixture of both, for frying

Periyali's Mixed Salad Greens, lightly dressed (see page 65)

Lemon wedges, for garnish

If necessary, clean the squid as described on page 301. Rinse the cleaned squid and pat dry on paper towels. You should have about 12 ounces of cleaned pouches and 4 ounces of tentacles. Cut the pouches crosswise into ¼-inch rings. Lightly season the rings and the tentacles with salt and pepper and dust lightly with the flour.

Pour the oil into a medium-size skillet to a depth of about ½ inch. Set the skillet over medium-high heat until the oil temperature registers about 365°F on a deep-fry thermometer. Carefully lower a few pieces of the squid into the hot oil. It will bubble and splatter, so be careful. As they fry, turn the pieces once or twice until they are pale gold. Remove from the oil with a slotted spoon to a plate lined with paper towels. Keep warm in a 200°F oven while frying the remaining squid. Serve over the greens and garnish with lemon wedges.

Snails with Garlic, Spinach, and Feta

YIELD: 4 FIRST-COURSE SERVINGS

Tons of Greek snails are shipped annually to France and Belgium. The Greeks love them, too, and serve snails every which way, sometimes stewed in a zesty tomato sauce, other times just steamed with a squirt of lemon juice. The following preparation appeals particularly to American diners, who are known to appreciate a few snails with their garlic.

---

1 can (7 ounces) of 24 snails,
  drained
2 tablespoons lemon juice
1 pound fresh spinach or 1 package
  (10 ounces) frozen chopped spinach,
  thawed

¼ cup extra-virgin olive oil
2 scallions, thinly sliced, including
  some of the green tops
4 large garlic cloves, minced
1 cup crumbled feta cheese
Lemon wedges, for garnish

Preheat the oven to 425°F. Thoroughly rinse the snails in a sieve under cool running water and pat dry on paper towels. In a small bowl, toss the snails with the lemon juice and set aside. Rinse the spinach in several changes of cold water and drain in a colander. Trim away any tough stems and chop coarsely. (If using frozen spinach, place the thawed spinach in a colander or sieve and press down on it with the back of a spoon to extract most of the liquid; set aside.) Lightly grease 4 individual gratin dishes and set aside.

Heat 2 tablespoons of the olive oil in a large skillet. When it is hot, add the scallions and cook over medium-high heat, stirring constantly, until softened. Stir in the garlic and cook 1 minute longer, or until softened. Add the spinach and cook over medium heat, stirring, for 1 minute. Remove from the heat and stir in the snails. Divide the snail mixture evenly among the prepared dishes. Sprinkle each serving with the remaining 2 tablespoons of oil and *feta* cheese, dividing evenly.

Bake for about 10 minutes, or until the cheese has melted and started to bubble. Serve immediately with crusty bread and wedges of lemon.

Steamed Clams from Kos

YIELD: 4 TO 6 FIRST-COURSE SERVINGS

These clams come from Kos and undoubtedly many other islands, too, where immaculately fresh, briny clams are steamed and served with a thick, lemony sauce instead of the melted butter most Americans consider mandatory.

---

*2 dozen littleneck clams, the smaller
  the better*
½ cup water

*1 cup Thick Lemon Sauce for Fish
  and Shellfish (see page 233)*

Scrub the clams with a brush under cold, running water. Place them in a large, heavy saucepan with a tight-fitting lid. Add the water, cover tightly, and bring to a boil over medium-high heat. Reduce the heat and steam for about 8 minutes, stirring occasionally, until the shells open wide. Drain the clams and place on a large platter, discarding any that do not open. Spoon a little sauce onto each clam and serve the remainder on the side. Any leftover lemon sauce can be stirred into the clam juices that accumulate in the bottom of the serving platter and mopped up with chunks of crusty bread.

Mussels Steamed with Ouzo
MYDIA NISSIOTIKA

❧❧❧❧

YIELD: 4 FIRST-COURSE SERVINGS

This is a favorite recipe for mussels on the Greek islands. It's the islanders' version of the French *moules à la marinière* and every bit as delicious, the anise-flavored *ouzo* being just as complementary to the mussels as a dry white wine, perhaps even more so. Little-neck clams can be substituted for the mussels with the same good results.

2¹/2 pounds small mussels
¹/2 cup extra-virgin olive oil
3 garlic cloves, thinly sliced

¹/2 cup ouzo
3 tablespoons chopped flat-leaf
   parsley

Rinse the mussels under cold running water. Scrape off any loose barnacles and the beards with a small, sharp knife. Place the mussels in a large bowl and cover with cold water. Set aside to soak for about an hour. Drain thoroughly just before cooking.

Heat the olive oil in a Dutch oven or other large, heavy saucepan over medium-high heat. When it is hot, add the garlic and cook, stirring, until soft and just ready to turn golden. Add the drained mussels to the oil mixture, stirring until well coated. Stir in the *ouzo* and parsley. Reduce the heat to medium-low. Cover and cook for about 5 minutes, stirring and shaking the pan occasionally until the mussels have opened, discarding any that have not. Spoon the mussels into shallow serving bowls. Ladle the sauce remaining in the pan over each serving, dividing evenly. Serve with chunks of crusty bread.

Soup

The soup in Greece always stands alone. Next to bread, it is probably the most important element in the Greek diet—but rarely as an appetizer or a first course. Soup is almost always the main dish, accompanied by a good loaf of chewy bread, pulled apart at the table. Of course, appetizers of some sort will always precede it, but when soup is served, the appetizer is often just a Greek salad, made with whatever appropriate ingredients happen to be on hand.

Greek soups usually have three things in common: They're simple, hearty, and inexpensive. Sometimes meat is added, but beans, lentils, rice, and small pastas usually form the backbone of these sturdy soups, which are most often seasoned with tomatoes, onions, and, of course, olive oil.

Egg and Lemon Soup
SOUPA AVGOLEMONO

YIELD: ABOUT 10 CUPS; 6 TO 8 SERVINGS

This is Greek chicken soup, with undoubtedly the same remarkable curative and restorative powers as chicken soups the world over. *Avgolemono* soups are all very much alike, except that Periyali's version includes semolina, minuscule pasta balls, which gives the soup body and an exquisite flavor that one reviewer described as being "spiked with sunshine." Although we don't recommend it, in a pinch you can substitute canned chicken broth for homemade, but if you do, take the time to freshen it as described in Basic Recipes, Ingredients, and Techniques.

10 cups Chicken Broth
  (see page 5)
½ cup semolina or medium-grain
  couscous (see page 300)
2 tablespoons cornstarch

⅓ cup lemon juice
3 egg yolks
White pepper
Salt, to taste

In a large saucepan, bring the broth to a boil. Very gradually add the semolina to the boiling broth, stirring rapidly with a whisk so that it doesn't clump. In a small bowl, stir the cornstarch into the lemon juice, then stir into the boiling broth. Continue to cook until the couscous is soft, about 5 minutes. In a small bowl, lightly beat the egg yolks. Stir a big spoonful of the hot broth into the yolks to temper them. Rapidly stir the yolk mixture into the broth. When the broth returns to a simmer, the soup is ready to serve. Adjust the seasoning, adding white pepper and a little more lemon juice and salt, if needed. Ladle the soup into warm bowls. A little chopped parsley can be sprinkled on each serving, but traditionally this soup is served ungarnished.

Fish Soup

KAKAVIA

YIELD: 6 SERVINGS

In Greece, as well as every other country touching the seafood-rich Mediterranean Sea, you can count on a robust fish soup being served in restaurants and homes. These soups, which are really more stewlike in composition, are all similar in content: a blend of local vegetables, fish, shellfish, and bivalves—whatever is freshest and most available—cooked in an aromatic fish broth and served with a coarse bread that is often dipped in a fruity olive oil.

4 cups Fish Broth (see page 7)

2 medium-size all-purpose potatoes, cut into ¾-inch cubes (about 2 cups)

2 medium-size carrots, cut on the diagonal into thin slices (about 1 cup)

3 small celery ribs, cut on the diagonal into thin slices (about 1 cup)

16 to 20 littleneck clams, scrubbed

2 pounds assorted firm-fleshed fish fillets (for example, snapper, striped bass, grouper, cod or scrod, monkfish or haddock), cut into fairly large chunks or strips

16 to 20 medium-size shrimp, peeled and deveined

16 to 20 mussels, debearded and scrubbed

Salt and freshly ground black pepper, to taste

¼ cup chopped flat-leaf parsley

In a soup pot or other large, heavy saucepan or Dutch oven, bring the broth to a slow boil. Add the potatoes, carrots, and celery. Cover and simmer for about 6 minutes, or until the vegetables are just starting to soften. Stir in the clams; cover and cook for 3 minutes. Stir in the fish, shrimp, and mussels. Cover and cook until the fish is firm and the clams and mussels have opened, about 5 minutes. (Discard any clams or mussels that remain tightly closed.) Adjust the seasoning, adding salt and pepper, if necessary, and stir in the parsley. Ladle into warm soup bowls, dividing the seafood and vegetables evenly.

White Bean Soup

FASSOLADA

YIELD: 12 CUPS; 8 SERVINGS

Charles uses a quick-soak method when he cooks the dry beans for this hearty soup, so it can easily come to the table in a couple of hours. However, like most soups, this one improves enormously if allowed to languish in the refrigerator overnight after it's cooked to give the flavors a chance to become better acquainted. Leftovers freeze well, so the soup can make a second appearance weeks, or even months, later.

2 cups dried cannellini (white kidney) beans

1/4 cup regular (not extra-virgin) olive oil

2 large onions, finely chopped (2 cups)

2 medium-size carrots, finely chopped (1 cup)

3 small celery ribs, finely chopped (1 cup)

2 or 3 large garlic cloves, minced

2 small bay leaves

4 tablespoons tomato paste

4 quarts water

1 tablespoon salt

1/4 teaspoon freshly ground black pepper

Chopped flat-leaf parsley, for garnish

Pick through the beans, discarding any that are shriveled or badly discolored. Rinse the beans with cool water and turn them into a large saucepan. Cover by about 3 inches with cold water. Bring to a boil over high heat. Reduce the heat and simmer, covered, for 30 minutes. Drain into a colander and rinse with cool water; set aside.

While the beans are simmering, heat the olive oil in a large soup pot. When it is hot, add the onions, carrots, celery, garlic, and bay leaves and cook over medium-high heat, stirring frequently, until the vegetables are softened. Stir in the tomato paste with about 1 cup of the water until well blended. Add the reserved beans, the remaining 15 cups water, salt, and pepper and stir to mix well. Bring to a boil over high heat. Reduce the heat and simmer, uncovered, for about 1 hour and 30 minutes, stirring occasionally at first and frequently toward the end of cooking time to prevent the beans from sticking to the bottom of the pot, until the beans are very soft, but not falling apart. Remove the bay leaves and ladle the soup into warm soup bowls. Sprinkle with parsley.

Lentil Soup

SOUPA FAKES

YIELD: 8 CUPS; 6 SERVINGS

*G*reek-Americans, who consider Periyali a home away from home, rarely pass up this humble but flavorful soup, considered by many to be mandatory Greek comfort food.

2 cups dry lentils

3 large celery ribs, finely chopped
  (2 cups)

1 large onion, shredded (1 cup)

1 medium-size carrot, shredded
  (½ cup)

2 large garlic cloves, minced

2 bay leaves

3 tablespoons tomato paste

½ cup regular (not extra-virgin)
  olive oil

5 teaspoons salt

⅛ teaspoon white pepper

10 cups water

¼ cup extra-virgin olive oil

¼ cup red-wine vinegar

Chopped flat-leaf parsley, for garnish

Pick through the lentils, removing any foreign matter. Place them in a large saucepan and cover by about ½ inch with cold water. Bring to a boil over high heat. Reduce the heat and simmer for 15 minutes. Drain the lentils in a strainer and rinse very well. Return the lentils to the pan. Add the remaining ingredients, except the extra-virgin olive oil, vinegar, and chopped parsley, and bring to a boil. Lower the heat and simmer, uncovered, for 45 to 50 minutes, or until the lentils are very soft. Stir in the extra-virgin olive oil and vinegar just before serving. Ladle into warm soup bowls and sprinkle with parsley.

Lamb and Fresh Vegetable Soup
LAHANOSOUPA ME ARNI

YIELD: ABOUT 8 CUPS; 4 TO 6 SERVINGS

This quick-cooking soup is a real showcase for fresh summer vegetables. A light sprinkling of grated hard cheese does interesting things for it.

1½ pounds stewing lamb, cut into
  1½-inch cubes
2 or 3 large garlic cloves, minced
  (1 tablespoon)
2 teaspoons salt
⅛ teaspoon white pepper
12 cups water
1 medium-size potato, diced (1 cup)
1 cup green beans or wax beans, cut
  into 1-inch pieces (about ¼ pound)
1 medium-size onion, chopped
  (½ cup)

1 cup fresh or frozen peas
1 large ripe tomato, peeled, cored,
  and coarsely chopped
  (about 1 cup)
½ cup tomato juice
2 cups broccoli florets
1 small zucchini, diced (about 1 cup)
1 tablespoon chopped flat-leaf parsley
Chopped flat-leaf parsley, for garnish

Place the lamb in a Dutch oven or other large, heavy saucepan. Cover with cold water and bring to a boil over high heat. Reduce the heat and simmer for 5 minutes. Drain the meat, rinse it in cool water, and return to the pan. Stir in the garlic, salt, pepper, and water. Bring to a boil. Reduce the heat and simmer gently, uncovered, for 45 minutes. Add the potato and green beans and simmer 10 minutes longer. Add the onion, peas, tomato, and tomato juice. Simmer 10 minutes more. Add the broccoli, zucchini, and parsley and continue to simmer for 5 minutes. Taste and adjust the seasoning, if necessary. Ladle into warm, shallow soup bowls and sprinkle with parsley. Serve with warm bread.

Fish and Seafood

The selection of seafood in Greece is vast, and the daily catches literally shimmer with freshness. The fish market is almost always the noisiest, most commotion-filled place in town, and it's fun to visit one or two of them, if only to find out who's who and what's going on under the Aegean and Ionian seas. Although the Greeks moan that the price of fish has gone out of sight, a telltale sign that it might not be quite so plentiful as it used to be, to most Americans it still seems like quite a bargain.

To really experience the soul of Greek fishing, you must go to a village quayside in the evening and witness firsthand the red- and blue-painted wooden fishing boats in their stately parade out to sea. If you arrive earlier in the day, you can watch the fishermen and their crews, and even a few of the younger family members, expertly making order out of piles of what look like hopelessly tangled wet nets, before mending and neatly refolding them.

If you visit Greece, undoubtedly you will be presented with many fishes, sometimes poached in a fragrant broth, other times baked in tomato sauce, but more often impeccably grilled; moist, flavorful, subtly smoky. The only adornment is a lavish sprinkling of parsley, sometimes, and big domes of lemon, always.

Most Greek recipes can be successfully duplicated if you view the fish as the Greeks do, as big, medium, or small. Big fish are almost always served whole, either baked or poached; medium fish are grilled, and little fish are fried. And is it necessary to mention

that the fish *always* comes to the table staring up at the diner? Heads and tails are *never* removed. The head is considered a delicacy, especially the little morsels of meat in the cheeks. Very large fish, tuna and swordfish, for example, are cut into steaks or fillets, which are baked or grilled, and very often end up as skewered chunks to be roasted with vegetables over a fire.

No one is ever expected to eat a fish that has not been inspected before it is cooked. In Greek homes, the host will invariably show off the fish that has been selected for you before it is cooked. In restaurants, the practice is to go directly into the kitchen, where the proprietor will allow you to paw through a large pan of well-iced fish and pick your own.

At Periyali the menu leans decidedly toward fish species that are indigenous to both Greek and American waters, but some Mediterranean varieties—for instance red mullet, anchovies, Mediterranean porgies, and the ugly but sweet-fleshed scorpion fish—arrive thrice weekly via Olympic Airways.

Mykonos-Style Poached Fish with Fish Broth Avgolemono

YIELD: 4 SERVINGS

Aromatic and unpretentious, this fish preparation came to our lunch table at a seafood *taverna* located at the end of a long, bumpy road on a desolate tip of Mykonos. The proprietors are a fisherman and his wife. She cooks, and various women relatives help out in the kitchen and wait on tables. The kids' main chores include clearing dishes and running out to the fish pen now and then to bring in gigantic spiny lobsters for the steam pot. Before our order was taken, we went into the kitchen to look over the day's catch and pick our fish. That done, the silvery specimen was plopped on

a scale and the charge computed by the kilo. Besides the fish, we also dined on poached spiny lobster, Greek salad, fried potatoes, and two kinds of homemade bread.

---

1 whole, firm-fleshed fish, such as
  striped bass, sea bass, or sea trout,
  weighing 3 to 3½ pounds, cleaned
  and gutted
4 cups Fish Broth (see page 7), made
  without tomato paste

2 egg yolks
½ cup lemon juice
Coarsely chopped flat-leaf parsley,
  for garnish
Lemon halves, for garnish

Measure a length of double-thickness cheesecloth that is about twice as long as the fish. Lay the fish lengthwise in the center of the cheesecloth. Make a knot in each end of the cloth to form a sort of "hammock" that will help maneuver the fish into and out of the poaching liquid and to keep it from breaking apart. Add enough water to the fish broth to measure 6 cups. Bring the broth to a boil in a fish poacher or other shallow, flameproof baking pan. Lower the fish into the poacher. Reduce the heat so that the broth barely simmers. Cover the pan tightly and poach very gently for about 7 minutes per pound, or until the fish flakes when tested with a fork. Remove the fish from the poacher, grasping the ends of the cheesecloth. Carefully remove the fish from the cheesecloth and place it on a serving platter. Sprinkle with plenty of parsley and garnish with lemon halves. Set aside in a warm place while finishing the broth. Pour the liquid in the poacher into a medium-size saucepan and set the pan over medium heat until the broth simmers. In a small bowl, beat the eggs with the lemon juice. Stir a big spoonful of the hot broth into the egg yolks to temper them, then slowly add the egg mixture to the broth, stirring rapidly with a wire whisk. Continue to cook and stir until the broth is slightly thickened. Do not allow the mixture to boil.

To serve, cut the fish into serving portions and place them in large, shallow soup bowls. Ladle the broth into the bowls with the fish, dividing evenly. Sprinkle with parsley and garnish with lemon halves. Serve with plenty of crusty, chewy bread.

Fish Fillets Wrapped in Grape Leaves

The flavor and rather coarse texture of the briny grape leaves against the silky fillets in this recipe are most unusual and intriguing. Serve these healthful wrapped fillets with rice and red Swiss chard that has been lightly sautéed in olive oil with garlic.

---

4 skinless snapper or sea bass fillets,
  weighing about 4 ounces each
8 large grape leaves (see page 14)
4 teaspoons lemon juice
2 teaspoons dried oregano
  leaves, crumbled
Freshly ground black pepper, to taste

1½ cups Chicken Broth or Fish Broth
  (see page 5 or 7)
Thick Lemon Sauce for Fish and
  Shellfish (see page 233) or
  2 tablespoons butter
Thinly sliced lemon, for garnish

Cut the fillets in half and set them aside. Prepare the grape leaves as directed in "How to Work with Grape Leaves" (see page 14). Lay one-half fillet in the center of each grape leaf. Sprinkle each half fillet with ½ teaspoon lemon juice and ¼ teaspoon oregano, and season with pepper. Fold up the bottom of each leaf, then the sides, and then the top around each fillet and secure with a wooden pick. Arrange the bundles, smooth side up, in a large skillet, and add the broth. It should come about halfway up the sides of the bundles. If not, add a little water. Bring the broth to a brisk simmer over medium-high heat. Reduce the heat and partially cover the skillet. Simmer gently for 10 minutes, basting the bundles 2 or 3 times with the broth. Remove the bundles to a serving platter and keep warm. Use 1 cup of the broth that remains in the pan to make Thick Lemon Sauce. Or, if you prefer, make a pan sauce by increasing the heat under the skillet and boiling the liquid until it is reduced and slightly syrupy. Off the heat, stir in the butter until melted. Remove the picks and spoon the sauce over the bundles, dividing evenly. Garnish with lemon slices.

Fillet of Snapper Baked with Tomato, Onion, and Garlic

PSARI PLAKI

YIELD: 6 SERVINGS

Plaki is one of the most famous and best-loved Greek fish recipes. It is served everywhere, and is one of the few dishes in which there is little variation, no matter where it's cooked, from Salonika to Santorini. Tomatoes, onion, garlic, and olive oil are the common denominators, and the fresher the fish, of course, the better it will be. Accompany the *plaki* with a salad or a plain green vegetable, and to soak up the extraordinary sauce, serve rice, or lots of bread.

⅓ cup plus 2 tablespoons regular (not extra-virgin) olive oil

1 large and 1 medium-size onion, finely chopped (1½ cups)

2 medium-size carrots, thinly sliced (1 cup)

3 garlic cloves, sliced

1¼ cups dry white wine

2 cans (14½ ounces each) whole tomatoes, undrained and chopped (see Note)

1 cup water

¼ cup chopped flat-leaf parsley

2 teaspoons salt

⅛ teaspoon freshly ground black pepper

6 fillets of red snapper, striped bass, or black sea bass, weighing 5 to 6 ounces each

Chopped flat-leaf parsley, for garnish

Heat ⅓ cup of the olive oil in a large, heavy skillet. When it is hot, add the onions, carrots, and garlic and cook over medium-high heat, stirring frequently, until softened. Add the wine and continue to cook, stirring occasionally, until most of the wine has evaporated and only the essence remains. Stir in the tomatoes, water, parsley, salt, and pepper. Bring to a boil, then reduce the heat and simmer, uncovered, for 15 minutes, stirring frequently. Set aside to cool slightly.

Preheat oven to 400°F. Rub both sides of the fish with the remaining 2 tablespoons of olive oil and season lightly with salt and pepper. Spoon about one-third of the tomato sauce into the bottom of a shallow baking dish that is just large enough to hold the fish fillets comfortably. Arrange the fish, skin side down, over the sauce. Spoon the remaining sauce over the fish. Bake for 10 to 15 minutes, or until the sauce is bubbling and the fish flakes when tested with a fork. Divide the fish and sauce evenly among dinner plates and sprinkle with chopped parsley.

NOTE: The easiest way to chop canned tomatoes is to use clean kitchen scissors and cut them up in the can.

Shrimp in Clay Pots
GARIDES YOUVETSAKI

YIELD: 4 TO 6 SERVINGS

Shrimp baked with tomatoes and *feta* cheese is said to have originated in a restaurant in Piraeus, the port of Athens. *Youvetsaki* refers to the small clay pots in which the shrimp are usually baked, but any shallow baking dish will work as well. We especially like to serve this for company, since it can be put together several hours ahead of time and baked at the last minute, coming to the table sizzling hot, with a positively ravishing aroma. Also offer a few easy appetizers, a green salad, a loaf of crisp, warm bread, and you've got all anyone could want.

---

2 tablespoons regular (not extra-virgin) olive oil

1 medium-size onion, finely chopped (1/2 cup)

3 cloves garlic, finely chopped

1 pound tomatoes, peeled, seeded, and chopped

Salt and freshly ground black pepper, to taste

1/4 cup brandy

1 1/2 pounds medium-size to large shrimp, peeled and deveined, tails left on

1/4 pound feta cheese, crumbled

18 Kalamata olives, pitted (see page 296)

1 tablespoon chopped flat-leaf parsley, for garnish

Preheat the oven to 425°F. Heat the olive oil in a large skillet. Add the onion and cook over medium-high heat, stirring occasionally, until softened. Stir in the garlic, tomatoes, salt, pepper, and brandy. Continue to cook, stirring frequently, until the sauce thickens but the tomatoes have not completely broken down, 5 to 10 minutes. Remove from the heat and set aside.

Arrange the shrimp in a shallow 8-cup baking dish that has been lightly greased or coated with nonstick spray. (You can substitute 6 individual gratin dishes.) Cover with the tomato mixture and sprinkle with the *feta* cheese and olives. (The dish can be prepared ahead up to this point and refrigerated, lightly covered, for several hours.) Bake for 10 to 15 minutes, or until the shrimp are firm and the cheese has melted. Be careful not to overcook the shrimp or they will become tough. Sprinkle with parsley and serve directly from the baking dish.

Fried Salted Cod with Skordalia

BAKALIAROS

~~~~~~

YIELD: 4 SERVINGS

This is primarily a winter dish in Greece, when fresh fish are not so plentiful. Dried cod, imported from more northerly European countries, has been used throughout the Mediterranean area for eons, and has always been an important Lenten food. Every country has its own pet method of preparing the hard, salted fish. In Greece, it is usually fried and served with *skordalia*. Dried cod is easy to find in Italian, Asian, Latin American, and, of course, Greek markets. Look for fillets with very white flesh. As it ages, the flesh becomes slightly yellowed. We think fried cod really needs the strong, garlicky flavor of the *skordalia,* so don't skip it.

---

1 pound dried salted codfish
1 cup all-purpose flour
1/4 teaspoon freshly ground black
 pepper
1 tablespoon regular (not extra-
 virgin) olive oil
1 egg, beaten

3/4 cup water
Regular (not extra-virgin) olive oil or
 vegetable oil, for frying
Nicola's Mother's Zakinthos-Style
 Skordalia (see page 231)
Lemon wedges, for garnish

Place the cod in a large bowl and cover with cold water. Soak the fish for at least 24 hours, or up to 2 days, changing the water 5, 6, or more times to soften it and remove some of the salt. The longer the fish soaks, the less salty it will be.

In a medium-size bowl, combine the flour and pepper. Stir in the olive oil and egg. Gradually add the water, beating constantly. The mixture should have the consistency of pancake batter. (Although the batter can be used immediately, it will be better if refrigerated for about 3 hours, or up to 24 hours. Stir to blend before using.)

Drain the cod and pick out any small bones. Scrape off any bits of fatty skin. Blot as dry as possible with paper towels and cut the fish into serving-size pieces.

Pour enough oil into a large skillet to measure about ¼ inch. Place the skillet over high heat until the oil ripples. Dip the pieces of fish into the batter and carefully slip them into the skillet. Cook, adjusting the heat as necessary, until golden brown on both sides, about 10 minutes total cooking time. Serve immediately with *skordalia* and plenty of lemon wedges.

Fish Filled with Fresh Herbs, Currants, and Nuts

Currants might not seem like exactly the right ingredient for a fish stuffing, but every element in this filling knows exactly what the other one is doing, and the result is a splendid fusion of flavors and textures that mingle beautifully with every bite of the fish.

---

1 whole fish, such as striped bass,
 sea bass, or sea trout, weighing
 4 to 4¹/₂ pounds
¹/₄ cup dried currants
¹/₄ cup lemon juice
1 teaspoon salt
4 tablespoons (¹/₂ stick)
 unsalted butter
3 tablespoons regular (not extra-
 virgin) olive oil
¹/₂ cup finely chopped flat-leaf
 parsley
¹/₄ cup finely chopped scallions,
 including some of the green tops

¹/₄ cup finely chopped fresh mint
 leaves or 1¹/₂ tablespoons dried mint
 leaves, crumbled
2 tablespoons minced tarragon or
 2 teaspoons dried tarragon leaves,
 crumbled
1 tablespoon chopped cilantro (fresh
 coriander)
1 large garlic clove, crushed
1 cup finely chopped walnuts
¹/₄ teaspoon freshly ground black
 pepper
Lemon slices and flat-leaf parsley
 sprigs, for garnish

Ask the fish merchant to butterfly the fish and remove the bones. Leave the head on or, if you must, have it removed. In a small bowl, mix the currants with the lemon juice and set aside for about an hour.

Preheat the oven to 350°F. Rinse the fish and pat it dry with paper towels. Sprinkle half of the salt evenly in the cavity. Heat 3 tablespoons of the butter and the olive oil in a large skillet over medium-high heat. When it is hot, add the parsley, scallions, mint, tarragon, and cilantro and cook, stirring frequently, until the scallions are softened. Stir in the garlic, walnuts, and reserved currants, the remaining salt, and pepper and remove from the heat. Stuff the fish with this mixture, spreading it evenly. Use small metal skewers to close the fish, or tie it in two or three places with kitchen string. Place the fish in a large, greased baking dish or roasting pan. Dot with the remaining tablespoon of butter. Add about 1 cup of water to the pan. Bake for 35 to 40 minutes, basting occasionally with the juices that accumulate, until the fish flakes with a fork. Arrange the fish on a serving platter and remove the skewers. Garnish with lemon slices and parsley sprigs. To serve, cut the fish into 4 equal portions and accompany with couscous or rice and a lightly sautéed green vegetable, such as broccoli, zucchini, or sugar-snap peas.

Shellfish Stew

YIELD: 4 SERVINGS

If you think you've eaten this stew in France, Italy, or Spain, you probably have, but food historians are convinced that most of the seafood stews so closely associated with these countries originally came from Greece, and not the other way around. This is a very casual dish, to be shared with good friends and a whole loaf of bread that can be broken off as needed to soak up the sauce. Paper napkins are also a good idea, since the shrimp are peeled at the table.

1/2 cup regular (not extra-virgin) olive oil

1 large onion, finely chopped (1 cup)

1 or 2 small celery ribs, finely chopped (1/2 cup)

1 medium-size carrot, finely chopped (1/2 cup)

3 pounds firm, ripe tomatoes (about 6 large), cored and chopped or 3 cans (14 1/2 ounces each), partially drained and chopped

1/4 cup red-wine vinegar

1 to 2 teaspoons salt

1 teaspoon dried oregano leaves, crumbled

1/4 teaspoon freshly ground black pepper

2 pounds small mussels

1 pound littleneck clams

1 pound medium-size unpeeled shrimp

1/4 cup extra-virgin olive oil

3 tablespoons chopped flat-leaf parsley

Chopped flat-leaf parsley, for garnish

Lemon wedges, for garnish

Heat the regular olive oil in a Dutch oven or other large, heavy saucepan over medium-high heat. When it is hot, add the onion, celery, and carrot and cook, stirring occasionally, until softened. Stir in the tomatoes, vinegar, salt, oregano, and black pepper. Reduce the heat, cover, and simmer slowly for 45 minutes, stirring occasionally. Uncover and continue to simmer for 45 minutes, stirring frequently. The mixture will be very thick.

While the tomato sauce is cooking, scrape the beards from the mussels with a small, sharp knife, then soak them in several changes of cold water for about an hour. Rinse the clams in a colander under cold running water. Rinse and drain the shrimp.

Stir the clams into the tomato sauce, along with the extra-virgin olive oil and parsley. Cover and cook over medium heat for 5 minutes. Stir in the mussels and shrimp and continue to cook for 5 to 10 minutes, stirring once or twice, until the clams have opened wide and the shrimp have turned pink.

To serve, ladle into large, shallow bowls, discarding any mussels or clams that have not opened. Sprinkle with parsley. Serve with lemon wedges, lots of crusty bread, and plenty of paper napkins.

Pan-Seared Swordfish with Garlic Brown Butter

FILETO XIFIA

YIELD: 4 SERVINGS

*N*early everybody enjoys the meaty texture and delicate flavor of swordfish, and since this impressive preparation also happens to be quick and simple, it's a good choice for unexpected guests. Begin with a simple green salad. If you're not in a rush, serve the fish with steamed spaghetti squash and Roasted Potatoes. Otherwise, Couscous Timbales and plain broiled tomato halves are faster.

---

2 center-cut swordfish steaks, each about 1 inch thick and weighing about 1 pound

Salt and freshly ground black pepper, to taste

2 tablespoons regular (not extra-virgin) olive oil

4 tablespoons (1/2 stick) butter

1 teaspoon minced garlic

1 tablespoon finely chopped flat-leaf parsley

1/2 teaspoon salt, or to taste

1/4 teaspoon white pepper

1/4 cup lemon juice

Flat-leaf parsley sprigs, for garnish

Lemon wedges, for garnish

Cut each swordfish steak in half to make two portions. Sprinkle lightly with salt and pepper. Heat the olive oil in a large skillet over medium-high heat. When it is very hot, carefully add the swordfish steaks. Cook until nicely browned on both sides, about 3 minutes on the first side and 2 minutes on the second side, adjusting the heat as necessary until done through. Remove the swordfish from the pan to a serving platter or dinner plates. Discard the oil left in the skillet and wipe with paper towels. Return the skillet to medium-high heat. Add the butter and cook, stirring, just until it begins to turn brown. Immediately stir in the garlic, parsley, salt, and pepper. Remove from the heat and stir in the lemon juice. Pour the sauce over the fish, dividing evenly. Garnish with parsley and lemon wedges.

Grilled Whole Fish

The grilled fish at Periyali is a little more upscale than its country cousin in Greece. There, little is done to the fish other than brushing it with plenty of olive oil and giving it a generous sprinkling of oregano. Onto the grill it goes and, if all proceeds according to plan, the skin is crisp and even blackened in some spots, and the meat flaky and succulent. On the table is a bowl of lemon juice mixed with olive oil, which is stirred up and spooned over the whole fish, and also over individual servings as it is eaten. Sometimes the fish is accompanied by big halves of lemon. In that case, the procedure is to spear the lemon halves on a fork, dip them into the drippings left on the plate recently occupied by a Greek salad, and rub and squeeze the flavored lemon juice over the fish. In lieu of the lemon juice and olive oil, this recipe calls for a simple, savory sauce made from the herb-flavored pan drippings. Serve the fish with couscous or rice and a green vegetable.

---

4 whole fish, such as red snapper, bass, or bluefish, weighing about 1 pound each, cleaned, gutted, and the fins removed

Lemon wedges, for garnish

MARINADE

1/2 cup regular (not extra-virgin) olive oil

1/4 cup extra-virgin olive oil

1 tablespoon minced chives or scallion tops

1 tablespoon minced flat-leaf parsley

1 1/2 teaspoons minced fresh thyme leaves or 3/4 teaspoon dried thyme leaves, crumbled

1 1/2 teaspoons minced fresh oregano leaves or 3/4 teaspoon dried oregano leaves, crumbled

Thin lemon slices

SAUCE

1 1/2 cups Chicken Broth or Fish Broth (see page 5 or 7)

1/2 cup extra-virgin olive oil

1/4 cup lemon juice

2 teaspoons minced chives or scallion tops

2 teaspoons minced flat-leaf parsley

1 teaspoon minced fresh thyme leaves, crumbled or 1/2 teaspoon dried thyme leaves

*1 teaspoon minced fresh oregano or
½ teaspoon dried oregano leaves,
crumbled*

*Salt and freshly ground black pepper,
to taste
1 teaspoon chopped flat-leaf parsley*

Make 3 shallow, diagonal slashes on each side of the fish. Mix the oils and herbs for the marinade in a shallow pan. Add the fish and rub inside and out with the marinade. Place a couple of lemon slices in each fish. Set aside at room temperature for about 30 minutes, or cover and refrigerate for up to 12 hours, turning the fish occasionally.

Prepare a bed of medium-hot charcoal and oil the grill. (The fish can also be grilled in an oiled wire basket.) Season the fish lightly with salt and pepper and place it on the grill about 4 inches above the coals for about 2 minutes on each side. Remove from the grill and place in a shallow baking dish, just large enough to hold the fish comfortably.

To make the sauce, in a medium-size bowl, mix the fish broth, extra-virgin olive oil, lemon juice, chives, minced parsley, thyme, and oregano and pour over and around the fish.

Preheat the oven to 400°F. Bake the fish for about 15 minutes, basting occasionally with the sauce, until it flakes easily. Remove the fish from the baking dish and keep it warm. Pour the juices in the baking dish into a small saucepan and bring to a boil. Reduce by about half. Season with salt and pepper and a little more lemon juice, if necessary. Stir in the chopped parsley. Arrange the fish on dinner plates. Spoon the sauce over the fish, dividing equally, and garnish with lemon wedges.

Grilled Tuna or Swordfish Salad

*W*hen you want something easy, unusual, and a little on the elegant side, this is an excellent choice. Most of the salad can be prepared ahead and assembled at the last minute, and the relatively small amount of tuna or swordfish needed to serve four makes this dish reasonable in price, too. If you know your dining companions to be somewhat adventuresome, you might consider serving icy *retsina*, especially if the meal is to be served outdoors and the weather is very warm.

---

1 tuna or swordfish steak, about
  1¼ inches thick and weighing
  about 1¼ pounds
¼ cup plus 2 tablespoons extra-
  virgin olive oil
¼ teaspoon dried oregano
  leaves, crumbled
¼ teaspoon dried thyme
  leaves, crumbled
3 tablespoons lemon juice
1 teaspoon minced fresh oregano or
  ¼ teaspoon dried oregano leaves,
  crumbled
1 teaspoon fresh minced thyme or
  ¼ teaspoon dried leaves, crumbled
½ teaspoon salt
About 5 turns of a pepper mill
1 medium-size red bell pepper,
  roasted and cut into ⅛-inch strips
  (see page 37)

1 large yellow bell pepper, roasted
  and cut into ⅛-inch strips
2 large ripe tomatoes (about
  1 pound), peeled, seeded, and
  coarsely chopped
1 medium-size red onion, cut into
  thin vertical slices (½ cup)
1 or 2 small celery ribs, thinly sliced
  (½ cup)
6 small radishes, thinly sliced
  (½ cup)
2 tablespoons drained capers
4 to 6 cups lightly packed mixed
  salad greens
16 Kalamata olives or a mixture of
  Kalamata and Amfissa olives
Chopped flat-leaf parsley, for garnish

Rinse the fish and pat it dry on paper towels. Mix 2 tablespoons of the olive oil, the dried oregano, and the thyme in a small bowl. Brush both sides of the steak with the oil mixture and set aside for 30 minutes at room temperature, or up to several hours in the refrigerator. Mix the remaining ¼ cup olive oil, lemon juice, fresh oregano and thyme, salt, and pepper in a small bowl and set aside.

Preheat the oven broiler. Broil the fish about 4 to 6 inches below the source of heat until just done, but still somewhat soft and juicy, about 4 minutes on the first side and 3 minutes on the second side. (Swordfish is best if cooked through, but tuna can be grilled for a slightly shorter time so that it is medium-rare or even rare, if you prefer.) Set aside to cool.

In a large bowl, toss the bell peppers, tomatoes, onion, celery, radishes, and capers. Pour the reserved dressing over the vegetables and toss gently to mix. Pull the skin from the swordfish. With a very sharp knife, cut the fish into ¾-inch pieces. (The recipe can be made ahead up to this point and refrigerated for a couple of hours.) Add the fish to the vegetable mixture, along with any juices that have accumulated in the pan with the fish. Toss again, very gently, so that the fish does not break apart. Divide the greens among 4 dinner plates. Spoon the salad over the greens, dividing evenly. Arrange 4 olives on each salad and sprinkle with parsley.

HOLLY GARRISON

Grilled Tuna
TONOS SCHARAS

*A*lthough this tuna can be marinated for as little as 30 minutes, it's really better to plan ahead and marinate it all day in the refrigerator, so that the flavor has a chance to subtly permeate the fillet. Try this with Potato Salad and *Horta*. A grilled tomato can also be added to the plate.

---

4 pieces tuna fillet, each weighing
  6 to 8 ounces and at least ¾ inch
  thick
Chopped flat-leaf parsley, for garnish
Lemon wedges, for garnish
MARINADE
2 tablespoons extra-virgin olive oil
2 tablespoons regular olive oil
2 teaspoons minced chives or
  scallion tops
2 teaspoons minced flat-leaf parsley
1 teaspoon minced fresh thyme or
  ½ teaspoon dried thyme leaves,
  crumbled
1 teaspoon minced fresh oregano or
  ½ teaspoon dried oregano leaves,
  crumbled

SAUCE
¾ cup Chicken Broth (see page 5)
¼ cup extra-virgin olive oil
1 tablespoon lemon juice
1 teaspoon minced chives or
  scallion tops
1 teaspoon minced flat-leaf parsley
½ teaspoon minced fresh thyme or
  ¼ teaspoon dried thyme leaves,
  crumbled
½ teaspoon minced fresh oregano
  leaves or ¼ teaspoon dried oregano,
  crumbled
Salt and freshly ground black pepper,
  to taste
½ teaspoon chopped flat-leaf parsley

Mix the olive oils and herbs for the marinade in a shallow pan. Add the tuna and turn until well coated. Set aside at room temperature for about 30 minutes, or cover and refrigerate for up to 12 hours, turning occasionally.

To make the sauce, mix the chicken broth, extra-virgin olive oil, lemon juice, chives, minced parsley, thyme, and oregano in a medium-size saucepan. Bring to a boil, then reduce the heat and simmer until reduced by about half. Remove from the heat and season with salt and pepper. Stir in the chopped parsley and set aside.

Prepare a bed of medium-hot charcoal and oil the grill. (The fish may also be grilled in an oiled wire basket.) Remove the tuna from the marinade and season lightly with salt and pepper. Place the fish on the prepared grill about 4 inches above the coals. Grill for 2 to 4 minutes per side, or until done as you like it, although these days the preference is for tuna to be a little rare. Arrange the fish on dinner plates. Reheat the sauce slightly and spoon it over the fish, dividing evenly. Sprinkle with parsley and garnish with lemon wedges.

HOLLY GARRISON

Grilled Shrimp with Herbs and Lemon

GARIDES SCHARAS

YIELD: 4 SERVINGS

Sometimes the easiest recipes are the best. Try this on a summer evening when you're in the mood for a no-frills but delicious meal.

---

32 medium- to large-size shrimp
  (1¾ to 2 pounds)
Chopped flat-leaf parsley, for garnish
Lemon wedges, for garnish
MARINADE
2 tablespoons extra-virgin olive oil
2 tablespoons regular (not extra-
  virgin) olive oil
2 teaspoons minced chives or
  scallion tops
2 teaspoons minced flat-leaf parsley
1 teaspoon minced fresh thyme or ½
  teaspoon dried thyme leaves,
  crumbled

1 teaspoon minced fresh oregano or
  ½ teaspoon dried oregano leaves,
  crumbled
SAUCE
¼ cup Chicken Broth (see page 5)
¼ cup extra-virgin olive oil
2 tablespoons lemon juice
Salt and freshly ground black pepper,
  to taste

Peel and devein the shrimp, leaving the tail shells attached. Rinse the shrimp and blot dry with paper towels. Mix the olive oils and herbs for the marinade in a shallow pan. Add the shrimp and toss until well coated. Set aside at room temperature for about 30 minutes, or cover and refrigerate for up to 12 hours, stirring occasionally.

To make the sauce, mix the chicken broth, olive oil, and lemon juice in a medium-size skillet. Bring to a boil, then reduce the heat and simmer until reduced by about half. Season with salt and pepper and set aside.

Remove the shrimp from the marinade. Thread 8 shrimp on 2 parallel 8-inch wooden skewers, running the shrimp lengthwise on the skewers as shown. Repeat with the remaining shrimp.

Prepare a bed of hot charcoal. Place the skewers on the grill 3 or 4 inches above the coals for 2 to 4 minutes, turning once, until the shrimp turn pink and feel firm to the touch. Be careful not to overcook them. Push the shrimp off the skewers onto dinner plates. Pour the sauce over the shrimp, dividing equally. Sprinkle with parsley and garnish with lemon wedges. At Periyali, each serving of shrimp is served with rice, a broiled tomato half, and Zucchini and Carrots.

Grilled Lobster with Olive Oil, Lemon, and Herbs
ASTAKOS

YIELD: 4 SERVINGS

The lobster presentation at Periyali is a far cry from the gigantic spiny lobster that travelers may enjoy in Greece, where the whole creature is steamed, dropped onto an immense platter, and brought forth to the table. Since the spiny lobster has no claws, only the tail is eaten. Although the meat is fluffy and white, it lacks the tenderness and sweetness of Maine lobster, its distant cousin. Grilling lobster to perfection is something of a chore, but the results are so utterly delectable that it's worth it. Because the lobster pieces are cooked separately, each part is done perfectly, something that can't be said about a lobster cooked whole, no matter how expertly it's prepared.

---

4 lobsters, weighing 1¼ pounds each
2 teaspoons coarsely chopped flat-leaf
  parsley
2 teaspoons coarsely chopped fresh
  chives or scallion tops
½ teaspoon dried oregano leaves

½ teaspoon dried thyme leaves
½ cup extra-virgin olive oil
¼ cup lemon juice
1 cup lobster broth (see Note) or
  Chicken Broth (see page 5)
Chopped flat-leaf parsley, for garnish

Kill each lobster by inserting the point of a heavy knife into the head just between the eyes. Separate the tail from the body by twisting the lobster at the point where the head and body meet the tail, and set these aside. Break off the large claws close to the body and set aside separately; break off the smaller claws and set aside separately. Break off the legs and set these aside with the head and body. (If you like, these pieces can be used to make a rich lobster broth; see Note.) The intestines can be removed by twisting the center fin on the tail and gently pulling it away from the tail. The long intestine, which is attached to it, should follow. If not, it can be removed later when the tail is split. Run two 6-inch wooden skewers lengthwise through each tail, starting from the body end. This prevents the tails from curling.

While preparing the lobsters, bring a large pot of unsalted water to a rolling boil. (The lobsters will be partially cooked in the water before they are grilled.) The lobster pieces must be boiled separately, since they require different cooking times.

Place the parsley, chives, oregano, and thyme on a cutting surface and chop together until very fine and well mixed. Place the chopped herbs in a small bowl and set aside.

Drop the lobster tails into the boiling water. When the water returns to a boil, reduce the heat and simmer for exactly 4 minutes.

Remove the tails with a slotted spoon and plunge into a basin of cold water to stop further cooking. Remove and set aside. Repeat this entire procedure with the large claws, simmering for exactly 7 minutes. Repeat again with the small claws, simmering for exactly 5 minutes.

Prepare a bed of hot charcoal. Remove the skewers from the tails. Cut the tails in half lengthwise with a sharp, heavy knife, and crack the claws. Brush the tail halves with some of the olive oil and sprinkle lightly with half the mixed herbs. Place the tails on the grill, meat side down, 2 or 3 inches above the hot coals. Arrange the claws around the tails. Grill for about 3 minutes, turning the claws once. This should be just enough grilling time to mark and flavor the pieces, but not quite enough to cook them through. Remove the lobster to a broiling pan with the tail halves meat side up.

Preheat the oven to 500°F. Sprinkle the lobster with the remaining herbs, olive oil, and lemon juice. Pour the chicken broth into the bottom of the pan. Just before serving, bake for about 5 minutes, or until sizzling. Arrange the lobster on serving plates, dividing evenly. If the sauce in the pan seems thin, reduce it over high heat. Pour over the lobster. Sprinkle with parsley and serve immediately with couscous and a plain, broiled tomato half or sautéed cherry tomatoes.

NOTE: To make lobster broth, cook the lobster bodies, heads, and legs in about 2 tablespoons olive oil over medium-high heat in a Dutch oven or other large, heavy saucepan until they turn bright red. Add ½ cup brandy and continue to cook, stirring, until only the essence of the brandy remains. Add 6 cups water, 1 tablespoon tomato paste, and 1 teaspoon *each* dried oregano, thyme, and tarragon leaves. Bring to a boil, then reduce the heat and simmer for 30 minutes. With a slotted spoon, lift the lobster shells and most of the vegetables from the broth and discard. Set the broth aside to cool. Strain through a colander lined with a double thickness of cheesecloth into a large bowl. Ladle the broth into containers with tight-fitting lids and refrigerate. The broth can also be frozen for up to 6 months. If freezing, allow about ½ inch of headspace for expansion in each container.

Great Barrels of Feta

Whether or not the Greeks consider it so, to the rest of the world *feta* is the national cheese of Greece, and has become so internationally popular over the years that it is now made in many other countries as well. No one knows how many different types of *feta* are produced on the Greek mainland and islands, but one thing is sure. Because the formula for making this brine-cured cheese has never been standardized, no two will ever taste quite alike.

Greek *fetas* (the word means "slice") are usually made from sheep's milk, occasionally from goat's milk, and sometimes from a combination of the two. (Cow's milk alone is also used in other countries, something most Greeks shudder to think about.) *Feta* ranges in density from rather soft to very firm. The flavors can vary subtly or remarkably, from region to region and season to season, and depending on which aromatic herbs and grasses the milk-producing sheep and goats have nibbled on.

The technique for making *feta* is simple, as cheeses go, and has remained unchanged for thousands of years. The process involves heating the milk, adding rennin (a milk-coagulating enzyme), and leaving the curds to drain. When enough of the whey (the liquid that has separated from the curds) has drained away for the milk to form a solid mass, the fresh cheese is cut into blocks or wedges, rubbed with sea salt, and put into wooden barrels to cure in its own whey. The longer it sits, the saltier, more pungent, and firmer it becomes.

Feta cheese appears on the table almost any time a Greek sits down to eat. It has many culinary applications, but very often it's eaten as is with bread and olives; other times it's soaked with olive oil and sprinkled with oregano. It is the quintessential ingredient in all Greek salads, and bubbles on top of many hot dishes, too.

For information about buying and storing *feta* cheese, see page 289.

Salmon Wrapped in Phyllo with Spinach-and-Feta-Cheese Filling

YIELD: 8 SERVINGS

There's no denying that salmon is one of the most popular fish in the market these days, but in our opinion, plain salmon can get tedious, and, if not cooked with great care, tends to be rather dry. To circumvent these problems while giving the salmon a decidedly Greek touch, top salmon fillets with the same versatile spinach-and-feta cheese filling that's used for the *tiropita*, then wrap it in layers of *phyllo* before baking it to tender, moist perfection.

8 pieces of salmon fillet, each
  weighing about 4 ounces
18 sheets ultra-thin phyllo
1 to 1½ cups (2 to 3 sticks) Clarified
  Melted Butter (see page 8)
3 tablespoons lemon juice
½ recipe of Spinach-and-Feta-
  Cheese Filling (see page 13)

MARINADE
1 tablespoon coarsely chopped
  flat-leaf parsley
1 tablespoon coarsely chopped fresh
  chives or scallion tops
1 teaspoon dried oregano leaves
1 teaspoon dried thyme leaves
½ cup extra-virgin olive oil

Before starting to make this, please read "How to Work with *Phyllo*" on page 12.

Rinse the salmon fillets and pat dry with paper towels.

To make the marinade, place the parsley, chives, oregano, and thyme on a cutting surface and chop together until very fine and well mixed. Sprinkle the herbs in a shallow pan and stir in the olive oil. Coat the salmon fillets in the marinade and set aside for about 30 minutes at room temperature, or for 1 or 2 hours in the refrigerator.

Preheat the oven to 375°F. Place 2 sheets of *phyllo* on a work surface, a long side facing you, and cut into 3 strips, each measuring about 5½ inches in width. Fold the strips in half, crosswise, and cut in half. (These pieces will be used as patches to reinforce the *phyllo* packets; there will be 4 patches left over.) Place 1 sheet of *phyllo,* a short side facing you, on a flat work surface. Brush with butter. Place another sheet of *phyllo* on top of the first and brush with butter. Place a patch of *phyllo* on the buttered *phyllo* as shown and brush with butter. Sprinkle the salmon fillets with lemon juice. Place 1 salmon fillet on the patch. Cover with ¼ cup of the spinach mixture. Fold the bottom of the *phyllo* over the salmon. Brush the folded portion with butter. Fold in the sides of the *phyllo* and brush with butter. Roll up the salmon in the *phyllo* to make a neat packet. Brush the top with butter, making sure to seal the end flap of the *phyllo* onto the packet. Repeat with the remaining ingredients to make 7 more packets. As they are finished, place the packets on 1 or 2 ungreased baking sheets.

Bake for about 15 minutes, or until golden brown. Remove from the oven and serve immediately with Roasted Potatoes and plain broiled tomato halves.

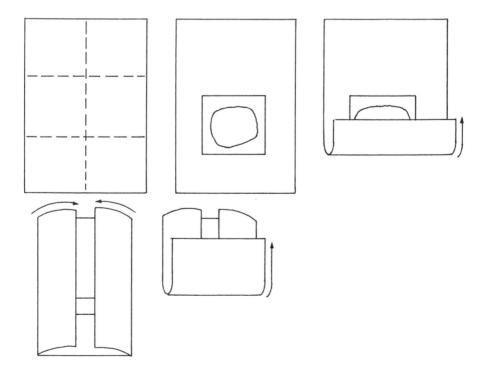

Meat and Poultry

Spit-roasted lamb is the meat most closely associated with Greece, where cooking meat over an open fire is a custom that has lasted for tens of centuries, or at least since the days when just the *aroma* of it was thought to be so special that it was offered up to the gods on Mount Olympus.

Considering the size of the country and the lack of decent grazing land, it's not surprising that meat from small, self-sufficient animals—lamb, pork, chicken, rabbit, sometimes goat, and game —is most commonly found on the Greek table. Or, at least it used to be. Nowadays, cattle are raised in the northern part of the country, and some beef is actually hung and aged in the American manner before it's served. Veal, at least as we know it, is a relative newcomer to the Greek table.

With the price of seafood constantly rising, for better or worse the Greeks have lately "discovered" red meat and eat it as much as they can afford to, while the rest of the Western world struggles to emulate the "old" Greek diet of vegetables, pasta, and fish, with meat reserved for special occasions.

But if the Greek diet is changing, the time-honored cooking methods have not. Stewing, braising, and similar techniques suitable for a pan over an open fire, and of course grilling, remain popular and have transcended the advent of electric ranges and stoves, harking back to the old days when the village breadmaker's oven was also the communal baking center.

Lamb Chops with Rosemary Grilled over Charcoal

PAIDAKIA THENDROLIVANO

YIELD: 4 TO 6 SERVINGS

The tiny, three-bite chops served at Periyali are cut from a rack of lamb in the restaurant kitchen, but you will undoubtedly find it easier to simply start with rib chops. The bone trimmings from the racks are used to make a rich-tasting, glossy sauce, known as a *demi-glace*. It's easy enough to make the sauce at home, and if you have the inclination and the time to do it, a small spoonful is a sublime addition to the chops.

---

12 or 16 lamb rib chops, each about
  ¾ inch thick
1 heaping tablespoon minced fresh
  rosemary
1 teaspoon salt

½ teaspoon freshly ground black
  pepper
½ cup Demi-glace *for Lamb Chops*
  (see page 236)
Rosemary sprigs, for garnish

With a small, sharp knife, scrape the chop bones clean (or have the butcher do this for you), then wrap them in foil so they don't burn during grilling.

Mix the rosemary, salt, and pepper in a small bowl, rubbing the mixture between your fingers to release the oils in the rosemary and give the mixture a somewhat pasty consistency. Rub some of this mixture into both sides of the chops. Set the chops aside for 30 minutes at room temperature, or cover and refrigerate for several hours.

Prepare a bed of medium-hot charcoal. Grill the chops about 6 inches from the coals for 4 to 5 minutes on each side, or until pink in the center. (The chops can also be oven-broiled about 4 inches below the source of heat for about 3 minutes per side.)

To serve, pull the foil off the bones. Arrange 3 or 4 chops on each dinner plate, and spoon a little of the *demi-glace* over each chop, dividing equally. Garnish with rosemary sprigs and serve with Roasted Potatoes and Broiled Tomatoes.

Shish Kabob of Lamb Grilled over Charcoal

SOUVLAKI ARNISIO

YIELD: 4 SERVINGS

*L*amb on a skewer is usually eaten as snack food in Greece; it is cut into small pieces, grilled until nearly incinerated, and served off street carts or in the tiny *"souvlaki* places" that dot every city and town. Occasionally the skewer includes vegetables, but it's not likely that you will ever find big, chunky pieces of marinated lamb, grilled just until the moment of juicy-pink perfection, with tender-crisp, grilled vegetables. This is one case, we think, where the Americanization of Greek folk food has definitely improved it.

½ teaspoon dried thyme leaves, crumbled

½ teaspoon dried oregano leaves, crumbled

2 or 3 large garlic cloves, minced (1½ teaspoons)

2 tablespoons dry red wine

2 tablespoons red-wine vinegar

2 tablespoons regular (not extra-virgin) olive oil

2 small bay leaves

2 pounds boneless leg of lamb cut into 1½-inch cubes (you will need 20 cubes)

1 large green bell pepper

1 large red bell pepper

1 large red onion

1 small zucchini

Salt and freshly ground black pepper, to taste

SAUCE

½ cup Chicken Broth (see page 5)

¼ cup extra-virgin olive oil

1 tablespoon lemon juice

Pinch fresh minced rosemary

Salt, to taste

In the bottom of a large bowl, mix the thyme, oregano, and garlic. Stir in the wine, vinegar, regular olive oil, and bay leaves. Add the lamb cubes, turning them until they are well coated. Cover and refrigerate for one to three days, stirring the mixture twice a day.

Core and seed the peppers. Cut each into 8 squares. Separate the onion into layers. Cut the layers into 1¼-inch squares to make 8 pieces. Cut the zucchini into 8 equal slices. Remove the lamb cubes from the marinade and pat dry. There will be 5 pieces of lamb on each of four 8-inch skewers, beginning and ending with the lamb. Between the cubes of lamb, skewer 2 pieces of red pepper, 2 pieces of green pepper, 2 pieces of onion, and 2 pieces of zucchini in an attractive, alternating pattern. Repeat with the remaining ingredients. Season the kabobs lightly with salt and pepper.

To make the sauce, simmer the chicken broth, extra-virgin olive oil, and lemon juice in a medium-size skillet until reduced by about half. Stir in the rosemary and season to taste with salt. Set aside and keep warm.

Prepare a bed of medium-hot charcoal. Grill the kabobs 4 to 6 inches from the coals for 12 to 15 minutes, turning frequently, or until pink in the center. The kabobs can be oven-broiled about 4 inches below the source of heat for about 6 minutes, turning once. Push the meat and vegetables off the skewer and onto dinner plates. Accompany the kabobs with rice and Okra or Green Beans with Tomatoes.

Roast Lamb
with Giant White Beans

*A*s the lamb roasts, the juices drip down into the beans, giving them an exquisite flavor. Make sure the lamb is well trimmed of fat so that the beans won't be greasy, especially if you prefer your lamb—as the Greeks do—a little on the well-done side.

4 large garlic cloves
1 cup flat-leaf parsley sprigs
1 recipe Giant White Beans (see page 9)
2 tablespoons tomato paste dissolved in 2 cups water
5 1/2- to 6-pound leg of lamb, trimmed of excess fat

2 tablespoons regular (not extra-virgin) olive oil
1 teaspoon dried oregano leaves, crumbled
1/2 teaspoon salt
1/4 teaspoon freshly ground black pepper

Preheat the oven to 450°F. Chop the garlic and parsley together until both are minced and well mixed. In a large bowl, stir the garlic mixture into the warm beans. Spoon the beans into a roasting pan that is just large enough to hold the lamb comfortably. Drizzle the tomato paste and water mixture over the beans. Rub the lamb with the olive oil, oregano, salt, and pepper and set it on top of the beans. Place the lamb in the oven and immediately reduce the heat to 325°F. Roast for 20 to 25 minutes per pound, or until a meat thermometer inserted in the center of the thickest part of the leg, without touching fat or bone, registers 140° for rare, 160° for medium, and 170° for well done. Remove the lamb from the oven. Cover the pan lightly with foil and set aside for about 20 minutes before carving. Carve the lamb into thin slices and arrange on dinner plates with the beans alongside. Serve with Periyali's Mixed Salad Greens.

Boneless Leg of Lamb Marinated in Yogurt

*C*ooked together or just served together, lamb and yogurt make one of the world's most perfect culinary couplings. Another time you can substitute a tablespoon or so of chopped fresh mint for the anise seed in the marinade. This is a perfectly grand dish for company or a family gathering. We like it served with plain broiled tomatoes, or a salad of Red Onions and Rocket, and Greek Fried Potatoes.

2-pound boneless butterflied leg of lamb

1/2 cup plain whole-milk yogurt, preferably sheep's-milk

2 tablespoons lemon juice

3 large garlic cloves, put through a garlic press

1/2 teaspoon anise seed, crushed

1/2 teaspoon salt

1/4 teaspoon white pepper

Spread the lamb out flat and trim as much of the fat as possible. In a small bowl, mix the yogurt, lemon juice, garlic, anise seed, salt, and pepper. Spoon about half of the yogurt mixture into the bottom of a shallow pan that is large enough to hold the lamb comfortably. Place the lamb in the pan. Spread the remaining yogurt mixture over the lamb. Cover and refrigerate for 8 to 24 hours, turning occasionally.

Preheat the oven to 500°F. Pat the lamb dry on paper towels and place it in a shallow baking pan, reserving the marinade. Roast the lamb for 12 minutes, basting once after 6 minutes with half of the remaining marinade. Turn and roast 12 minutes longer, basting again after 6 minutes. Remove the lamb to a carving board and let it rest for 10 minutes before cutting into thin slices to serve. The thicker parts of the lamb will be medium-rare and the thinner parts will be more well-done.

Nicola's Mother's Lamb with Rice and Yogurt

ARNAKI ME RIZI KE YAOURTI

The idea here is to stir the cold yogurt into the lamb, sauce, and rice after it arrives at the table. You might also want to try stuffing the lamb and yogurt into split rounds of Fried Bread Dough or warm pita bread.

1/4 cup regular (not extra-virgin) olive oil

2 large onions, chopped (2 cups)

2 large garlic cloves, minced

2 pounds lamb stew meat, cut into 1-inch cubes

2 cups water

1 can (14 1/2 ounces) whole peeled tomatoes, chopped with their juice (see Note)

2 tablespoons chopped flat-leaf parsley

2 teaspoons salt

1/4 teaspoon freshly ground black pepper

3 cups hot cooked rice

1 cup sheep's milk or other whole-milk yogurt (see page 303)

Chopped flat-leaf parsley, for garnish

Heat 2 tablespoons of the olive oil in a large, heavy skillet or sauté pan. When it is hot, add the onion and garlic and cook over medium-high heat, stirring frequently, until golden. Remove with a slotted spoon to a plate and set aside. Heat the remaining 2 tablespoons of oil in the skillet. Stir in the lamb and cook briefly, just until the meat has lost its raw look. Add the water, stirring up the crust and brown bits that cling to the bottom of the pan. Stir the onion and garlic back into the skillet with the lamb. Bring the mixture to a boil. Reduce the heat, partially cover, and simmer for 35 to 40 minutes, or until the lamb is tender, stirring occasionally. Stir in the tomatoes, parsley, salt, and pepper. Bring the mixture back to a simmer and cook, uncovered, for 5 to 10 minutes, stirring frequently, until the sauce has reduced slightly. It should not be

Place the lamb shanks in a 6-quart saucepan or Dutch oven. Cover with water and bring to a boil over high heat. Reduce the heat and simmer for 5 minutes. Drain the shanks, rinse them in cool water, and set aside. Rinse the saucepan and dry it. Heat the olive oil in the saucepan. When it is hot, add the onion and garlic and cook over medium-high heat, stirring frequently, until the onion is softened. Add the red and white wines and cook at a fast simmer, stirring occasionally, until most of the liquid has evaporated. Stir in the tomatoes, water (only if using fresh tomatoes), bay leaf, salt, and pepper. Add the lamb shanks, turning to coat them with the sauce. Bring the mixture to a boil. Reduce the heat, cover, and simmer gently for 50 to 60 minutes, occasionally spooning the sauce over the shanks, until they are very tender. Remove the shanks from the sauce. Remove the bay leaf and discard it. If the sauce seems thin, reduce it over high heat for several minutes. Serve the lamb shanks on orzo or rice, with the sauce spooned over the meat and pasta. Sprinkle with parsley and accompany with Zucchini and Carrots.

NOTE: The easiest way to chop canned tomatoes is to use clean kitchen scissors and cut them up in the can.

Victor Gouras's Sautéed Breast of Chicken with Lemon Sauce
KOTOPOULO LEMONATO

YIELD: 6 SERVINGS

A first-class Greek restaurant is about the last thing one would expect to find in a mountaintop village on the out-of-the-way island of Patmos. But there it is, complete with terrace and flowering vines, set in Victor and Irene Gouras's ancient stone house in the village of Hora. This intimate little restaurant came to the attention of American tourists a few years ago, after the couple helped to develop the menu at Periyali. When we dined there recently, we sampled a number of the restaurant's specialties, including these delicate chicken breasts, which came to the table flawlessly cooked and glistening with a light coating of lemon sauce.

Victor and Irene serve only the fresh vegetables they grow themselves in a tiny garden several miles away from the restaurant. In a space not half as large as a tennis court, they grow everything from grape leaves and zucchini to plum trees and herbs. There's even a chicken coop in the corner where fresh eggs are gathered daily.

---

1 cup Chicken Broth (see page 5)
1/2 cup dry white wine
1 tablespoon minced shallot
8 tablespoons (1 stick) unsalted
  butter, softened
Lemon juice, to taste
3 whole chicken breasts, skinned,
  boned, and cut in half

2 eggs
Salt and white pepper, to taste
Granulated flour (see page 291),
  for dredging chicken
Regular (not extra-virgin) olive oil,
  for frying
Chopped flat-leaf parsley, for garnish

Combine the broth, wine, and shallot in a small, heavy saucepan. Cook over medium heat for about 20 minutes, or until the mixture has been reduced to about 2 tablespoons. Remove from the heat and gradually beat in the softened butter with a whisk. (The first tablespoon or so of butter will undoubtedly melt when beaten into the hot reduction, but the remaining butter should soften, not melt, into the sauce.) Add the lemon juice to taste. Set the pan aside away from the heat. The sauce will cool and thicken slightly, but will warm up and thin out when spooned over the cooked breasts.

Lightly pound the breast halves between sheets of waxed paper with a smooth meat mallet or rolling pin until they are of even thickness. Lightly beat the eggs in a pie plate or other wide, shallow dish and season to taste with salt and pepper. Sprinkle the flour on a sheet of waxed paper. Just before cooking, lightly dredge the breasts in flour, shaking off the excess. The coating should not be heavy. Dip the floured breasts into the beaten egg.

Heat a scant ⅛ inch of olive oil in a large, heavy skillet. When it is hot add the breast halves and cook over medium-high heat until light golden on both sides and firm, but not hard, to the touch, about 1½ to 2 minutes per side. Arrange 1 half breast per serving on dinner plates. Spoon the sauce over the breasts, dividing evenly. Sprinkle with chopped parsley and serve immediately with rice.

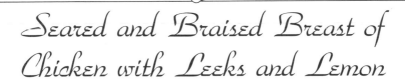

Seared and Braised Breast of Chicken with Leeks and Lemon Cream Sauce
KOTOPOULO LEMONATO ME PRASSA

YIELD: 4 SERVINGS

*T*his is a recipe you'll find yourself turning to frequently when you want to serve something stylish and easy. At Periyali, the sauced chicken is presented with plain broiled tomatoes and Rice Pilaf that's been turned out of a little fluted mold onto the dinner plate.

---

6 small leeks (no more than 1 inch in diameter)

2 cups Chicken Broth (see page 5)

2 tablespoons lemon juice

4 large chicken breasts, skinned, boned, and cut in half

Salt and freshly ground black pepper, to taste

Granulated flour (see page 291), for dredging chicken

¼ cup regular (not extra-virgin) olive oil

1 cup dry white wine

1 cup heavy cream

Chopped flat-leaf parsley, for garnish

HOLLY GARRISON

Trim off the green leaves and the roots from the leeks. Rinse the leeks thoroughly, then cut them into ¼-inch slices (about 2½ cups). Place the leeks, chicken broth, and lemon juice in a medium-size saucepan. Bring to a boil. Reduce the heat and simmer until the leeks are tender, 3 to 5 minutes. Remove from the heat and set aside.

Make 3 shallow, diagonal slashes on the top side of each breast half. Lightly pound the breast halves between sheets of waxed paper with a smooth meat mallet or rolling pin until they are of even thickness. Season lightly with salt and pepper. Sprinkle the flour on a sheet of waxed paper. Dredge the chicken in the flour, shaking off the excess. Heat the olive oil in a large skillet. When it is hot add the breast halves and cook over medium-high heat until light golden, about 1½ to 2 minutes per side. (The breasts will finish cooking later.) Remove the breasts from the skillet and set aside. Discard the oil in the skillet. Add the wine to the hot skillet and boil for 1 minute, stirring constantly. Add the leek mixture and cook over high heat, stirring frequently, until most of the liquid has evaporated. Whisk in the cream and bring the mixture to a simmer. Add the reserved breasts and continue to simmer slowly until the breasts feel firm, 4 to 5 minutes. Remove the breasts from the skillet to dinner plates. Reduce the cream mixture in the skillet over high heat until it achieves a thick, saucelike consistency. Spoon the sauce over the breasts, dividing equally. Sprinkle with parsley and serve as suggested above.

Pot-Roasted Chicken and Potatoes with Vinegar Sauce

YIELD: 4 SERVINGS

*J*ust when we thought there was nothing new under the sun to do with a chicken, up pops a very old Greek recipe with all the elements that make it exactly right for today's busy cook.

---

1 broiler-fryer chicken, weighing
  about 3½ pounds
¼ cup extra-virgin olive oil
¼ cup red-wine vinegar
1 garlic clove, put through a
  garlic press
½ teaspoon dried thyme
  leaves, crumbled

½ teaspoon salt
⅛ teaspoon freshly ground
  black pepper
6 to 8 new potatoes
¼ cup Chicken Broth (see page 5)
Sprigs of fresh thyme or flat-leaf
  parsley, for garnish

Rinse the chicken and pat dry with paper towels. Pull out and discard the lumps of fat just inside the cavity. Place the chicken, neck end first, in a plastic bag. Make a marinade by mixing the olive oil, 2 tablespoons of the vinegar, garlic, thyme, salt, and pepper in a 1-cup measure. Pour some of the marinade into the cavity of the chicken and the rest around it. Close the bag tightly and rub the marinade over the chicken. Set aside at room temperature for about 30 minutes, or refrigerate for up to 12 hours, the longer the better, turning the bag occasionally.

Preheat the oven to 375°F. Remove the chicken from the bag, leaving the marinade in the bag and reserving it. Fold the wing tips behind the back and tie the drumsticks together. Place the chicken breast side up on an oiled rack in a Dutch oven or other large heavy stewpot. Drop the potatoes into the bag containing the marinade. Turn the potatoes in the bag until well coated. Arrange the potatoes around the chicken. Pour the chicken broth into the bottom of the roasting pan. Cover and roast for 1 hour. Uncover and continue to roast for about 30 minutes, turning the potatoes and basting the chicken occasionally with pan juices, until the chicken is golden and the potatoes are soft. Remove the chicken and potatoes and keep warm on a serving platter. Spoon off and discard the excess fat in the pan. Set the pan over high heat and add the remaining 2 tablespoons of vinegar. Bring to a boil, stirring almost constantly, until the sauce has reduced and thickened enough to lightly coat the spoon. Carve the chicken and serve with the potatoes and pan sauce. Garnish the serving platter with sprigs of thyme or parsley. One or two grilled vegetables would be very tasty accompaniments.

Nicola's Mother's Stuffed Roasted Chicken

YIELD: 4 SERVINGS

Stuffing chicken with highly seasoned ground meat and liver is a typical Greek preparation. What makes Nicola's mother's roast chicken a little different is that she scatters small chunks of hard cheese around the chicken. The cheese melts among the potatoes as they roast and eventually becomes rather crisp and pleasantly chewy, so make sure everyone gets some of it when you dish up the potatoes.

1 broiler-fryer chicken, weighing
  about 3½ pounds
Salt and freshly ground black pepper
1 tablespoon regular (not extra-
  virgin) olive oil
3 garlic cloves, finely chopped
½ pound ground veal, pork, lamb,
  or beef
¼ pound chicken livers, chopped
1 small tomato, chopped (½ cup)

1 tablespoon dried oregano
  leaves, crumbled
1 teaspoon softened butter
1¼ pounds (about 4) all-purpose
  potatoes, peeled and cut
  into quarters
1 tablespoon melted butter
¼ pound hard cheese, such as
  graviera, kasseri, or kefalotiri,
  cut into ½-inch pieces

Rinse the chicken and blot dry with paper towels. Sprinkle the
cavity lightly with salt and pepper and fold the wing tips behind
the back. Heat the olive oil in a large skillet over medium-high
heat. Stir in the garlic and immediately add the ground meat and
livers. Cook over medium heat, stirring frequently, for about 5
minutes, or until most of the liquid has evaporated. Stir in the
tomato, oregano, ½ teaspoon salt, and ¼ teaspoon pepper until
well blended. Remove from the heat and cool slightly.

Preheat the oven to 350°F. Fill the chicken cavity lightly with
stuffing. Set the remaining stuffing aside. Tie the legs together and
set the chicken on a rack in a shallow roasting pan. Rub the chicken
with the softened butter. Arrange the potatoes around the chicken.
Spoon any remaining stuffing over and around the potatoes. Drizzle the melted butter over the potatoes. Tuck pieces of cheese here
and there between the potatoes. Roast for about 1½ to 1¾ hours,
basting once or twice with the pan drippings as they accumulate,
until the chicken is golden and the juices run clear when the thigh
is pierced with a kitchen fork or the tip of a knife. Carve the chicken
and serve with Nicola's Mother's Beans Stewed in Tomato Sauce.

Charles Bowman's Tips for Perfect Charcoal Grilling

One of the most frequently asked questions at Periyali is why the charcoal-grilled meat, poultry, and fish are so moist, flavorful, and evenly cooked, when similar results are so difficult to achieve at home.

Perfect charcoal grilling has always been a chef's secret, although Charles has always been happy to share this bit of professional wisdom with anyone who asks.

Part of the problem when preparing restaurant recipes at home lies with the cooking equipment, or lack thereof, in the home kitchen. One such piece of equipment is the lava rock grill, which constantly and effortlessly maintains the blistering temperature of red-hot charcoal with just the flick of a dial. To impart the flavor and well-defined grill marks associated with charcoal cooking, marinated meat, poultry, or fish is first seared briefly on the grill and then transferred to the oven to finish cooking under more controlled conditions.

It's easy enough to do this at home, but most cooks simply don't want to bother lighting *both* the charcoal grill and the oven. Grilling a thick, well-marbled piece of red meat, which can more or less take care of itself over a charcoal fire, is one thing, but trying to maneuver an irregularly shaped chicken or, even trickier, a delicate, lean fish in such capricious heat conditions so that it's perfectly and evenly cooked is difficult, even for the best grill chef.

To circumvent the need to light a fire, you can sear the meat under an oven broiler, in a sizzling hot skillet, or on an electric kitchen grill or range-top grill before it is oven-finished. The flavor of an open fire is sacrificed, of course, but the brief alliance with intense heat does a good job of sealing in the flavor and natural juiciness of the meat.

Oven-Grilled Chicken

The chickens one tastes in the *souvlaki* places in Greece are almost always crisp-skinned, deep-flavored, and, for the most part, plenty juicy, with a distinct lemony tang. However, none of the cooks will ever give you even the tiniest clue as to how the chicken is marinated. Greek restaurant owners tend to be very close-mouthed about their recipes. Nevertheless, the method that follows for grilling chicken in the oven comes very close to the flavor of a chicken that has been spit-roasted over an open fire. By the way, if you want to add a clove or two of crushed garlic to the marinade, go ahead, although it is not customary to do so.

---

1 broiler-fryer chicken, weighing	½ teaspoon salt
2¾ to 3 pounds	⅛ teaspoon freshly ground
2 tablespoons lemon juice	black pepper
1 tablespoon extra-virgin olive oil	

Preheat the oven to 500°F. Rinse the chicken and pat dry with paper towels. Pull out and discard the lumps of fat just inside the cavity. With poultry shears, cut out the backbone. Spread the chicken out, skin side up, and flatten it as much as possible with the palm of your hand. In a small bowl, mix the lemon juice, olive oil, salt, and pepper. Use this mixture to brush the chicken on both sides. Arrange the flattened chicken on the rack of a broiling pan, skin side up.

Roast, without turning, for 35 to 40 minutes, or until the chicken is dark brown and crusty and the juices run clear when the thigh is pierced with a fork or the tip of a knife. Cut the chicken in halves or quarters to serve. Spoon off and discard some of the fat left in the roasting pan and serve the remaining juice with the chicken. Serve with Potato Salad and *Horta* or Beets with Beetgreens.

Grilled Scallops of Venison Marinated with Herbs and Olive Oil

ELAFI PSYTO

YIELD: 4 TO 6 SERVINGS

*W*e know lots of people who thought they didn't like venison—until they finally agreed to have a bite of it off someone else's plate at Periyali. To make sure that the venison you serve is as good as this, buy it from a reliable purveyor. If the meat comes straight from the hunter, make certain that it has been properly handled and dressed. A bad piece of venison can ruin the pleasure of eating it for life. Good venison is not particularly "gamey," but it is extremely lean, so some fat must be put into it during cooking. In the case of these thin scallops, the oil in the marinade does it, and they will be very juicy and tender as long as they are not over-cooked.

---

*1 1/2 to 2 pounds venison scallops
(about 2 ounces each) from the loin
or top round of the leg
Salt and freshly ground black pepper,
to taste
Chopped flat-leaf parsley, for garnish*

*MARINADE
1 tablespoon coarsely chopped
flat-leaf parsley
1 tablespoon coarsely chopped fresh
chives or scallion tops
1 teaspoon dried oregano leaves
1 teaspoon dried thyme leaves
1/2 cup extra-virgin olive oil
3 tablespoons red-wine vinegar*

SAUCE
2 teaspoons red-wine vinegar
2 cups Beef Brown Stock
  (see page 4)
2 tablespoons extra-virgin olive oil
2 teaspoons minced chives or scallion
  tops
2 teaspoons minced flat-leaf parsley
1 teaspoon minced fresh thyme leaves
  or ½ teaspoon dried thyme leaves,
  crumbled

1 teaspoon minced fresh oregano
  leaves or ½ teaspoon dried oregano
  leaves, crumbled
Salt, to taste, depending on the
  saltiness of the stock
⅛ teaspoon freshly ground
  black pepper
1 to 2 tablespoons butter, softened

Lightly pound the pieces of venison between sheets of waxed paper with a smooth meat mallet or rolling pin until they are of an even thickness, about ¼ inch.

To make the marinade, place the parsley, chives, oregano, and thyme on a cutting surface and chop together until very fine and well mixed. Mix the chopped herbs, olive oil, and vinegar in a large, shallow baking dish. Add the venison, turning in the marinade until well coated. Set aside at room temperature for 30 minutes, or cover and refrigerate for up to 24 hours, the longer the better.

To make the sauce, heat a large skillet. When it is hot, add the vinegar, then immediately stir in the brown stock, olive oil, chives, parsley, thyme, and oregano. Cook over medium heat until reduced by about half. Season with salt and pepper and set aside.

Prepare a bed of medium-hot charcoal. Season the venison to taste with salt and pepper. Place the meat on the grill 3 or 4 inches from the coals and cook briefly on both sides until done to your liking; most people prefer it medium. The venison can also be cooked in a very hot skillet (see Note). Transfer to dinner plates, dividing evenly, about 3 or 4 slices per serving. Rewarm the sauce. Remove from the heat and swirl in the butter. Pour over the venison and sprinkle with chopped parsley. Serve with Roasted Potatoes and Okra or Green Beans and Tomatoes.

NOTE: If you sear the venison in a skillet, the sauce can be used to deglaze the skillet after the meat has been removed.

Grilled Scallops of Veal with Oregano and Olive Oil

MOSCHARI SCHARAS ME RIGANI

YIELD: 4 SERVINGS

Because these veal scallops are evenly thin, they take well to cooking over charcoal. They need only the briefest time over the fire to be just cooked through, the best way, we think, to serve veal.

1/2 cup regular (not extra-virgin) olive oil

2 teaspoons dried oregano leaves, crumbled

1 1/2 to 2 pounds veal scallops

Salt and freshly ground black pepper, to taste

Extra-virgin olive oil

Lemon juice

Chopped flat-leaf parsley, for garnish

Mix the regular olive oil and oregano in a shallow pan. Dip the veal scallops into the oil mixture to coat them evenly and set aside at room temperature for 30 minutes, or refrigerate for up to 24 hours, the longer the better.

Prepare a bed of medium-hot charcoal, or heat a large skillet until it is very hot. Season the veal lightly with salt and pepper. Place the meat on the grill about 4 inches above the medium-hot charcoal and grill for about 2 minutes on each side, or until just done through. Be careful not to overcook or the meat will toughen. If cooking in a hot skillet, blot the veal dry before seasoning it with salt and pepper, then sear it for about 2 minutes on each side. Place the veal on dinner plates, dividing evenly. Drizzle each serving with a little extra-virgin olive oil and lemon juice and sprinkle with parsley. Serve with Roasted Potatoes and Zucchini and Carrots or Crisp Snow Peas.

Sautéed Calf's Liver with Red Onion and Vinegar Sauce

SIKOTI MOSCHARI

YIELD: 4 SERVINGS

The greatest injustice that can be done to this dish is to overcook the liver, which is easy to do, since such thin slices can cook through and start to curl almost before you know it. Although the liver should not be served rare, it should have a distinct pinkness in the center.

---

3 tablespoons regular (not extra-virgin) olive oil

2 large red onions, cut into vertical slices (2 cups)

Granulated flour (see page 291), for dredging liver

1½ pounds calf's liver, cut into 8 thin slices

Salt and freshly ground black pepper, to taste

1 tablespoon plus 2 teaspoons butter

2 tablespoons red-wine vinegar

1½ cups Beef Brown Stock (see page 4)

1 tablespoon chopped flat-leaf parsley

Heat 1 tablespoon of the olive oil in a large skillet. When it is hot, add the onion and cook over medium-high heat, stirring frequently, until soft and just starting to brown. Remove to a small bowl with a slotted spoon and set aside.

Sprinkle the flour on a piece of waxed paper. Season the liver with salt and pepper, then dredge lightly in flour on both sides, shaking off the excess. Add another tablespoon of oil and 1 teaspoon of butter to the skillet. When it is hot, add half of the liver slices and cook over medium-high heat for about 2 minutes on each side for medium done. Remove from the skillet and keep warm in a 200°F oven. Add the remaining tablespoon of oil and 1 teaspoon of butter to the skillet. When it is hot, add the remaining liver slices and cook as before. Remove the liver slices and stir in the vinegar. Add the stock and cook over high heat, stirring frequently, until the sauce is reduced to about ½ cup. Remove from the heat. Season with salt and pepper, if necessary. Swirl in the remaining tablespoon of butter. Place the liver on dinner plates, dividing evenly, and arrange the reserved onion on top. Spoon the sauce over the liver and onions and sprinkle with parsley. Serve with Roasted Potatoes and *Horta*.

Rabbit Stew

KOUNELI STIFADO

YIELD: 4 SERVINGS

A good *stifado* can't have too many little white onions. This is Greek comfort food at its best. The word *stifado* means stew and, as you might guess, the same preparation technique can be used to cook many things besides rabbit. Chicken, big beef cubes, and duck are all good candidates for the *stifado* pot. All you need with this is plenty of good bread to help sop up the last drop of broth left in the bottom of the bowl.

MARINADE
1 small carrot, coarsely chopped
1 celery rib, coarsely chopped
1 small onion, coarsely chopped
2 small bay leaves
1 sprig fresh rosemary
1 sprig flat-leaf parsley
1 garlic clove, cut into 3 slices
½ teaspoon salt
⅛ teaspoon freshly ground
  black pepper
¼ cup dry red wine
2 tablespoons red-wine vinegar

RABBIT
1 frying rabbit, weighing about
  3 pounds, cut into pieces (see Note)
Salt and freshly ground black pepper
8 ounces (about 2 cups) tiny
  pearl onions
1 can (14½ ounces) whole tomatoes
2 tablespoons tomato paste
½ cup regular (not extra-virgin)
  olive oil
1 or 2 large garlic cloves, minced
1 sprig fresh rosemary
2 small bay leaves

4 whole allspice

4 whole cloves

¼ cup red-wine vinegar

½ cup dry red wine

2 tablespoons butter

Mix the vegetables and the dry ingredients for the marinade in a large bowl. Stir in the red wine and vinegar. Rinse the rabbit and pat dry with paper towels. Add the rabbit to the marinade and stir to coat well. Cover and refrigerate for at least 24 hours, or up to 3 days, stirring occasionally.

When ready to cook, remove the rabbit from the marinade and pat dry with paper towels. Season with salt and pepper and set aside. Place the pearl onions in a saucepan of boiling water for about 1 minute. Drain and add cold water to the onions in the pan. Remove the onions from the water, trim off the roots, and slip off the skins. Drain the tomatoes, reserving the juice. Add enough water to the tomato juice to make 2 cups. Place the tomatoes, tomato paste, and tomato juice in a food processor and process until smooth.

Heat ¼ cup of the olive oil in a Dutch oven or other large, heavy saucepan. Add the rabbit pieces and brown on all sides over medium-high heat. Remove from the pan and set aside. Discard the oil remaining in the pan. Heat the remaining ¼ cup oil in the same pan. When it is hot, add the pearl onions and cook over medium-high heat, turning frequently, until lightly browned. Reduce the heat, then add the garlic and cook, stirring, for a few seconds. Add the rosemary, bay leaves, allspice, cloves, vinegar, and wine. Cook, stirring, until the liquid has partially evaporated and is somewhat syrupy. Stir in the processed tomato mixture, butter, ½ teaspoon salt, ⅛ teaspoon pepper, and the browned rabbit pieces. Bring to a boil over medium-high heat. Reduce the heat so that the mixture barely simmers. Partially cover and simmer slowly for about 35 minutes, stirring occasionally, until a leg is tender when pierced with a fork. Arrange the rabbit pieces in shallow bowls. Remove the bay leaves and rosemary from the sauce. Ladle the sauce and onions over each serving, dividing equally. Serve with crusty bread.

NOTE: Charles cuts the rabbit into 7 pieces. He removes all 4 legs and cuts the loin into 3 parts. The ribs are not served at the restaurant, but Charles suggests including them, since the rib meat is tender and delicious, if a little difficult to get at.

Duck Stew Substituting a 5- to 6-pound duck for rabbit makes this a quicker preparation, since the duck is not marinated.

Eliminate the marinade ingredients; also the olive oil and butter called for in the list of ingredients for Rabbit Stew.

Preheat the oven to 400°F. Rinse and dry the duck. Trim off and discard the wing tips, the tail, and the flap of neck skin, and pull out and discard the fat from inside the cavity. With poultry shears or a meat cleaver, cut the duck in half lengthwise. Cut out the backbone and cut the duck into quarters. Prick the skin on each piece many times with the tines of a fork, being careful not to penetrate the meat. Arrange the duck pieces, skin side up, on a high rack in a roasting pan. Roast for 45 minutes to 1 hour, or until the fat beneath the skin has been rendered, the skin is very crisp, and the juices run clear when the thigh is pierced with a fork or the tip of a knife. Remove the duck from the roasting pan and season with ½ teaspoon salt and ⅛ teaspoon pepper.

Proceed with the recipe for Rabbit Stew from the point of preparing the onions. (There is no need to brown the duck, since it has already been roasted.) Continue with the recipe, eliminating the butter in the sauce and simmering for the same length of time, or until the leg and thigh are very tender. Arrange the duck quarters in shallow bowls. Remove the bay leaves and rosemary from the sauce. Ladle the sauce and onions over each serving, dividing equally. Serve with crusty bread.

Roast Pheasant

FASIANOS STO FOURNO

YIELD: 4 SERVINGS

Although it has a pleasing flavor, pheasant, whether it's domestically raised or comes straight from the wild, is always a little on the dry side and even a little chewy, so it's important not to overcook it. In Greece, pheasant is usually oven-roasted, or cooked on a spit, and served more or less plain, with no more than a squirt of lemon juice for a touch of piquancy. At Periyali the bird is moistened with a very simple sauce made from the wing tips and giblets.

---

1 farm-raised pheasant, weighing
  about 3 pounds
Salt and freshly ground black pepper,
  to taste
6 sprigs flat-leaf parsley
2 lemon wedges
2 bay leaves
2 garlic cloves, each cut into 3 slices
1 branch fresh thyme or 1/2 teaspoon
  dried thyme leaves, crumbled
2 tablespoons regular (not extra-
  virgin) olive oil
SAUCE
2 tablespoons extra-virgin olive oil

3 small celery ribs, coarsely chopped
  (1 cup)
1 small onion, coarsely chopped
  (1/2 cup)
1 medium-size carrot, coarsely chopped
  (1/2 cup)
1 cup Chicken Broth (see page 5)
1 cup water

2 tablespoons butter
1 tablespoon lemon juice
1 teaspoon chopped flat-leaf parsley
Salt, to taste

Remove the neck and giblets from the pheasant and cut off the wing tips. Refrigerate the pheasant until ready to roast.

To make the sauce, heat the extra-virgin olive oil in a medium-size saucepan. When it is hot add the wing tips and giblets, except for the liver, which can be discarded or saved for another use. Cook over medium-high heat, stirring frequently, until nicely browned.

Stir in the celery, onion, carrot, chicken broth, and water. Cover and simmer for about 1 hour. Strain the broth into a small bowl and set aside. You should have about 1 cup. If more, boil to reduce slightly; if less, add water or chicken broth to make up the difference.

Preheat the oven to 400°F. Rinse the pheasant and pat dry with paper towels. Lightly season the inside with salt and pepper; season the outside with salt. Stuff the body cavity with the parsley sprigs, lemon wedges, bay leaves, garlic, and thyme. Tie the legs together with string. Fasten the wings to the body with small skewers. Heat the regular olive oil in a Dutch oven or other large, heavy saucepan. When it is hot, add the pheasant and brown on all sides, adjusting the heat as necessary. With the breast side up, place the pheasant, still in the browning pan, in the oven and roast, uncovered, for about 35 to 40 minutes, or just until the juices run clear when the thigh is pierced with a fork or the tip of a knife. Remove the pheasant to a platter or carving board and keep warm while finishing the sauce.

Discard the fat from the roasting pan and set the pan over medium-high heat. Stir in the reserved broth, butter, and lemon juice. Cook at a brisk simmer until the liquid is reduced by about half. Stir in the parsley and season with salt. Carve the pheasant into pieces (the same way a chicken is carved), or cut it into quarters and serve with the sauce. At Periyali, the pheasant is usually accompanied by Rice Pilaf and a green vegetable.

Chicken and Potatoes
Baked in Phyllo

Exohikon means leftovers. In Greece, when things are left over, instead of just heating them up, the women wrap them in *phyllo* and bake them. You can use fresh or leftover chicken for this recipe. The result, either way, is quite delicious.

---

4 slices chicken breast, each weighing
  3 to 4 ounces
Salt and freshly ground black pepper,
  to taste
Granulated flour (see page 291),
  for dredging chicken
1/4 cup regular (not extra-virgin)
  olive oil
1 tablespoon butter
6 small new potatoes, thinly sliced
  (about 1 pound)

2 small onions, sliced and the slices
  separated into rings
1/2 cup dry white wine
2 tablespoons regular (small-curd)
  cottage cheese
1/4 cup crumbled feta cheese
1 tablespoon chopped flat-leaf parsley
10 sheets ultra-thin phyllo
1/2 to 3/4 cup (1 to 2 1/2 sticks)
  Clarified Melted Butter (see
  page 8)

Before starting to make this recipe, please read "How to Work with *Phyllo*" (see page 12).

Pound the cutlets lightly between sheets of waxed paper with a smooth mallet or rolling pin until they are of an even thickness. Season to taste with salt and pepper. Sprinkle the flour on a sheet of waxed paper. Just before cooking, lightly dredge the cutlets in flour, shaking off the excess.

Heat 2 tablespoons of the olive oil and the butter in a large skillet. When it is hot, add the cutlets and cook over medium-high heat until they are barely colored and still rare on the inside. (They will finish cooking later.) Remove from the skillet to a plate. Cover lightly and refrigerate until cooled.

In the same skillet, heat 1 tablespoon of the remaining oil. When it is hot, add the potatoes and cook over medium heat, stirring frequently, until soft and lightly browned. Remove to a plate and set aside. Add the remaining tablespoon of oil to the skillet. When it is hot, add the onion rings and cook over medium heat, stirring frequently, until soft. Add the wine and cook, stirring, until it is nearly evaporated and the onions are lightly caramelized. Off the heat, return the potatoes to the skillet and stir gently until well blended. Add the cheeses and parsley and toss gently; set aside.

Preheat the oven to 375°F. Place 2 sheets of *phyllo* on a work surface, a long side facing you, and cut into 3 strips, each measuring about 5½ inches in width. Fold the 3 strips in half, crosswise,

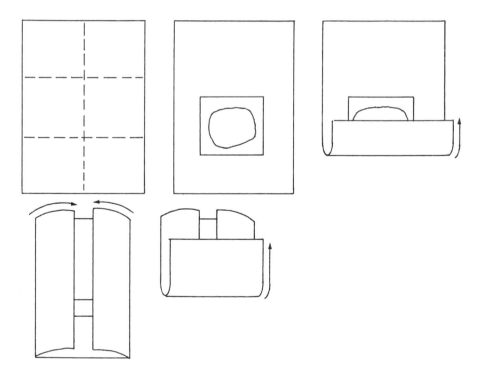

and cut in half. (These pieces will be used as patches to reinforce the *phyllo* packets; there will be 2 patches left over.) Place 1 sheet of *phyllo*, a short side facing you, on a flat work surface. Brush with butter. Place another sheet of *phyllo* on top of the first and brush with butter. Place a patch of *phyllo* on the buttered phyllo as shown and brush with butter. Place a piece of chicken on the patch. Cover with about ½ cup of the potato mixture. Fold the bottom of the *phyllo* over the chicken and potato mixture. Brush the fold with butter. Fold in the sides of the *phyllo* and brush with butter. Roll up to make a neat packet. Brush the top with butter, making sure to seal the end flap of the *phyllo* onto the packet. Repeat with the remaining ingredients to make 3 more packets. As they are finished, place the packets on an ungreased baking sheet.

Bake for 12 to 15 minutes, or until golden brown. Remove from the oven and serve immediately. Serve with *Horta*.

Nicola's Mother's Meatballs

KEFTEDES

YIELD: 24 TO 30 MEATBALLS; 4 TO 6 SERVINGS

Tradition says that for *keftedes* to be good they must contain fourteen ingredients. Nicola's mother's recipe for meatballs, which is so delicious that you will have to forcibly drag yourself away from the platter to keep from overindulging, calls for only thirteen ingredients, probably because she doesn't use the small quantity of milk called for in many recipes. The cheese is optional and we can never decide if we like the *keftedes* better with it or without it. If you're as indecisive about this as we are, you can compromise and use cheese in half the meatballs and leave the other half of them plain.

2 slices firm white bread, torn into
  small pieces (about 1 cup)
1½ pounds lean ground beef or
  ¾ pound lean ground beef and
  ¾ pound lean ground lamb
2 eggs, lightly beaten
1 large onion, minced (1 cup)
2 large garlic cloves, minced
¼ cup finely chopped fresh mint
  leaves
2 tablespoons chopped flat-leaf
  parsley
1 teaspoon dried oregano leaves,
  crumbled

1½ teaspoons salt
½ teaspoon freshly ground black
  pepper
¼ teaspoon ground allspice
1 cup finely chopped graviera or
  Parmesan cheese
Water, if needed
Granulated flour (see page 291),
  for dredging meatballs
Regular (not extra-virgin) olive oil,
  for frying
Mint leaves, for garnish

In a small bowl, soak the bread briefly in water. Remove the bread
and squeeze to remove most of the water. Set the bread aside. In a
large bowl, mix the ground meats, damp bread, eggs, onion, garlic,
mint, parsley, oregano, salt, pepper, and allspice. Add the cheese
and mix gently until well blended. The mixture should be rather
loose. If not, add a little cool water and mix gently. Shape into
small patties measuring about 2 inches in diameter (about 1½
measuring tablespoonfuls of the meat mixture per patty). Sprinkle
the flour on a sheet of waxed paper and coat the patties on both
sides. Place the floured patties on a floured platter, separating the
layers with sheets of waxed paper. Cover lightly and refrigerate for
at least 1 hour before frying. Just before frying, coat the patties
with flour once again so that they will have a thick crust.

Add enough olive oil to a large skillet just to coat the bottom.
Set the skillet over high heat. When the oil is very hot, fry the
patties over medium heat, in batches, until nicely browned. (Keep
the fried meatballs warm in a 200°F oven.) Garnish with mint
leaves and serve with Tomato and Red Onion Salad.

NOTE: These meatballs can also be served as a hot appetizer. In that
case, roll the mixture into ¾-inch balls. Proceed with the recipe as given
above, and serve hot, speared with cocktail picks.

Casserole of Eggplant and Ground Lamb

MOUSSAKA

YIELD: 8 TO 10 SERVINGS

*T*his is Periyali's rendition of quite probably the best-known of all Greek dishes. Like most old and popular recipes, it will almost always change slightly from region to region and cook to cook. One thing that *never* varies is the topping of thick, creamy béchamel sauce, sprinkled with cheese, which everybody loves and kids (of all ages) scrape off and eat first.

---

1 slender eggplant, weighing about
  1½ pounds
Salt
All-purpose flour, for dredging
  eggplant slices
Regular (not extra-virgin) olive oil
2½ pounds lean ground lamb
1 medium-size onion, finely chopped
  (½ cup)
2 large garlic cloves, minced
2 bay leaves
3-inch cinnamon stick
4 whole allspice
1 cup whole, peeled, canned tomatoes,
  chopped
1 cup dry white wine

2 tablespoons tomato paste
Freshly ground black pepper, to taste
½ cup grated graviera *or Parmesan*
  cheese
2 tablespoons chopped flat-leaf
  parsley
¼ teaspoon ground nutmeg
BÉCHAMEL SAUCE
6 tablespoons butter
6 tablespoons all-purpose flour
1 quart milk
1 teaspoon salt
½ teaspoon ground nutmeg
⅛ teaspoon white pepper
2 eggs

Trim and peel the eggplant and cut it into ⅓-inch slices. Lightly sprinkle the slices with salt and set aside on paper towels to drain for about 30 minutes. Grease a 13-by-9-inch baking dish and set aside.

Preheat the oven to 400°F. Sprinkle the flour on a sheet of waxed paper. Lightly coat the eggplant slices with flour, shaking off the excess. Pour just enough olive oil into a jelly-roll pan or other shallow roasting pan to lightly coat the bottom. Place the pan in the oven to heat the oil. When it is hot, add the eggplant slices in one layer, sprinkling each slice with a few drops of oil. Bake, turning once, to brown lightly on both sides, 10 to 15 minutes per side. Remove from the oven and set aside. Reduce the oven heat to 375°F.

Heat a large, heavy skillet over medium-high heat. When it is hot, add the ground lamb and cook, stirring, over medium heat until it is lightly browned and most of the fat has cooked out. With a slotted spoon, remove the lamb to a large plate lined with several thicknesses of paper towels. Discard the fat remaining in the skillet and wipe the skillet with paper towels. Return the lamb to the skillet. Stir in the onion, garlic, bay leaves, cinnamon stick, allspice, tomatoes, wine, and tomato paste. Simmer the meat sauce, uncovered, for about 35 minutes, or until most of the liquid has been absorbed. Remove the bay leaves, cinnamon stick, and allspice. Season to taste with salt and pepper.

Arrange the eggplant slices in one layer in the prepared baking dish. Sprinkle evenly with ¼ cup of the *graviera* and parsley. Spoon the meat sauce over the eggplant, spreading evenly, and set aside.

To make the sauce, in a heavy, 3-quart saucepan, melt the butter over medium heat. Stir in the flour. Cook, stirring, until the mixture bubbles. Off the heat, with a whisk, briskly stir the milk into the flour mixture all at once. Return to medium heat and cook, stirring constantly with the whisk, until the mixture bubbles. Reduce the heat slightly, and continue to cook for about 10 minutes, stirring constantly. The sauce should be quite thick. Remove from the heat and stir in the salt, nutmeg, and pepper until well blended. Beat the eggs in a small bowl. Stir a big spoonful of the hot sauce into the eggs to temper them, then whisk the egg mixture into the sauce. Pour the sauce over the eggplant smoothing the top. Sprinkle with ground nutmeg and then the remaining ¼ cup of cheese.

Bake for about 25 minutes, or until hot through. Set aside for 10 to 15 minutes before cutting. Serve the *moussaka* with a green salad.

Giant White Beans with Sausage

*G*iant white beans, for all their great texture, are rather bland-tasting, but they really shine when put to their best use: acting like a sponge for foods that are more richly endowed with flavor.

---

1 recipe Giant White Beans (see page 9)
2 tablespoons extra-virgin olive oil
1 large onion, chopped (1 cup)
2 large garlic cloves, minced
2 medium-size tomatoes, coarsely chopped or 1 can (about 14¹/₂ ounces) whole tomatoes, chopped with liquid (see Note)
¹/₂ to 1 pound hard beef sausage, cut into bite-size pieces (see page 300)

¹/₂ teaspoon dried thyme leaves, crumbled
2 tablespoons chopped flat-leaf parsley
¹/₂ teaspoon salt
Freshly ground black pepper, to taste
1 cup water (or ¹/₂ cup if using canned tomatoes)
Coarsely chopped flat-leaf parsley, for garnish

Drain the cooked beans into a colander, then turn them into a bowl and cover with plastic wrap pressed directly onto the beans to keep them from drying while preparing the rest of the ingredients.

Preheat the oven to 350°F. Heat the olive oil in a Dutch oven or other large, heavy saucepan over medium-high heat. When it is hot, add the onion and cook, stirring frequently, until soft. Stir in the garlic and cook 1 minute longer. Stir in the tomatoes, sausage, thyme, parsley, salt, and pepper. Stir in the water until well blended. Bring to a simmer and cook, stirring occasionally, for 10 minutes. Add the beans, stirring gently until they are well combined with the tomato mixture. Cover tightly and bake for about 30 minutes, or until hot and bubbly. Sprinkle with parsley and serve directly from the casserole. All that's needed to make this a meal is a good salad and bread.

NOTE: The easiest way to chop canned tomatoes is to use clean kitchen scissors and cut them up in the can.

Pork with Celery
HIRINO ME SELINO

YIELD: 6 SERVINGS

*W*hether this rib-sticking winter stew is more like "celery with pork" or the other way around usually depends on how much pork there is and how many mouths there are to feed. Young celery root, thinly sliced, is more typical in this stew than celery ribs and can be substituted for the ribs if you like.

*2 pounds lean pork, cut into
  1-inch cubes
½ cup granulated flour (see
  page 291), for dredging pork
2 teaspoons salt
¼ teaspoon freshly ground black
  pepper
¼ cup regular (not extra-virgin)
  olive oil*

*2 large onions, chopped (2 cups)
1 cup beer
1½ cups water
7 or 8 large outer celery ribs
  with leaves
2 egg yolks
1 tablespoon cornstarch
¼ cup water
¼ cup lemon juice*

Pat the pork cubes dry with paper towels. Mix the flour, 1 teaspoon of the salt, and pepper on a sheet of waxed paper. Roll the pork cubes in the flour mixture to coat them lightly.

In a Dutch oven or other large, heavy saucepan, heat the olive oil over medium-high heat. When it is hot, add the pork cubes in two or three batches and cook over medium heat, turning frequently, until lightly browned on all sides. Remove the pork with a slotted spoon to a plate and set aside. Add the onions to the fat remaining in the pan and cook, stirring almost constantly, until softened. Add the reserved pork cubes to the pan, stirring to blend them with the onions. Stir in the beer and then the water and bring to a boil over high heat. Reduce the heat to low, then cover tightly and simmer for 1 hour.

Meanwhile, rinse the celery ribs and trim the root ends. Cut the ribs, with the leaves, into 1½-inch pieces. There should be about 6 cups. Stir the celery and the remaining teaspoon of salt into the stew and continue to cook, covered, for about 30 minutes, or until the celery is very tender.

Beat the egg yolks in a small bowl. Stir the cornstarch into the water and add to the yolks along with the lemon juice. Rapidly stir a large spoonful of the hot pork broth into the yolk mixture to temper the yolks, then stir the yolk mixture into the stew. Continue to stir over very low heat until the sauce has thickened slightly, but do not allow it to boil. Serve with crusty bread.

Tripe Soup with Egg and Lemon Sauce

PATSAS

YIELD: ABOUT 12 CUPS

A very garlicky soup that is eaten just about everywhere in Greece with great gusto, usually early in the morning after a night out, when its special powers are believed to cure the common hangover and almost everything else. The things that go into a pot of *patsas* vary drastically, but all *patsas* include tripe as a main ingredient, and many include pigs' feet as well. The soup is cooked forever and served with red vinegar heavily laced with raw garlic. This version of *patsas,* minus the pigs' feet and with more meat than most, appeals more to the American taste.

2 pounds chicken wings	1 tablespoon salt
2 pounds veal shank, sawed crosswise into 2 or 3 pieces	1/2 teaspoon peppercorns
2 1/2 pounds honeycomb tripe	1 teaspoon dried thyme leaves
2 large ribs celery and leaves, coarsely chopped	2 bay leaves
2 large carrots, coarsely chopped	16 cups water
1 large onion, coarsely chopped	3 egg yolks
8 garlic cloves, or more to taste, peeled and lightly crushed	3 tablespoons cornstarch
	3/4 cup lemon juice
	Red-Wine Vinegar and Garlic Sauce (see page 234)

Combine the chicken wings, veal shank, and tripe in an 8-quart soup pot and add cold water to cover. Bring to a boil; lower the heat and simmer for 5 minutes; drain the meats in a colander and rinse thoroughly. Rinse the soup pot and return the meats to it. Add the celery, carrots, onion, garlic, salt, peppercorns, thyme, bay leaves, and 16 cups of cold water. Bring to a boil. Reduce the heat, cover, and simmer very gently for 3 hours. Uncover and continue to simmer slowly for 1 hour longer. Set aside to cool. Remove the chicken wings, shank pieces, and tripe and set them aside. Strain the liquid through a fine sieve into a large bowl, pressing down lightly on the vegetables to extract most of the liquid. There should be about 10 cups of broth. Remove 1 cup of the broth and set it aside. Cut the tripe into slivers. Remove the meat from the chicken wings and veal shanks and shred it or cut it into small bits, discarding the bones and any bits of skin or gristle. Rinse the soup pot and return the broth and meat. (The dish can be prepared ahead up to this point and refrigerated until ready to serve.)

Just before serving, bring the soup to a simmer. In a small bowl, beat the egg yolks with the cornstarch, reserved broth, and lemon juice. Stir a big spoonful of the hot broth into the egg mixture to temper the yolks, then slowly add the egg mixture to the soup, stirring rapidly with a whisk, until the soup is hot and slightly thickened. Ladle into warm soup bowls and serve with Red-Wine Vinegar and Garlic Sauce, which is added to taste at the table. Leftovers can be refrigerated and reheated *very gently*.

Vegetables: Mainstays of the Greek Table

The Greek word *ithaca,* loosely translated, means "fit for goats," and aside from the fertile plains, it aptly describes the Spartan growing conditions in much of Greece, especially on the smaller islands, where the thin topsoil supports very little—*except* goats.

Most of the produce in Greece is still grown on tiny family plots, divided and subdivided through the years by inheritances and dowries, the theory being that a little bit of everything is a lot better than a big single crop that fails. Farming families live together in villages and go out every morning, on donkey back or tractors, to tend the fields.

Fortunately, because of its temperate climate, the growing season in Greece—two of them, actually, interrupted by the hot, dry summer—is a long one, and if a crop fails in the spring, well, there's a good chance that it won't in the fall. Beside every highway in Greece, old women, shrouded in black, sit in straight-backed chairs like sentinels of the season, selling just-picked produce grown in the fields or orchards behind them. They will undoubtedly insist—with hand gestures, if you don't speak Greek—that you taste before you buy.

Vegetables make up a big part of the Greek diet, and vegetarian meals are served more often than not. Should you have the chance to stroll through a city or village market during the height of the growing season, it's easy to understand why. Looking at the immense variety of artistically arranged, perfectly proportioned fruits

and vegetables, in a profusion of colors that could easily rival a flower market, one has to marvel at the ingenuity of farmers who can coax harvests like these from such stubborn soil.

Vegetable cookery in Greece has remained very much the same for hundreds of years. Because these people are particularly resistant to changes of any kind, processed foods and out-of-season produce have made few inroads into the old ways, and most cooks have yet to embrace the brief, simple vegetable cooking techniques that are so favored by Americans these days. Vegetables are usually slow-cooked in traditional combinations, bathed in either tomato sauce or the much-loved *avgolemono* sauce. Sometimes they're roasted with a little olive oil and herbs until they achieve a soft, almost caramel-like consistency and intense flavor.

As we mentioned earlier, side dishes, as such, are simply nonexistent in Greek menus. Although the recipes that follow are intended to conform to the Western preference for a selection of several complementary tastes and textures to accompany the main course, many of these can just as easily come to the table as main dishes themselves. Other vegetable recipes suitable for side dishes can be found in the chapters on appetizers and first courses.

Potatoes are the exception to the no-side-dish rule. Fried potatoes appear almost automatically with grilled meat and fish, and are frequently oven-baked alongside the meat. New potatoes, or anything other than plain, all-purpose potatoes, are still a rarity in Greece. But the flavor of freshly dug potatoes more than makes up for the lack of variety.

Roasted Potatoes with Oregano

PATATES STO FOURNO
RIGANATES

YIELD: 4 SERVINGS

The secret to the crisp, brown crust, tender interior, and deep flavor of these roasted potatoes is very slow baking and frequent, gentle turning. Although the Greeks use all-purpose potatoes for this and for almost everything, Periyali substitutes red or white new potatoes, which are much better for roasting, since they can cook and cook without falling apart. If you like, some chopped onion can be roasted with the potatoes.

---

12 small red or white new potatoes (about 1 pound), peeled or unpeeled and cut into quarters

2 tablespoons extra-virgin olive oil

2 teaspoons lemon juice

½ teaspoon salt

¼ teaspoon dried oregano leaves, crumbled

4 or 5 turns of a pepper mill

Preheat the oven to 350°F. Place the potatoes in a shallow pan just large enough to hold them all comfortably. Add the olive oil, lemon juice, salt, oregano, and pepper and toss until well coated. Roast for about 1½ hours, turning frequently, until soft and richly browned.

Greek-Fried Potatoes

YIELD: 3 TO 4 SERVINGS

No plate of grilled meat, fish, or poultry in Greece can be considered complete without a few fried potatoes on the table, too. These are to the Greeks what French fries, to which they bear a close resemblance, are to Americans. Generous pre-salting is important, so don't skimp.

---

1 pound russet or other baking
   potatoes

Regular (not extra-virgin) olive oil,
   for frying
Salt

Peel the potatoes and cut them into pieces resembling large French fries. Place the cut potatoes in a bowl of cold water to prevent them from darkening until ready to fry. Pour the olive oil into a large skillet until it measures about ¼ inch. Set the skillet over high heat until the oil ripples and is on the verge of smoking. Meanwhile, drain and blot the potatoes with paper towels, then sprinkle them generously with salt, tossing until they are well coated on all sides. Carefully slip the potatoes into the hot oil, which will bubble around them. Cook over high heat, turning and moving the potatoes about, until they are crisp and golden, about 10 minutes. Remove from the skillet with a slotted spoon onto paper towels to drain. Transfer to a platter and serve very hot.

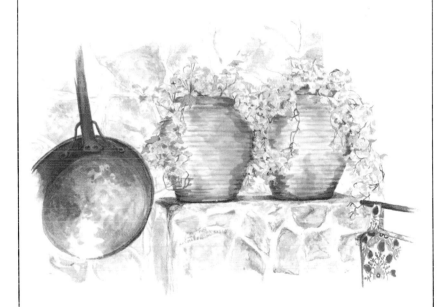

Vegetables of the Day

Zucchini and Carrots

YIELD: 4 TO 6 SERVINGS

*T*his is the vegetable combination that most frequently accompanies the main dishes at Periyali. To make it as the restaurant does, you really need a mandoline (a French implement that cuts vegetables into slices, shreds, julienne, or whatever else the cook needs fast). At Periyali, the mandoline cuts the zucchini and carrots into neat, long "shoestrings," which can also be done by hand.

Depending on what's available at the produce market, Charles may also pan-braise snow peas to serve as the vegetable *du jour*. Although snow peas may not strike you as being particularly Greek, they are very similar to immature pea pods, a spring delicacy in Greece.

---

2 medium-size zucchini trimmed (about 1 pound)

2 or 3 medium-size carrots scraped and trimmed (about 1/2 pound)

2 tablespoons regular (not extra-virgin) olive oil

1/4 cup Chicken Broth (see page 5) or water

1/4 to 1/2 teaspoon salt (depending on the saltiness of the broth)

1/8 teaspoon freshly ground black pepper

2 teaspoons chopped flat-leaf parsley

Cut the zucchini and carrots into 2-inch lengths; cut the lengths into 1/4-inch slices, and the slices into 1/4-inch strips. Heat the olive oil in a large skillet over medium-high heat. When it is hot, add the vegetables, stirring until they are well coated with the oil. Stir in the chicken broth and cover tightly. Cook over medium heat for about 5 minutes, or until tender. Stir in the salt, pepper, and parsley and serve immediately.

Crisp Snow Peas

YIELD: 4 SERVINGS

1 pound snow peas or sugar-snap peas	Salt and freshly ground black pepper, to taste
1/2 cup Chicken Broth (see page 5)	1 tablespoon butter

Trim the tips of the peas and remove the string that runs along one or both sides. Bring the chicken broth to a boil in a large skillet. Drop in the peas and cook, partially covered, shaking the pan occasionally, just until the peas are crisp-tender, about 5 minutes. Stir in the salt, pepper, and butter and serve immediately.

Oven-Baked Mixed Vegetables
BRIAM

YIELD: 8 TO 10 SERVINGS

Slow cooking and red, ripe summer tomatoes are the two main requirements for this excellent Greek version of *ratatouille*. If you serve it at room temperature, add a splash or two of red-wine vinegar or balsamic vinegar and a few drops of extra-virgin olive oil.

4 pounds firm ripe tomatoes, cut into
  1/4-inch slices or 5 cans (14 1/2
  ounces each) whole plum tomatoes,
  drained and sliced
Salt, to taste
Freshly ground black pepper, to taste
Crumbled dried oregano leaves,
  to taste
1 pound red or white new potatoes,
  cut into 1/4-inch slices
1 pound small zucchini, cut into
  1/4-inch slices
2 small slender eggplants (about 1/2
  pound each), cut into 1/4-inch slices

1 pound small okra, trimmed
1 large red onion, finely chopped
  (1 cup)
1 small red bell pepper, cored, seeded,
  and finely chopped (1/2 cup)
2 or 3 large garlic cloves, minced
2 tablespoons chopped
  flat-leaf parsley
2 tablespoons tomato paste dissolved
  in 2 tablespoons warm water
1 cup extra-virgin olive oil

Preheat the oven to 350°F. Lightly grease a shallow 6-quart casserole or roasting pan. Lay half of the tomato slices in the bottom of the casserole and sprinkle generously with the salt, pepper, and oregano. Arrange the potato slices over the tomatoes. Toss the zucchini and eggplant slices and okra together in a large bowl. Add the mixed vegetables in layers to the casserole, sprinkling each layer generously with salt, pepper, and oregano. Lay the remaining tomato slices over the vegetables. Mix the onion, bell pepper, garlic, and parsley together and scatter over the tomatoes. Sprinkle with salt, pepper, and oregano. Stir the tomato paste mixture and olive oil together and pour over the vegetables. Cover tightly and bake for 1 hour and 15 minutes. Uncover and continue to bake for about 45 minutes, or until the vegetables are very soft. Toward the end of the baking time, spoon some of the juices that have accumulated in the bottom of the casserole over the top. The *briam* can be served warm or at room temperature. Leftovers taste wonderful the next day or the day after, and reheat very nicely in a microwave oven.

Broiled Tomatoes

*W*e suggest you don't waste your time making these unless the tomatoes you plan to use are red, ripe, and luscious. Tomatoes prepared this way are also excellent served as a main dish, and you can sprinkle them with a little grated hard cheese before they're baked, if you like.

---

3 large, ripe tomatoes (8 to 10 ounces each)

Salt and freshly ground black pepper, to taste

1 cup fresh bread crumbs

1/4 cup chopped flat-leaf parsley

2 large garlic cloves, minced

1 1/2 teaspoons minced fresh oregano or 1/2 teaspoon dried oregano leaves, crumbled

3 tablespoons extra-virgin olive oil

Preheat the oven to 400°F. Cut the tomatoes in half and remove just the seeds that can be gotten at easily with the tip of a small spoon (a grapefruit or demitasse spoon works well). Place the tomatoes cut side up in a shallow baking dish. Sprinkle lightly with salt and pepper and set aside.

In a small bowl, mix the bread crumbs, parsley, garlic, oregano, and salt and pepper to taste. Stir in the olive oil until well blended. Spoon the bread-crumb mixture over the tomatoes, dividing evenly and pushing some of it down into the seed cavities. Bake for 15 to 20 minutes, or until the tomatoes are hot and slightly soft and the topping is lightly browned.

Sliced Tomatoes with Spinach-and-Feta-Cheese Filling

Sometimes great recipes just happen. During the testing for this book, we found ourselves with an unbelievable number of good things left over. The filling that's used primarily in the Spinach-and-*Feta*-Cheese Pies was one of these, and, so that it wouldn't go to waste, we piled it on thick tomato slices and baked them. Suffice it to say that the tomatoes were barely out of the oven before they went into the cookbook.

---

2 cups Spinach-and-Feta-Cheese
Filling (see page 13)

8 thick tomato slices

Preheat the oven to 400°F. Spread about ¼ cup of the filling on each tomato slice. Arrange the slices on the rack of a broiling pan. Bake for 3 to 5 minutes, or until the tomato slices are warm, but still firm. Run under the broiler for a minute or so until the filling is hot and lightly browned.

Grilled Greek Vegetables

As just about everyone knows, the Greeks were the civilized world's first outdoor cooks, grilling meat over open fires for thousands of years. On the other hand, *vegetable* grilling can hardly be considered a time-honored Greek cooking technique, with the possible exception of the vegetables that are cooked in combination with meat and seafood on a kabob. But lately, as more Greeks visit relocated relatives and friends in the United States and other parts of the Western world, a few of the more daring and progressive Greek cooks have gradually, and sometimes grudgingly, started integrating some of the cooking methods they've learned about on these trips back home.

Now a visitor to Greece may be treated to a few intensely flavored grilled vegetables (mostly eggplant and green bell peppers) that come with the appetizers. Doused with olive oil and lemon juice, they are simply wonderful when eaten along with the ubiquitous grilled fish and other seafood that one feasts on at least once a day, every day. Adhering to the Greek philosophy that a little overcooking is better than a little undercooking, the vegetables come to the table soft and smoky-tasting, nicely caramelized with their own natural sugar.

Grilling vegetables over a charcoal fire (or an electric kitchen grill, if you have one) is about the easiest thing you'll ever do. Most vegetables, except for those that are very dense (artichokes, for instance) and may require some pre-cooking, can go straight onto the grill in their raw state. On the other hand, vegetables that are very fragile or have a high water content (tomatoes and mushrooms, for example) cook especially fast. Because they contain no fat to make them self-basting, it's always a good idea to oil-marinate vegetables briefly before grilling. The easiest way to do this is to make up a mixture of olive oil with lemon juice or vinegar to taste. Garlic and chopped fresh or dried herbs can be added. The grill should also be brushed with oil first as added insurance against sticking.

There are no firm guidelines for knowing just when grilled vegetables are done to a turn, but most will take between 10 and 20 minutes over medium-hot coals. Or, start them over high heat and move them to the edge of the grill to finish cooking. When they are soft and brown, the vegetables are usually done. To make sure, test for softness with a skewer or long-tined fork.

Large vegetables can be cooked directly on the grill, but smaller ones should be either skewered or cooked in a hinged basket to keep them from falling through the grids. The hinged basket is also good for preventing fragile vegetables from falling apart.

ARTICHOKES: Baby artichokes can be grilled whole. Large artichokes must be halved or quartered. Trim and steam until tender. Marinate and grill for 10 to 15 minutes, or until brown.

BELL PEPPERS: Skewer squares of pepper, or slice into rings, cut in half, or leave whole. Marinate squares, rings, or halves before grilling. Brush whole peppers with marinade during grilling. Grill for 10 to 20 minutes, or until slightly charred and tender.

CARROTS. Brush unpeeled medium-size carrots, or halved large carrots, with marinade. Grill for 20 to 25 minutes, turning frequently, until soft and brown.

CORN ON THE COB: Grilled is the only way corn is eaten in Greece, at least by humans. In the late summer it is sold by the same vendors who sell roasted chestnuts in the winter. Pull the husk down and discard the silk. Brush the corn with marinade. Pull the husk up and tie the tops tightly with string. Soak in water for 10 to 15 minutes before grilling. Grill for 15 to 20 minutes, turning frequently, until the husks are charred. Brush with marinade to serve.

EGGPLANT AND JAPANESE EGGPLANT: Cut large eggplants into ½-inch rounds or lengthwise slices; cut small Japanese eggplants in half or leave whole. Marinate before grilling. Grill for 5 to 7 minutes per side, or until soft and brown.

FENNEL: Cut in half or into thick, lengthwise slices. Marinate briefly before grilling. Grill for 10 to 20 minutes per side, or until brown and tender.

LEEKS: Cut large leeks in half, leaving enough of the root intact to hold the halves together. Marinate briefly before grilling. Grill for 10 to 15 minutes, turning frequently, until soft and brown.

MUSHROOMS: Large mushrooms can be cooked directly on the grill; skewer small mushrooms. Do not marinate, but brush with marinade during grilling. Grill for 5 to 10 minutes, turning frequently, until soft.

ONIONS: Quarter or slice large onions; skewer small onions. Marinate briefly before grilling. Grill for 10 to 30 minutes, or until brown, glossy, and soft.

POTATOES: Slice large potatoes into ½-inch slices or quarter them. Small potatoes can be grilled whole. Marinate slices or quarters before grilling. Rub the skins of whole potatoes with marinade, then prick the skins. Grill for about 15 minutes per side, or until soft. Small whole potatoes will take about 30 minutes, with frequent turning.

SCALLIONS: Leave whole with a few inches of the green leaves and marinate before grilling. Grill for about 10 minutes, or until brown and tender.

SUMMER SQUASH: Small zucchini can be grilled whole; cut larger ones in half; skewer slices or pieces. Prepare yellow squash the same way, but allow more grilling time since yellow squash has a denser texture. Marinate slices and pieces; rub skins of whole or halved squashes with marinade. Grill slices or pieces for 10 to 15 minutes; 20 to 30 minutes for whole squashes and halves.

TOMATOES: Skewer cherry tomatoes; cut larger tomatoes into slices or quarters. Plum tomatoes can be cut in half or grilled whole. Brush with marinade during grilling. Grill for 3 to 5 minutes, or just until hot.

Couscous (Semolina) Timbales

*C*harles gives this vegetable-studded semolina a few restaurant airs by packing it into timbales (or little soufflé dishes or custard cups) and turning it out onto dinner plates, a nice little touch for home cooks to know about. In Greece, however, the semolina would probably be more at home if it were piled into a big earthenware bowl and served as the main course after an assortment of appetizers. You can do the same, but you might want to double the amount of the vegetables to give the semolina a little more color and crunch.

---

3 tablespoons regular (not extra-
  virgin) olive oil
1 small red bell pepper, cored, seeded,
  and finely chopped (about ¹/₂ cup)
1 small green bell pepper, cored,
  seeded, and finely chopped (about
  ¹/₂ cup)
1 small red onion, finely chopped
  (¹/₄ cup)

3 scallions, thinly sliced, including
  some of the green tops (about
  ¹/₄ cup)
2 cups Chicken Broth (see page 5)
¹/₂ teaspoon salt
¹/₈ teaspoon freshly ground black
  pepper
1¹/₄ cups medium-grain semolina
  (see page 300)

Heat 1 tablespoon of the olive oil in a medium-size skillet over medium-high heat. Add the bell peppers, onion, and scallions and cook, stirring frequently, until softened. Remove from the heat and set aside.

Bring the broth to a boil in a medium-size saucepan. Stir in the remaining 2 tablespoons of oil, salt, and pepper. Gradually add the semolina, stirring constantly, until the mixture boils. Remove from the heat and set aside, covered, until the semolina has absorbed all of the liquid, about 5 minutes. Fluff with a fork, then gently stir in the reserved vegetables. Press the semolina mixture into timbales or ½-cup soufflé dishes or custard cups and turn out onto dinner plates.

Rice Pilaf

PILAFI

YIELD: 4 TO 6 SERVINGS

This is a good, basic pilaf that can be served alongside just about anything. To add a little color, you can substitute chopped red or green bell pepper for half of the onion, or stir in a little finely chopped tomato a few minutes before the pilaf has finished cooking.

2 tablespoons extra-virgin olive oil
1 medium-size onion, finely chopped
   (½ cup)
1 cup regular long-grain or converted
   raw rice
2 cups Chicken Broth (see page 5) or
   water

¼ to ½ teaspoon salt (depending on
   the saltiness of the broth)
⅛ teaspoon freshly ground black
   pepper
1 bay leaf
2 teaspoons finely chopped
   flat-leaf parsley

Heat the olive oil in a heavy, medium-size saucepan until it is hot. Add the onion and cook over medium-high heat, stirring frequently, until softened. Add the rice and cook until it is opaque, stirring constantly. Stir in the chicken broth. Add the salt, pepper, and bay leaf and bring to a boil. Reduce the heat until the mixture barely simmers. Cover and cook for 15 to 20 minutes, or until the rice is tender and the liquid is absorbed. Remove the bay leaf and stir in the parsley before serving.

Eggplant and Semolina

At Periyali, this popular Greek combination is often used to garnish appetizer plates, although you will also find it quite useful as a side dish with cold roast chicken, a green salad, and a loaf of warm bread. It is also great served as a meatless main dish. And leftovers just keep getting better and better.

½ cup medium-grain semolina
  (see page 300)
¾ cup plus 2 tablespoons water
¼ teaspoon salt
½ cup regular (not extra-virgin)
  olive oil
2 medium-size green bell peppers, cut
  into ⅜-inch cubes (about 2½ cups)
2 medium-size red bell peppers, cut
  into ⅜-inch cubes (about 2½ cups)
3 large celery ribs, diagonally cut into
  ⅛-inch slices (about 2 cups)

1 medium-size red onion, cut into
  ⅜-inch cubes (about ½ cup)
2½ pounds eggplant, cut into
  ½-inch cubes (about 10 cups)
Chopped flat-leaf parsley, for garnish
Lemon wedges, for garnish
DRESSING
¼ cup extra-virgin olive oil
¼ cup lemon juice
½ teaspoon dried oregano leaves,
  crumbled
2 teaspoons salt

Place the semolina in a small bowl. Bring the water with the salt to a boil and stir into the semolina. Let stand for 5 minutes, then fluff with a fork and set aside.

Heat 2 tablespoons of the regular olive oil in a large, heavy skillet. Add the bell peppers and cook over medium-high heat, stirring frequently, until soft and beginning to brown. Remove to a large bowl and set aside. Heat another tablespoon of oil in the skillet. Add the celery and cook, stirring frequently, until softened. Remove to the bowl. Heat another tablespoon of oil in the skillet. Add the onion and cook, stirring frequently, until softened. Remove to the bowl. Add the remaining ¼ cup of oil to the skillet.

When it is very hot, add the eggplant and cook, stirring and tossing constantly until very soft. (If the eggplant begins to stick to the skillet, add about ½ cup of water.) Remove to the bowl. Crumble the semolina into the vegetables and toss gently to blend.

To make the dressing, in a small bowl stir together the extra-virgin olive oil, lemon juice, oregano, and salt. Pour over the warm vegetables and toss gently to blend. Cover lightly and set aside for an hour or two to allow time for the flavors to mingle. Serve sprinkled with parsley and garnished with lemon wedges.

Okra or Green Beans with Tomatoes

YIELD: 4 SERVINGS

*W*hen choosing okra, the rule of thumb is just that: the okra should be no larger than a man's thumb. The pods should be green, firm, and very fresh-looking. In Greece, during the warm weather, this dish is often served chilled.

---

1 pound okra or green beans
¼ cup red-wine vinegar
1 tablespoon regular (not extra-virgin) olive oil
2 tablespoons finely chopped onion
1 small garlic clove, minced
1 large tomato, finely chopped with the juice

1¼ cups water
1 tablespoon chopped flat-leaf parsley
2½ teaspoons salt
⅛ teaspoon freshly ground black pepper
1 fat lemon wedge plus 1 teaspoon lemon juice

Preheat the oven to 375°F. Rinse and drain the okra. Trim off the stems and the tips. (If using green beans, trim and cut them into

2-inch pieces.) Place the okra or beans in a shallow baking pan and toss with the vinegar. Bake for 10 minutes, stirring after 5 minutes. Remove from the oven; rinse in a colander and set aside.

Heat the olive oil in a Dutch oven or other large, heavy saucepan. When it is hot, add the onion and cook over medium-high heat, stirring frequently, until the onion is softened. Add the garlic and continue to cook, stirring, for about 30 seconds. Add the tomato, water, parsley, salt, and pepper and bring to a boil. Stir in the okra or green beans. Squeeze the juice from the lemon wedge into the okra or green beans. Add the lemon wedge and additional lemon juice and bring to a boil. Reduce the heat, cover, and simmer gently for about 20 minutes, or until the okra or green beans are very tender, but still hold their shape. Remove the lemon wedge before serving.

Baby Artichokes with Potatoes, Pearl Onions, and Carrots

YIELD: 4 TO 6 SERVINGS

Artichokes and onions are two of the vegetables most closely associated with Greek cooking, and this combination of the two with carrots in a creamy egg and lemon sauce is quite traditional. Sometimes meat is added to make a kind of fricassee. In that case, add oil-browned pieces of stewing veal or chicken parts at the same time the broth and artichokes are added and cook until the meat is tender.

10 baby artichokes (see Note)

3 tablespoons regular (not extra-
  virgin) olive oil

1 cup tiny pearl onions, peeled

1 large carrot, cut into ½-inch
  cubes (1 cup)

2 tablespoons lemon juice

2 tablespoons dry white wine

2 tablespoons butter

3 tablespoons all-purpose flour

2 tablespoons chopped fresh dill

3 cups Chicken Broth (see page 5) or
  water, or a mixture of both

1 medium-size potato, cut into
  ½-inch cubes (about 1 cup)

1 egg yolk

Chopped flat-leaf parsley, for garnish

Rinse and drain the artichokes. Bend back the outer green leaves and snap them off at the base until you reach a point where the leaves are half green (at the top) and half yellow. Cut off the top cone of leaves at the point where the yellow color meets the green. Trim off the stem even with the base. Rub the exposed areas of the artichoke with lemon juice.

Heat the olive oil in a Dutch oven or other large, heavy sauce-pan. Add the onions and carrot and cook over medium-high heat for 2 minutes, stirring constantly. Stir in the lemon juice and wine and continue cooking and stirring until most of the liquid has evaporated. Add the butter. When it has melted, stir in the flour and the dill and cook over low heat, stirring constantly, for 3 minutes. Add the chicken broth and the artichokes. Cover and simmer gently for 15 minutes. Add the potato and simmer, uncovered, for 20 minutes longer, or until the artichokes and potato are tender and the sauce has thickened. Beat the egg yolk in a small bowl. Stir a large spoonful of the hot cooking liquid into the yolk to temper it, then stir the egg mixture into the broth. Continue to cook over low heat, stirring constantly, for 2 minutes. Serve sprinkled with parsley.

NOTE: When baby artichokes are not available, a package or two of thawed, frozen artichoke hearts can be substituted.

Great Greens

Except during the height of summer, spinach is available in Greece (and almost everywhere else in the world) year-round and at the right price, so many of the most enduring Greek recipes are based on this vitamin-rich green. One of the most popular is *spanokorizo,* which is actually lots of dishes, since there are about as many variations of it as there are cooks. Each cook adds special little touches, passed down from mother to daughter and sometimes to son—Periyali's version is actually Steve's mother's version and includes tomato sauce and dill.

Two varieties of fresh spinach come to market: savoy and semi-savoy, the former being the most familiar one with dark green, very crinkled leaves. Semi-savoy spinach is slightly less crinkled and a slightly paler shade of green; this is the variety that Charles prefers to use. For all practical purposes, the taste is identical and the two can be used interchangeably. The important thing when buying spinach is to choose bunches with crisp leaves that show no traces of rot or bruising. Only the main, tough stems should be trimmed away, and the leaves should be rinsed in several changes of water to remove the sand that lurks stubbornly in every crease.

Although never as desirable as fresh, frozen spinach is always an acceptable substitute when good fresh spinach is not available, or when time—or lack of it—is an important factor. In that case, figure on one 10-ounce package of frozen spinach for each pound of fresh spinach.

Spinach with Rice in Dill-Flavored Tomato Sauce

YIELD: 6 TO 8 SERVINGS

12 cups very tightly packed fresh
  spinach leaves (about 2 pounds) or
  2 packages (10 ounces each) frozen
  whole-leaf spinach, thawed and
  drained
¼ cup regular (not extra-virgin)
  olive oil
3 large onions, finely chopped
  (3 cups)
6 scallions, thinly sliced, including
  some of the green tops

¼ cup plus 1 tablespoon chopped
  fresh dill
⅓ cup converted raw rice
¼ cup water
3 tablespoons tomato paste
1 tablespoon salt
⅛ teaspoon freshly ground black
  pepper

Trim away any tough stems from the spinach leaves. Rinse the leaves in several changes of cold water and drain in a colander. Heat the olive oil in a large pot with a tight-fitting lid. When it is hot, add the onions, scallions, and ¼ cup of the dill and cook over medium-high heat, stirring frequently, until the onions are softened. Add the rice and cook 1 minute, stirring constantly. Stir in the water, tomato paste, salt, and pepper. Add the spinach and stir to combine. Cover and cook over low heat for several minutes, stirring occasionally, until the spinach has wilted down. Continue to cook over very low heat for about 30 minutes, or until the rice is nearly tender. Stir in the remaining dill and cook for about 5 minutes, or until the rice is tender. Cover and set aside until ready to serve.

Spinach with Rice

SPANAKORIZO

YIELD: 4 TO 6 SERVINGS

½ cup regular long-grain raw rice

2 pounds fresh spinach or 2 packages (10 ounces each) frozen chopped spinach

3 tablespoons regular (not extra-virgin) olive oil

3 large cloves garlic, peeled and thinly sliced

3 tablespoons lemon juice

1 tablespoon extra-virgin olive oil

½ teaspoon salt

¼ teaspoon freshly ground black pepper

Kalamata olives, for garnish

Lemon slices, for garnish

Cook the rice as the package directs and set aside. Rinse the spinach in several changes of cold water and drain in a colander. Trim away any tough stems and chop the spinach coarsely. Heat 1 tablespoon of the regular olive oil in a Dutch oven or other large, heavy saucepan. Add the garlic and cook, stirring, over medium heat until lightly browned. Remove the garlic with a slotted spoon and set aside. Add the remaining 2 tablespoons of regular olive oil to the pan. When it is hot, start adding spinach in large handfuls, stirring each addition until it is wilted down. (If using frozen spinach, cook as the package directs and drain well in a colander; cook in the oil until heated through.) Stir in the reserved rice and garlic, lemon juice, extra-virgin olive oil, salt, and pepper. Cook over medium heat, stirring, until heated through. Serve warm, at room temperature, or chilled. Garnish with olives and lemon slices.

Rice with Garlic

SKORDORIZO

❧❧❧❧

YIELD: 4 SERVINGS

*I*f you really like garlic, add more. The Greeks usually do. The quantity can be doubled or even tripled. They also drizzle a little more extra-virgin olive oil over the rice just before serving.

---

2 tablespoons extra-virgin olive oil
4 large garlic cloves, finely chopped
1 cup long-grain raw rice
2 cups water

1 teaspoon salt
2 tablespoons finely chopped flat-leaf
  parsley

Heat the olive oil in a 2-quart saucepan over medium heat. When it is hot, add the garlic and cook over low heat, stirring, until softened and very lightly browned. Stir in the rice until well coated. Add the water and salt and bring to a boil. Lower the heat until the mixture barely simmers. Cover tightly and cook for about 15 minutes, or until all of the water is absorbed. Remove from the heat and set aside, covered, for 5 minutes. Stir in the parsley and serve immediately.

Caramelized Onions

A touch of honey makes these onions extra-sweet, soft, and brown, so that they almost melt in your mouth. They're also easy to prepare and are the best accompaniment we know of for grilled meat and poultry.

---

1 pound tiny pearl onions
1/2 cup water
2 tablespoons butter

2 tablespoons honey (see page 293)
1/4 teaspoon salt

To loosen the skins, place the onions in a saucepan of boiling water for about 1 minute. Drain and add cold water to the onions in the pan. Remove the onions from the water and slip off the skins.

Place the onions in a large skillet with the water, butter, honey, and salt. Bring to a boil, then reduce the heat to medium and cook, stirring almost constantly, until the onions are caramelized and golden. A little water will probably have to be added to the skillet from time to time toward the end of the cooking time so that the onions caramelize evenly and don't stick to the skillet.

Nicola's Mother's Beans Stewed in Tomato Sauce

YIAHNI

❦❦❦❦

YIELD: 4 TO 6 SERVINGS

Despite its simple ingredients, this homey dish has lots of good, deep flavor. In the summertime it's good served at room temperature, or leftovers can be gently reheated.

1 pound mature (late-summer)
   wax or green beans
1 tablespoon regular (not extra-
   virgin) olive oil
1 tablespoon butter
1 medium-size onion, chopped
   (½ cup)
2 large garlic cloves, minced

1 medium-size all-purpose potato,
   peeled and cut into ½-inch cubes
½ cup canned tomato sauce
½ teaspoon dried oregano leaves,
   crumbled
½ teaspoon salt
¼ teaspoon freshly ground
   black pepper

Trim the beans and cut them into 1½-inch pieces. Heat the olive oil and butter in a large skillet. Add the onion and garlic and cook over medium heat, stirring frequently, until softened. Add the beans and the potato, stirring until well coated with the oil mixture. Stir in the tomato sauce, oregano, salt, and pepper. Add enough water to just cover the vegetables. Bring to a boil, then reduce the heat until the mixture simmers. Cook, uncovered, stirring occasionally, until the vegetables are tender and the pan juices have reduced to a fairly thick sauce, 20 to 25 minutes.

Flowers to Eat

Greek gardeners have always known that the squash vine—from acorn squash to zucchini—produces *two* bumper crops: the squash, of course, and the delicate yellow-orange blossoms, an edible bonus with a subtle flavor that's hard to describe.

Both the male and the female blossoms are edible, and if you handle them properly, you can have your blossoms and eat squash too. The male blossoms grow directly from the stem. They don't produce fruit, but about half of them should be left on the vine to provide the necessary pollination. Female blossoms grow at the end of the baby squash. If you separate the blossoms carefully from the squash, the vegetable will continue to develop.

Because they open only briefly and then stay closed, female blossoms are easier to handle, and are preferred for frying and stuffing. Male blossoms tend to stay open as showy, five-pointed flowers. Uncooked, both blossoms make an attractive plate garnish or salad ingredient. The male flower can also be used as a cup to hold a dip or a salad.

Squash blossoms should be picked soon after they have opened, while they are still dewy and fresh. You must handle them reasonably gently, but they aren't as fragile as they look. Trim away the green stem. Reach into the center of the blossom and pinch out the stamens or the pistils. Rinse under cold water to remove any dirt or tiny bugs that may be making a home there. Turn upside down on paper towels to drain. If not using immediately, place the blossoms in one layer on a paper-towel-lined tray and cover tightly with plastic wrap. Refrigerate for no more than a day or two.

If you live in the city, squash blossoms don't bloom outside the back door, as they do for both Steve's and Nicola's mothers. If you are also garden-less, I suggest you check your local farmers' market, or ask the produce manager at your market to order them. Nowadays, with all the interest in edible flowers, squash blossoms are becoming easier to find.

Squash Blossoms Lightly Stewed in Butter

KOLOKITHOKORFADES

❧❧❧❧

YIELD: 3 TO 4 SERVINGS

*A*s a side dish or first course, this is quite tasty and certainly unusual, and invariably leads to a long conversation about the cultivation of squash blossoms. If you have enough blossoms to do it, you might also like to serve this for a light lunch on a warm summer afternoon. Accompanied by a glass of chilly, dry white wine and a loaf of good bread, this homey Greek dish suddenly becomes elegance personified.

---

18 female squash blossoms,
  3 to 4 inches long
4 tablespoons butter
10 scallions, thinly sliced, including
  some of the green tops (about 1 cup)

1 large tomato, seeded and coarsely
  chopped (about 1½ cups)
Freshly ground black pepper, to taste
2 tablespoons freshly grated
  kefalotiri *or Parmesan cheese*

Prepare the blossoms as described on page 181. Twist the tips gently to close. Melt the butter in a large skillet over medium-high heat. When it foams, add the scallions and cook, stirring frequently, until they are starting to soften. Gently stir in the blossoms and the tomato until well blended. Cover and cook over medium heat for 1 minute. Uncover and continue to cook, stirring gently, until most of the liquid has evaporated. Stir in the pepper and serve immediately, sprinkled with cheese.

A Platter of Beets and Beetgreens

YIELD: 4 TO 6 SERVINGS

If they had to make a choice, most Greeks would sooner throw out the beets than the beet greens. They even save the red cooking water and give it to children as a health drink. Greeks believe that beet juice cleanses the blood. This preference for beet greens, and sometimes very tiny beets, is based on a certain amount of necessity, because the topsoil in most of Greece is too thin to support the full development of the root.

This is a salad to be made only in the very early summer, when small, tender beets with their fresh, shiny, red-veined greens come to the market. In Greece, this salad would undoubtedly be served as an appetizer, but Americans will probably find it more useful as an accompaniment to the main course.

---

2 pounds small (about 1½ inches in diameter) beets with fresh leaves
2 teaspoons salt

½ cup Olive Oil and Lemon Dressing (see page 233)

Cut the greens from the beets, leaving about 1 inch of the stems on each beet. Rinse and scrub the beets and place them in a large saucepan with the salt and enough water to cover by about an inch. Bring to a boil. Cover and boil gently over medium heat for about 15 minutes, or until the beets are slightly tender. Meanwhile, wash the greens in several changes of cold water. Trim the stems to about 4 inches below the greens. Add the greens to the beets, pushing them down into the simmering liquid. Lower the heat slightly and simmer, covered, for about 20 minutes longer, or until the beets are very tender. With tongs, remove the greens to a colander to drain; drain the beets. Trim off the roots and stems, then rub off the skins under cold running water. Thinly slice and set aside. Arrange the beet greens and beet slices on a large, shallow platter. Drizzle with Olive Oil and Lemon Dressing. Serve immediately, or cover and set aside to be served later at room temperature. The salad can be made a day ahead and stored, tightly covered, in the refrigerator, but it is better if eaten the same day it's made.

Potato Salad

PATATOSALATA

YIELD: 4 SERVINGS

Although the Greeks serve a potato salad called *rossiki* that's remarkably like the one your American grandmother used to make, incorporating cooked vegetables, hard-boiled eggs, chopped dill pickle, and *lots* of mayonnaise, this *patatosalata* is the one that many Greek grandmothers make, and the one that is served warm at Periyali. It is also good served at room temperature or chilled.

¾ pound small red or white new potatoes, rinsed and cut into quarters

3 scallions, thinly sliced, including some of the green tops

¼ cup extra-virgin olive oil

2 tablespoons red-wine vinegar

2 tablespoons balsamic vinegar

1 teaspoon salt

⅛ teaspoon white pepper

2 medium-size firm tomatoes, cored and each cut into 6 wedges

1 tablespoon chopped flat-leaf parsley

In a medium-size saucepan, cook the potatoes, covered, in lightly salted, boiling water for 10 to 15 minutes, or until just tender. Drain and turn into a large bowl. Add the scallions and toss gently until well mixed. In a small bowl, mix the olive oil, vinegars, salt, and pepper. Drizzle over the warm potatoes and toss gently. If serving warm, add the tomatoes and parsley, toss gently, and serve immediately. If serving at room temperature or chilled, add the tomatoes and parsley after the potatoes have cooled to room temperature.

Horta: Steve's Story

Like most Greeks, I have very special feelings about *horta*. I was born during World War II, and when I was a little boy Greece was occupied by the Germans, even our insignificant little village in the mountains. As I remember, the only people left in town were the women and children, the old men, and, of course, German soldiers. The younger men were off fighting in the resistance or were in labor camps.

One day when I was about five years old, the German commandant ordered all of us out into the square. I think a German officer had been killed the night before and the commandant wanted to know who did it. I don't know if he really intended to have us shot, but I do remember the soldiers all around us with pointed guns. I have never been so afraid in my life. I was sure I was going to die and I hid my face in my mother's skirt. Just then, the priest came out of the church and had a short conversation in German with the commandant. None of us understood what they said, and we never did find out. I only know that the commandant motioned for all of us to go quickly. We were all so frightened that we ran up into the mountains, where we stayed for several days before we gradually started returning to our homes. During that time we lived on wild things, mostly *horta*, the wild field greens that the Greeks have been eating since only God knows when.

All that was very long ago. Things have changed and I try to forgive and forget. But when I go to Greece and visit my parents, my mother still makes *horta* for me.

—Steve

Wild Field Greens

HORTA

*I*t takes years of experience to know just which of the hundreds of wild greens that grow in Greece will make the best *horta*. The *horta* served in Greece is almost always too bitter for American tastes. At Periyali, Charles makes up his own blend of the milder greens suggested below. If you want a little more bitterness, substitute an equal part of dandelion greens for one of the more mellow varieties.

2¼ pounds mixed greens,
  such as escarole, mustard greens,
  red or green Swiss chard, or
  dandelion greens
3 quarts water

2 tablespoons salt
1 tablespoon red-wine vinegar
Lemon wedges, for garnish
Extra-virgin olive oil (optional)

Trim the greens and rinse them in several changes of cold water. In a large pot, bring the water, salt, and vinegar to a boil. Stir in the greens. When the water returns to a boil, reduce the heat and simmer for about 15 minutes, or until the greens are very tender. Drain into a colander, pressing down lightly with the back of a spoon to remove most of the cooking liquid. Spoon the greens into a serving dish. Serve hot with lemon wedges. A little extra-virgin olive oil can also be drizzled over the greens.

Easter in Greece and at Periyali

When the planes leave for Greece the week before Easter, no matter from where in the world they depart, there's rarely a spare seat to be found. Even if Easter falls early in the calendar, thus almost guaranteeing a cool and possibly rainy Easter week, especially in the more northerly regions, nothing can dampen the spirits of these ebullient travelers. This is the most joyous and important holiday of the year for all Greeks, and they are going home to celebrate—with gusto!

Inside every Greek, big and small, there is a Zorba waiting to get out, and never is this more apparent than at Easter, when forty days of fasting and somber introspection during Lent rapidly turn into feasting and festivities. If you've ever been fortunate enough to experience Easter in Greece, it's not likely that you will ever forget this moving and impressive spectacle.

The celebration begins on the evening of Good Friday, when a solemn procession takes place, and the symbolic body of the crucified Christ is carried through the streets to the sound of funeral music. The bearers walk slowly past silent crowds holding lighted yellow funeral candles, and every city, town, and village is hushed throughout Greece as the faithful mourn their dead Savior. Even in Athens, normally one of the noisiest cities in the world, all is eerily quiet.

On the following night, a most awe-inspiring service takes place. Everyone gathers at church in his or her best clothing, now holding tall, slim, white candles. When the service begins, the church is dimly lit, symbolizing the darkness of Christ's tomb. Even these lights are extinguished just before midnight. As the clock strikes twelve, the door of the church sanctuary swings open and the priest appears, holding a single lighted candle and chanting, *"Christos anesti"* ("Christ is risen"). The worshipers respond in one voice, *"Alithos anesti"* ("He is risen, indeed"). The light of resurrection is then passed from candle to candle until the church is blazing with the brightness of hundreds of candles. Church bells ring out wildly, fireworks explode in the sky, and everyone exchanges kisses. Soon after, the crowd moves off toward home, shielding the candles to keep them alight. If the flame is not extinguished before reaching home (or sometimes, these days, a restaurant), it's a good omen for the coming year.

Breaking the Fast

Not a moment too soon for most, the long fast is broken with midnight supper. The first course is a bowl of red-dyed eggs, the color symbolizing Christ's blood. This is the first egg eaten since the one that was consumed the night Carnival ended, and cracking the eggs open is a high-spirited traditional game. Each person taps the pointed end of an egg against another's egg until one cracks. The one whose egg doesn't crack is presumably blessed with good luck for the coming year. But it doesn't end there. Each winning egg is tested against other winners at the table, and rarely does one egg survive for long.

The rest of the meal consists of *mageritsa,* soup made from the innards of the lamb that will be roasted the next day, thickened with the traditional mixture of egg and lemon juice. There are also rich cheese pies wrapped in flaky *phyllo,* a bowl of fresh fruit, and freshly baked loaves of *tsoureki,* the traditional holiday bread decorated with more red-dyed eggs, although these are not eaten.

But Easter is the day that food- and fun-loving Greeks live for. The first light of dawn is hazy with the smoke of countless charcoal-pit fires, and the aroma of whole lambs, roasting on spits, wafts through the air. Cooking the lambs is men's work, and quite

A Typical Greek Easter Dinner

A Bowl of Red-Dyed Eggs
Traditional Easter Bread
Fish Roe Salad   Eggplant Salad   Cucumber Salad
Cheese Pies and Spinach Pies
Greek Country Salad or Easter Salad
Oven-Roasted Leg of Lamb
Roasted Potatoes   Horta
Warm Rice-Stuffed Grape Leaves with Thick
Avgolemono Sauce
Whole-Wheat Country Bread
Easter Cookies
Nuts, Strawberries, and Other Fresh Fruit
Greek Coffee

Dinner Wine: Hatzi Michalis Cabernet Sauvignon
Dessert Wine: Samos Muscat Wine and Brandy

a social event it is, too, since everyone who isn't busy in the kitchen stands around sniffing and watching the men performing this age-old ceremony. While one turns the spit, another bastes the lamb with a mixture of lemon juice, olive oil, and herbs. At some point bottles of wine are opened, which are consumed with chunks of *feta* cheese, olives, and a good, coarse bread.

Easter at Periyali

Every spring, Periyali serves dinner after church on Easter eve, a pleasant and welcome custom for many Greek-Americans in the New York City area. Nicola and Steve alternate spending the holiday in Greece, so that one of them is always at the restaurant on this night to wish their patrons a happy Easter.

For this most important of all holidays—in a country where celebrating saints' days makes literally every day a holiday of sorts —Greek-Americans from the New York area, joined by more than a few adventuresome non-Greeks, come to Periyali soon after midnight, carrying the traditional tall candles, ready to break the long meatless, eggless, and cheeseless Lenten fast. The menu is a combination of a typical midnight supper and Easter dinner, all accompanied by generous quantities of wine. After dinner, nearly everyone lingers over thick Greek coffee and sweet wine and brandy until the restaurant closes near dawn.

All of the recipes in the accompanying menu are given here or can be found in the index.

Oven-Roasted Leg of Lamb
ARNAKI FOURNOU

YIELD: 8 TO 10 SERVINGS

Slow-roasting a leg of lamb in the oven, while basting it frequently with lemon juice and olive oil, is as close as we can come to the technique the Greeks use of roasting a whole lamb over a charcoal pit. However, weather permitting, you just may want to go outdoors and cook the lamb on a spit over the charcoal grill. Balancing a bone-in leg of lamb on a spit is tricky, so you might want to consider a boneless rolled leg.

This is the one meal of the year when pink lamb is not served at Periyali. Greeks who have learned to enjoy their lamb less well done every other day of the year won't put up with it at Easter.

6- to 9-pound leg of lamb
2 or 3 large garlic cloves, cut
  into slivers
1/2 cup regular (not extra-virgin)
  olive oil
1/2 cup lemon juice
2 teaspoons dried oregano
  leaves, crumbled
1 teaspoon salt

1 1/2 teaspoons fresh rosemary,
  chopped
1/2 teaspoon freshly ground
  black pepper
1/2 cup hot water
Lemon wedges, for garnish
Lemon leaves, for garnish
Pink eggs, for garnish (see Note)

With the tip of a small, sharp knife, cut many slits in the skin of the lamb. Insert the garlic slivers into the slits. In a small bowl, combine the olive oil, lemon juice, oregano, salt, rosemary, and pepper. Brush the lamb generously with this mixture. Place the lamb in a shallow roasting pan. Cover and refrigerate for 24 hours. Cover the remaining basting mixture and set aside.

Uncover the lamb and bring to room temperature. Preheat the oven to 325°F. Roast the lamb for 1 hour. Drain off any fat that has accumulated in the bottom of the pan. Pour the hot water into the pan. Continue to roast the lamb, basting every 20 minutes, first with the remaining basting sauce, then with the juices that accumulate in the pan. Allow about 20 minutes per pound, or until a meat thermometer inserted in the thickest part of the lamb, without touching fat or bone, registers 140° for rare, 160° for medium, or 170° for well done. Remove the lamb from the oven and set aside, lightly covered, for about 20 minutes before carving. Skim the fat from the juices in the pan and serve the pan drippings with the lamb.

Place the lamb on a large platter and garnish it with lemon wedges and lemon leaves (usually available from a florist) or other bright greens. Sometimes whole, halved, or quartered red eggs are also used to decorate the platter.

NOTE: Hard-cook eggs in the usual way and peel them. Place the warm eggs in a bowl and pour beet juice that has been mixed with a little water over them. Cover and refrigerate for about a day, turning the eggs occasionally, until they are bright pink.

Leg of Lamb in Pita Breads with Yogurt Sauce

YIELD: 4 SERVINGS

*N*o matter how perfectly done and delectable the paschal lamb may be, there will always be leftovers, and this and the following recipe are great ways to use them.

¾ cup plain whole-milk yogurt,
  preferably sheep's-milk
  (see page 303)
1 tablespoon chopped fresh dill
½ teaspoon salt
1 medium-size red onion, cut into
  thin vertical slices (1 cup)
1 cup very thinly sliced unpeeled
  English cucumber, lightly salted and
  drained (see page 291)

2 tablespoons regular (not
  extra-virgin) olive oil
2 garlic cloves, put through a
  garlic press
4 cups small pieces of leftover leg
  of lamb
4 pita breads (6-inch size), cut in
  half to make 8 pockets (see Note)

In a medium-size bowl, mix the yogurt, dill, and salt. Fold in the onion and cucumber until well blended and set aside. Heat the olive oil in a large skillet over medium-high heat. Stir in the garlic, then add the lamb. Cook, stirring and tossing, until the meat is hot

and well coated with oil and garlic. Spoon ¼ cup lamb and ¼ cup
vegetable mixture into each pita-bread pocket. Serve immediately.

NOTE: Pita bread can be loosely wrapped in aluminum foil and warmed
in a 300°F oven for about 10 minutes.

Roasted Lamb Salad

YIELD: 4 SERVINGS

3 cups cooked lamb, cut into
  matchstick pieces
½ cup Olive Oil and Lemon
  Dressing (see page 233), omitting
  parsley and substituting ½ teaspoon
  minced fresh thyme or a pinch of
  dried thyme leaves, crumbled
4 to 6 toursi pickled peppers, cut into
  very thin crosswise slices
  (see page 302)

2 tablespoons plus 2 teaspoons finely
  chopped mint leaves
1 English cucumber (see page 291)
1 medium-sized red onion
Rocket (arugula) leaves
Mint leaves, for garnish

In a large bowl, toss the lamb with the dressing. Add the pepper
slices and 2 tablespoons of the mint and toss again until well
blended. Cover lightly and set aside to marinate at room temperature for 30 minutes, or chilled for several hours.

Cut the cucumber in half. Tightly wrap half the cucumber and
reserve for another use. Cut the remaining unpeeled cucumber in
half lengthwise; cut each half into very thin crosswise slices. Cut
the onion in half vertically, then cut the vertical halves into very
thin vertical slices.

Just before serving, add the cucumber and onion to the lamb and
toss until well blended. Serve the salad on a bed of rocket (arugula)
leaves, sprinkled with the remaining 2 teaspoons of chopped mint
and garnished with mint leaves.

Steve's Sister's Easter Cookies

KOULOURIA

Steve's sister makes these cookies year-round and keeps them on hand for snacking and dunking into the strong, medium-sweet Greek coffee she serves to virtually every visitor. At Easter, the cookies are put on the table with fresh fruit for dessert, and are simply celestial dipped into sweet wine or sherry.

2¾ cups all-purpose flour

1 teaspoon baking powder

½ teaspoon salt

¾ cup sugar

½ cup (1 stick) unsalted butter, softened

2 eggs

1 tablespoon ouzo

⅓ cup orange juice

½ teaspoon vanilla extract

2 drops lemon extract (optional)

1 egg yolk beaten with 1 teaspoon cold water, for brushing on cookies

---

In a large bowl, mix the flour, baking powder, and salt with a wire whisk until well blended.

In the large bowl of an electric mixer, beat the sugar and butter until creamy. Add the eggs, one at a time, beating well after each addition. Beat in the *ouzo,* orange juice, and extracts. (The mixture will look curdled.) Gradually stir the flour mixture into the butter mixture. Cover the bowl and chill for 1 hour.

Preheat the oven to 375°F. Cover 2 large baking sheets with foil and set aside. Tear off walnut-size pieces of the cold dough (about 1½ ounces each). Roll each piece into an 8-inch rope—about the length and thickness of a new pencil. Twist into traditional shapes as shown on the opposite page. As the cookies are formed, place them on the prepared baking sheets. Brush the tops of the cookies with the egg yolk mixture. Bake for about 30 minutes, or until light golden. Remove the cookies from the baking sheets and cool on wire racks. Store in a tightly covered container. The cookies can also be frozen for longer storage.

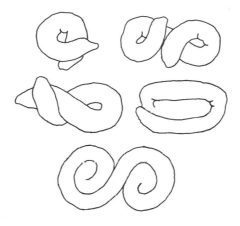

Steve's Sister's Traditional Easter Bread

LAMBROPSOMO

One reason for the popularity of this slightly sweet, rich bread may be the copious use in the recipe of butter and eggs, two foods strictly forbidden during Lent. It is similar to the French *brioche,* and is always baked in a twist or a braid. Although the bread is eaten all year, except during fast times, at Easter red-dyed eggs are nestled into the braids. Be sure to leave yourself plenty of time to bake Easter bread, since the rising times alone total ten hours!

Follow the directions for making Steve's Sister's Festive Bread. Just before the bread goes into the oven, and after it has been sprinkled with sesame seeds, nestle 2 or 3 red-dyed, hard-cooked eggs down into the braid. The quicker and easier recipe for New Year's Bread can also be made into Easter Bread.

Easter Salad

Salads are designated in Greece for spring, summer, and winter, a custom dictated by the simple matter of what's in season and what's out. The famous Greek salad technically contains no lettuce, because by the time the tomatoes, cucumbers, and bell peppers are ripe, the lettuce is long gone. This salad is served all through the spring, when *kos* (romaine) lettuce and scallions are plentiful. The addition of hard-cooked eggs makes it Easter salad.

---

1 head romaine lettuce (about
1¼ pounds)
1 bunch scallions (about 6)
3 tablespoons chopped fresh dill
⅓ cup extra-virgin olive oil

3 tablespoons lemon juice
Salt and freshly ground black pepper,
to taste
2 hard-cooked eggs, coarsely chopped

Cut out the ribs from the larger lettuce leaves. Stack a few leaves on a work surface and cut them into very narrow, lengthwise strips. Trim the scallions and cut them into lengthwise shreds, including some of the green tops. Combine the lettuce, scallions, and dill in a large bowl, tossing until well mixed. Beat the olive oil, lemon juice, salt, and pepper in a small bowl. Just before serving, pour the dressing over the greens and toss again until the greens are evenly coated with dressing. Spoon the salad onto a large platter. Scatter the eggs over the top and serve immediately.

Eggs and Pasta

Greeks eat more pasta than any people in the world—except the Italians. And more than half of the pasta eaten in Italy comes from Greece.

Pasta consumption in Greece, however, has not quite evolved into the culinary art form that it has become in Italy. The Greeks don't fuss much with their pasta, sometimes cooking it a good bit beyond the *al dente* stage, serving it with simple tomato-, cheese-, and yogurt-based sauces—or whatever else happens to be in the saucepot. They don't bother to distinguish among different shapes of pasta, either. It all goes under the casual, blanket term of *makaronia*. The pastas they use include most types of short, thick macaroni, orzo, and spaghetti, usually bucatini or perciatelli (a kind of thick, hollow spaghetti), and minuscule noodle squares called *hilopites,* as well as wide egg noodles.

Noodles are still made at home (at least in the country), using freshly milled, unbleached flour and newly laid eggs filched from the nests in the henhouse out back. Chickens, like goats, range far and wide over the countryside, hunting and picking, which may account, at least partly, for the rich flavor and deep color of the yolks in their eggs.

Although the Greeks are perfectly content with a breakfast that consists of not much more than coffee and a piece of dry toast (later on in the morning they'll have a snack to get them through until an early-afternoon meal), Americans in Greece usually opt

for something more substantial before another hard morning of trudging through ruins. A typical Greek-American breakfast might consist of eggs, big and brown, less than a day old, either soft- or hard-cooked, served with thick slices of very lightly toasted Country Bread, rich yogurt, and aromatic honey, and huge cups of steaming, strong coffee. If you're lucky, there might also be an assortment of spoon sweets to sample.

Greek families eat pasta two or three times a week, and eggs are freely consumed, many more per person in a given period than are eaten here these days. Greek cooks stir them into breads, cakes, and sauces, especially the quintessential *avgolemono* sauce, and serve them plopped on top of other things, too: tomatoes, tomato sauces, and potatoes, for example. Still, the Greeks have a remarkably lower rate of cardiovascular disease than we do. Some experts attribute this to the healthful benefits of olive oil, which is also used abundantly, and a diet that, for all the roasted spring lambs, is still largely based on fresh vegetables, fruit, pasta, and seafood. It may also have something to do with the Greek attitude of taking life as it comes. Despite a close proximity to the Western world, the Greeks seem to have resisted getting sucked into stressful lifestyles, especially on the islands and in the rural areas of the mainland, where life goes on pretty much as it has for hundreds of years.

Peasant Omelet

*C*olorful vegetables and shiny black olives stud the surface of this extremely pretty omelet. It's cooked flat and served cut into wedges, which means there's no tricky flipping or folding involved.

---

1 tablespoon regular (not
   extra-virgin) olive oil
2 small red onions, thinly sliced and
   the slices separated into rings
   (½ cup)
½ cup very thin red bell pepper strips

4 eggs, beaten
⅓ cup pitted Kalamata olives
2 ounces feta cheese, cut into ¼-inch
   cubes (about ⅓ cup)
Chopped flat-leaf parsley, for garnish

Preheat the oven broiler. In a large skillet, heat the olive oil over medium-high heat. When it is hot, add the onion and cook, stirring almost constantly, until lightly browned. Remove with a slotted spoon and set aside. Add the pepper strips and cook, stirring, until softened. Remove the pepper strips with a slotted spoon and set aside with the onion. Add the eggs and immediately sprinkle the reserved vegetables, olives, and cheese over the top. Cook just until set around the edge. Place the skillet in the oven about 6 inches below the source of heat. Broil until the eggs are just set on top. Cut into wedges, sprinkle with parsley, and serve immediately.

Eggs over Spinach-and-Feta-Cheese Filling

*I*n Greece they say "eyes" to refer to eggs that are fried or otherwise cooked so that the yolks are served whole. Steve says that when he first came to the United States and spoke one word of English ("yes"), he'd point to his eyes when he wanted fried eggs up and wondered why nobody understood.

---

2 cups Spinach-and-Feta-Cheese
  Filling (see page 13)

4 eggs
Freshly ground black pepper, to taste

Preheat the oven to 400°F. Butter 4 individual gratin dishes and place them on a baking sheet. Spread ½ cup of the cheese filling in each dish. Place the dishes, on the baking sheet, in the oven and bake for about 10 minutes, or until the spinach is hot. Remove from the oven and carefully break 1 egg over the spinach mixture in each dish. Bake for about 15 minutes longer, or until the eggs are set as you like them. Sprinkle with pepper and serve immediately.

Eggs in Tomato Sauce

*W*hen there's nothing handy to put over or under the sauce in the skillet, most Greeks will follow the path of least resistance and break an egg over it. And not a bad idea, either, since the eggs fortify the sauce and make it substantial enough to serve for a quick supper with a couple of slices of *paximadi* and a salad.

Half of the recipe for tomato sauce, as given in Pasta with Chopped Tomatoes and Cheese (see page 207), omitting the pasta and 2 tablespoons of the olive oil

4 to 8 eggs

Cook the tomato sauce as directed in a large skillet. Carefully break the eggs over the simmering sauce. Cover and cook, basting a couple of times with the sauce, until the eggs are done as you like them. Carefully transfer servings to a shallow bowl or a plate. Serve hot, sprinkled with the cheese.

Cheese Sunday and Clean Monday

Cheese Sunday ends what can be as long as three weeks of revelry and copious eating before Lent begins. During this time Greeks eat massive quantities of all the things that are forbidden during the forty-day fast before Easter, mainly meat, cheese, and eggs. These weeks are referred to as Carnival, and the festivities include parades and dressing up in costume as well as feasting. Nowadays, Carnival rarely goes on for more than a week, and sometimes it lasts just a few days.

The last thing eaten on Cheese Sunday is a hard-boiled egg, a reminder that there will be no more eggs until the fast ends with the eating of red-dyed eggs just after midnight on Easter.

When I was young, we usually spent Cheese Sunday with my grandparents on Zakinthos. I remember the food that day as being nearly all white: for instance, *pastitsio,* sweet and savory cheese pies, especially milk pie, and rice pudding.

Although Steve says he's never heard of it, and thinks it may be a dish unique to Zakinthos, my mother also serves a dish for breakfast that she makes out of spaghetti cooked with milk and sugar until the sauce is very thick and syrupy. It sounds strange, doesn't it? But it's really very good.

On Monday, the first day of Lent, everything changes. This day is called Clean Monday, because that's the day Greeks cleanse their bodies, their spirits, and their kitchens after the excesses of Carnival. Clean Monday still has a very festive air about it, but the food changes dramatically to such things as unleavened bread, pickled vegetables, and fish.

Children love Clean Monday, because it often means a picnic, and, for some reason, it's also the day that almost everybody in Greece goes out and flies a kite!

—Nicola

Nicola's Mother's Macaroni Pie

PASTITSIO

छ॰छ॰छ॰छ॰

YIELD: ABOUT 16 SERVINGS

*T*his recipe makes a really *big* pan of *pastitsio,* so big, in fact, that it's the perfect party dish. If you wish to serve lesser numbers, the quantities can be cut in half (in that case use either 2 or 3 eggs) and baked in a 13-by-9-inch glass baking dish. Or, if you want to make the whole thing and don't have a large enough pan, use two 13 by 9 inch dishes. By the way, don't dispose of leftovers too rashly. They reheat well and are delicious a day or two later.

¼ cup regular (not extra-virgin) olive oil

1 large and 1 medium-size onion, finely chopped (about 1½ cups)

3 large garlic cloves, minced

2 pounds lean ground beef

1 tablespoon dried oregano leaves, crumbled

1 teaspoon salt

¼ teaspoon freshly ground black pepper

1 can (8 ounces) tomato sauce

1 4-inch cinnamon stick

1 package (16 ounces) bucatini or perciatelli (thick, hollow spaghetti), broken in half

1 cup grated kefalotiri or Parmesan cheese

1 cup paximadi or Zwieback crumbs (see page 225)

BÉCHAMEL SAUCE

1 cup (2 sticks) butter

1 cup all-purpose flour

3 quarts (12 cups) milk

5 eggs

2 teaspoons salt

¼ teaspoon white pepper

Heat the olive oil in a large skillet or Dutch oven. When it is hot, add the onions and cook over medium-high heat, stirring frequently, until the onions are softened. Add the garlic and stir rapidly for about 5 seconds. Add the ground beef and cook, breaking up the meat with the side of a spoon, until it is crumbled and no trace of pink remains. Stir in the oregano, salt, and pepper until well blended. Stir in the tomato sauce and cinnamon stick. Cover and cook at a slow simmer over medium-low heat for about 20 minutes. Uncover and continue to cook until most of the liquid has evaporated or been absorbed into the meat. Remove from the heat and set aside.

While the sauce simmers, cook the pasta in a large pot of lightly salted water until barely tender, slightly less than *al dente,* about 10 minutes. Drain in a colander and rinse very well with cold water. Set aside.

To make the béchamel sauce, melt the butter in a Dutch oven or other large, heavy saucepan. Add the flour and cook over medium heat, stirring constantly, until the mixture bubbles. Rapidly stir in the milk and continue to cook until the sauce simmers and is thick and smooth. Remove from the heat. Beat the eggs in a medium-size bowl. Stir a couple of big spoonfuls of the hot sauce into the eggs to temper them, then rapidly stir the egg mixture into the sauce with a whisk. Season with the salt and pepper.

Preheat the oven to 350°F. Grease a shallow 6-quart baking dish or roasting pan. Arrange half of the pasta in the bottom of the pan and sprinkle with half of the cheese. Remove the cinnamon stick and spoon all of the meat sauce over the cheese. Add the remaining pasta and sprinkle with the remaining cheese. Spoon the sauce over the top, smoothing it lightly with the back of a spoon. Sprinkle evenly with the crumbs.

Bake for about 30 minutes, or until hot and bubbly. Remove from the oven and let stand for about 20 minutes before cutting into serving portions.

Metsovo-Style Noodles

For Greek-cooking enthusiasts, the mere mention of Metsovo brings to mind the soft, white, unsalted *hloro mizithra* cheese that comes from this pretty little town in the northwestern part of Greece, known for its handicrafts, the preservation of its architecture, and townspeople who still dress in traditional clothes. *Mizithra* is similar in flavor and texture to soft-curd ricotta cheese, which can be used in place of it. Greeks come from all over central Greece to pick up their supplies of *mizithra* in Metsovo, which is really saying something, since this cheese keeps for only a few days. Metsovo-Style Noodles are hearty enough to serve for dinner. Start with Greek Country Salad.

---

8 ounces broad egg noodles (about 3 cups)

3 tablespoons regular (not extra-virgin) olive oil

1/4 pound bacon strips, cut into 1-inch pieces

1 medium-size onion, finely chopped (1/2 cup)

2 large garlic cloves, minced

4 medium-size tomatoes, peeled and chopped or 1 can (14 1/2 ounces) undrained whole tomatoes, chopped (see Note)

1/2 cup water (only if using fresh tomatoes)

1/8 teaspoon freshly ground black pepper

1/2 cup soft mizithra or ricotta cheese (see page 290)

Cook the noodles in lightly salted, boiling water as the package directs. Drain into a colander; rinse with cold water and drain thoroughly. Turn the noodles back into the pan in which they cooked and toss with 1 tablespoon of the olive oil; set aside.

Place the remaining 2 tablespoons of oil and the bacon in a Dutch oven or other large, heavy saucepan and cook over medium-high heat, stirring almost constantly, until the bacon is crisp and lightly browned. Add the onion and garlic. Continue to cook over medium heat, stirring frequently, until the onion and garlic are golden. Stir in the tomatoes, water (only if using fresh tomatoes), and pepper. Add the reserved noodles, stirring gently until well blended. Lower the heat and barely simmer for about 10 minutes, stirring frequently, until the noodles are thickly coated with sauce. Onto each serving, spoon some of the *mizithra,* which is then stirred into noodles before they are eaten.

NOTE: The easiest way to chop canned tomatoes is to use clean kitchen scissors and cut them up in the can.

Short Pasta with Yogurt and Cheese

KOFTO MAKARONAKI ME YAOURTI KE TIRI

YIELD: 2 TO 4 SERVINGS

Some people think of this as the Greek version of fettuccine Alfredo, but you won't feel nearly as guilty when you eat it. If you like, you can add a substantial amount of minced garlic, stirring it in for a few seconds after the onion has browned.

½ pound short tubular pasta, such as macaroni, penne, cut ziti, rigatoni, etc.
4 tablespoons (½ stick) butter
1 medium-size onion, chopped (½ cup)

1 cup Thickened Yogurt (see page 11)
Grated kefalotiri *or Parmesan cheese*

Cook the pasta in lightly salted water until tender. Drain in a colander, then turn into a large bowl.

While the pasta is boiling, heat the butter in a medium-size skillet over medium-high heat. Add the onion and cook, stirring frequently, until lightly browned. Stir the browned onions and the yogurt into the hot pasta and toss until the strands are evenly coated. Serve immediately, sprinkled with lots of cheese.

Pasta with Chopped Tomatoes and Cheese

YIELD: 4 SERVINGS

*A*n unpretentious dish, but absolutely impeccable when garden-ripe tomatoes are the main ingredient, and surprisingly good even when canned tomatoes are substituted. You may be tempted to add a little fresh basil, although the herb is almost never used in Greece for culinary purposes. Large pots of it can be spotted growing everywhere, often next to a door or on a windowsill, since its strong, minty odor, especially when the leaves are crushed, presumably repels flies.

¼ cup plus 2 tablespoons extra-virgin olive oil
4 large garlic cloves, minced
2 pounds ripe tomatoes, peeled, seeded, and coarsely chopped with their juice or 2 cans (14½ ounces each) undrained whole tomatoes, coarsely chopped (see Note)

½ teaspoon dried oregano leaves, crumbled
1 pound pasta (see page 299)
8 ounces shredded kefalotiri cheese (about 2 cups)

Heat ¼ cup of the olive oil in a Dutch oven or other large heavy saucepan. When it is hot, add the garlic and cook over medium-low heat, stirring, until softened. Add the tomatoes and their juice and oregano and cook over medium heat, stirring frequently, until somewhat reduced. Meanwhile, cook the pasta in a large pot of boiling, salted water until tender and drain thoroughly. Toss the hot pasta with the remaining 2 tablespoons of oil. Divide the pasta among dinner plates and top with equal amounts of the hot sauce. Sprinkle with some of the shredded cheese and serve the remainder on the side to be sprinkled on the pasta as it is being eaten.

N O T E : The easiest way to chop canned tomatoes is to use clean kitchen scissors and cut them up in the can.

Pasta with Olives and Cream

YIELD: 2 TO 4 SERVINGS

*I*f you like zesty pasta sauces, you'll enjoy this one. It's easy to make and special enough to serve for company. To accompany it, we'd suggest a platter of Red Onions and Rocket or sliced tomatoes and a good loaf of bread. If appetites are hearty you might want to precede the pasta with Steamed Mussels with *Ouzo*.

*½ pound bucatini or perciatelli
  (thick, hollow spaghetti)
⅔ cup heavy cream
3 tablespoons butter
½ cup pitted Kalamata olives (see
 page 296)*

*½ cup finely chopped ham
½ cup grated* kefalotiri *or
  Parmesan cheese*

Cook the pasta in a large pot of lightly salted, boiling water until tender. Drain in a colander, then turn into a large bowl.

While the pasta is boiling, simmer the cream in a small saucepan until it is reduced by about half and set aside. In a medium-size skillet, heat the butter over medium-high heat. Add the ham and the olives and cook, stirring frequently, until the ham is lightly browned. Remove from the heat. Stir the ham and olives into the hot pasta until well blended. Add the cheese and the reduced cream and toss gently until each strand of pasta is evenly coated.

Breads: Savory and Sweet

A lot of the bread eaten in Greece is still baked at home, although electric ovens have brought about drastic changes in some of the charming, but laborious, Greek bread-baking traditions.

In the old days, on Saturday, the wood-burning ovens were lit and bread baking began, but not before the kids were sent out to collect a donkey-load of kindling.

Friday was wheat-grinding day, when some of the family's own supply of wheat was taken to the village miller, who ground it between gigantic millstones, often powered by the wind as it turned several winglike arms covered with sailcloth protruding from the side of a tower. (Many of these tall windmills still stand in Greece, mostly on the islands. The great majority are no longer in operation, and many have been converted to summer residences.) Back home, the flour was sifted through a horsehair sieve to remove any large bits of bran.

Little wonder that not even a scrap of bread was wasted, and so many of the old Greek recipes call for bread crumbs, most notably *taramosalata* and *skordalia*. Little wonder, too, that the Greeks have been more than a little inventive when it comes to baking bread over an open fire or using other techniques that don't involve heating the oven.

The one store you can count on, even in the most remote Greek village, is a bakery—more accurately a bread store, since pastries, as well as other confections, are sold at sweet shops, or *zakharoplas-*

tia. All of these bread stores are exactly alike: short on charm, but long on good smells and mouthwatering merchandise. The fragrant breads, ranging from dull pale brown to shiny deep golden, some heavily coated with sesame seeds and others studded with olives and other good things, are arranged hodgepodge in glass-front cases behind the counter. Around one o'clock, these places buzz with activity, as men (mostly) stop in to pick up loaves of freshly baked bread to accompany their midday meals.

Whole-Wheat Country Bread

YIELD: 2 LOAVES

This is the bread that is truly the staff of life for most Greek families. The women bake it on Saturday using a piece of dough from the previous week's batch as a starter. There's a very interesting story about starter that Nicola tells. You can choose whether to believe it or not. On Ascension Day, the priest specially blesses some water and gives a little of it to every woman who wants it. The women take it home, mix it with a little flour, and it becomes a bread starter. With enough faith anything is possible, so who knows?

1 package active dry yeast
2 cups very warm water
 (105 to 115°F)
4 cups all-purpose flour
1¹/₄ cups whole-wheat flour
1 tablespoon light brown sugar

2 teaspoons salt
2 tablespoons regular (not extra-
 virgin) olive oil
Regular (not extra-virgin) olive oil,
 for brushing on bread

Sprinkle the yeast over the warm water in a small bowl and stir until it is dissolved. In a large bowl, mix 2 cups of the all-purpose flour, all of the whole-wheat flour, the brown sugar, and the salt. Stir in the dissolved yeast and olive oil and mix thoroughly with a large spoon. Stir in another cup of the all-purpose flour. Turn the dough out onto a work surface that has been dusted with some of the remaining all-purpose flour. Knead for 10 minutes, adding only enough of the remaining flour to keep the dough from sticking. Cut the dough in half and shape each half into a round loaf. Set the loaves on a lightly floured baking sheet. Cover with oiled plastic wrap and let rise in a warm place for 1 to 1½ hours, or until doubled in size.

Preheat the oven to 425°F. Gently brush the risen loaves with olive oil. Wait for a minute or two and sprinkle lightly with whole-wheat flour. With a single-edged razor blade or the tip of a sharp knife, make 3 long, shallow cuts in the top of the bread in one direction; repeat in the opposite direction. Bake for 10 minutes. Lower the oven heat to 400°F and continue to bake for about 20 minutes, or until the bread is brown and sounds hollow when tapped on the side. Cool on a wire rack.

Patmos and Old-Fashioned Ovens

I think Patmos is one of the loveliest places on earth. I've spent time almost everywhere in Greece, and when I decided to have a summer house there, I never seriously considered any other island. Heaven knows, one must really *want* to come to Patmos, because it's not an easy place to get in and out of, and anyone brave enough to visit off-season—that is any time except summer—may find himself or herself stuck indefinitely waiting for the wind to subside long enough for the boat to go.

My white, stucco-covered stone house is typical of those in the village of Hora. It was built in the mid-sixteenth century and faces a very narrow, crooked street. From my rooftop I can see the orange tile roofs of the houses nearby, two rickety windmills, the monastery of St. John directly above, the mountains on the farthest side of the island, and the sea beyond. The house has no number and the street has no name. If you were to come to visit me, and you didn't know exactly where I lived, you'd simply have to keep asking until someone who knows me led you to my door. One of the things I love most about Hora is that the people who live here have not become indifferent to foreign visitors—there aren't that many—and they are all very friendly and helpful to strangers.

I was fortunate to find a house. Hora is a place where the homes have been inhabited by generations of the same family, so they rarely become available. And I was luckier still to find one in such good, original condition. I did add a few modern conveniences, but I tried to integrate them carefully so as not to disturb the antiquity. I think if the family who built this house were to come back today, they would feel quite at home.

One of the rooms I like the most is the large kitchen (as compared to my shoe-box kitchen in New York) with a wavy-patterned Patmos-tile floor, and the original "cool box" and two ovens built into the thick stone walls. In one of the oven niches I had an electric cooktop installed, and in the firebox beneath it, an oven. I left the other oven just as I found it, presumably all ready for a weekly bread-baking session such as Greek women had in the old days, but I haven't actually tried it.

Many of the women on Patmos still bake their own bread (mostly in electric ovens, these days), but just as many visit one of the sweet-smelling bakeries on the island, which still make the bread the way the Greeks have been doing it for centuries.

Along with olive oil and olives and cheese, bread is probably the most important single food in the Greek diet. I often say, the Greeks eat something with their bread, rather than eating their bread with something.

—Nicola

White Bakery Bread

YIELD: 1 LOAF

A thin, crisp crust and chewy interior make this bread similar in taste and texture to French bread, and it is very much like that sold every day in the bakeries of every city and town in Greece. Although making and baking it is an all-day affair, there's very little actual hands-on time, so you can be doing other things during the time it takes for three full risings, just as long as you're around when it needs attention. If you have to stop unexpectedly, the dough can go into the refrigerator at any point, which will slow the rising to a snail's pace.

---

1 package active dry yeast
2 teaspoons sugar
1 teaspoon salt

1 cup very warm water
(105 to 115°F)
2½ to 3 cups all-purpose flour

In a large bowl, stir the yeast, sugar, and salt into the warm water. Continue to stir until all three have completely dissolved. Stir in 2¼ cups of the flour, mixing with a large spoon. Sprinkle a work surface with some of the remaining flour. Turn the dough onto the floured surface. Knead for 15 minutes, adding only as much of the remaining flour as necessary to keep the dough from sticking. The dough should be slightly sticky. Place the dough in a large, ungreased bowl. Cover the bowl tightly with plastic wrap and set aside in a warm place until doubled in size, about 1 hour and 15 minutes. Punch the dough down in the bowl and knead it a few times to expel any air bubbles. Cover tightly again and let rise until doubled in size, about 1 hour. At the end of the second rising, turn the dough out onto a lightly floured surface and knead it a few times. Shape the dough into a rounded, oblong loaf. Set the loaf on a baking sheet that has been lightly greased or coated with nonstick vegetable spray. Cover with oiled plastic wrap and let rise until the loaf has doubled in size, about 1½ hours.

Preheat the oven to 400°F. Using a single-edged razor blade or the tip of a sharp knife, slash the loaf with 3 diagonal slits about ¼ inch deep. Bake for 30 to 40 minutes, or until the bread is lightly browned and sounds hollow when tapped on the side. Slide the bread onto a wire rack to cool completely before slicing.

Steve's Sister's Everyday Bread
PSOMI

YIELD: 1 LOAF

Eleteria Strouseas and her husband, Peter, have lived in the United States for more than twelve years, but she has yet to buy a loaf of bread for her family's daily consumption, even from the Greek bakeries that dot her ethnic neighborhood. This bread is very simple to make, she says, and one that beginning breadmakers should not be afraid to try. As long as the yeast is active (check the date on the package) and the water is not too hot or too cold (use a thermometer, if you have doubts), the bread will come out of the oven, crusty, tender, and a little bit chewy, every time.

2 packages active dry yeast
2 cups very warm water
 (105 to 115°F)
5 cups all-purpose flour
1 teaspoon sugar
1 teaspoon salt

2 teaspoons regular (not extra-virgin) olive oil
Regular (not extra-virgin) olive oil, for brushing on bread
Sesame seeds, for sprinkling on bread

In a small bowl, sprinkle the yeast over the warm water and set aside to soften for about 5 minutes.

Meanwhile, combine the flour, sugar, and salt in a large mixing bowl and stir with a whisk until well blended. Make a well in the center of the flour and add the yeast mixture. With your fingertips, gently mix the dry ingredients toward the center into the yeast until a stiff dough forms. Knead briefly in the bowl. Add the olive oil and knead until it is completely incorporated.

Form the dough into a ball and place in an 8-inch round pie or cake pan that has been lightly greased or coated with nonstick vegetable spray. Cover with oiled plastic wrap and let rise in a warm place for about an hour, or until doubled in size.

Preheat the oven to 300°F. Gently brush the risen loaf with olive oil. Wait for a minute or two and sprinkle to taste with sesame seeds. Make 4 shallow slits in the top of the dough with a single-edged razor blade or the tip of a very sharp knife. Place in the center of the oven and immediately increase the temperature to 400°F. Bake for 35 to 40 minutes, or until the loaf is nicely browned and sounds hollow when the side is lightly tapped.

Kalamata Olive Muffins from Crete

YIELD: 12 MUFFINS OR 24 MINI-MUFFINS

Most people who try these muffins for the first time mistake the olives for raisins and expect an entirely different flavor when they bite into one. We like these savory muffins served warm, spread with plain Fresh Yogurt Cheese. The muffin batter can also be baked in twenty-four mini-muffin cups (decrease the baking time 8 to 10 minutes, in that case) and served on the appetizer table, since they go wonderfully well with wine and other drinks.

---

2 cups all-purpose flour
2 teaspoons baking powder
½ teaspoon salt
2 eggs
2 tablespoons regular (not extra-virgin) olive oil

1 cup Kalamata olives, pitted and chopped (see page 296)
½ cup milk

Preheat the oven to 350°F. Grease twelve 2½-inch muffin cups and set aside. In a medium-size bowl, mix the flour, baking powder, and salt with a whisk until well blended and set aside. In a large bowl, beat the eggs until light and frothy. Stir in the olive oil and the olives. Add the flour mixture and milk, stirring just until blended. Do not overmix. Divide the batter evenly among the prepared muffin cups. (The cups will be fairly full.) Bake for 25 minutes, or until the muffins are golden brown and a wooden pick inserted in the center comes out clean. Turn out onto a wire rack to cool. Serve warm or at room temperature. The muffins can be reheated, loosely wrapped in foil, in a 250°F oven for 5 to 6 minutes.

Steve's Sister's Festive Bread

TSOUREKI

YIELD: ONE 2-POUND LOAF

Rich with eggs and butter, this braided, glossy bread is more familiar as Easter bread, or *lambropsomo,* when it is decorated with red eggs, and sometimes bits of dough that have been rolled into thin ropes and fashioned into springtime motifs. At Christmas the bread reappears, studded with raisins, almonds, and sometimes chopped candied or dry mixed fruit. However, it is also baked and eaten throughout the year—sans red eggs and fruit—usually on Sunday and other special occasions. Steve's sister's bread is the best we've ever eaten—fragrant, flavorful, and pleasingly moist. It also keeps well, freezes beautifully, *and* makes the world's greatest toast.

Now that your mouth is watering, we must tell you that this is not necessarily the easiest bread to make, and it certainly isn't the quickest, with ten hours of total rising time! The dough is extremely soft and difficult to handle, but if Eleteria's instructions are carefully followed, you'll be surprised how quickly you get the hang of it. Of course, she says, more flour could be added to the batter to make the dough easier to work, but that defeats the purpose, since it's the soft dough that makes the bread so light and moist. Eleteria makes the bread 12 loaves at a time, using a round stainless-steel bowl that is only slightly smaller than a child's wading pool. She has strong, finely shaped hands, and it's a pleasure to watch her deftly scoop out a handful of the soft dough, just exactly the amount needed for one loaf of bread, twirl it into a fancy shape, and plop it onto the baking sheet in three swift motions.

After the bread is completely cooled, it can be tightly wrapped and frozen. Thaw at room temperature and reheat at about 300°F for 10 to 15 minutes. To toast the bread, cut the number of slices needed from the still-frozen bread with a serrated knife, return the bread to the freezer, and toast the slices in a toaster or toaster oven. Spread the warm toast with soft butter, honey, or fruit jam.

⅓ cup milk	2 tablespoons ouzo
½ cup very warm water	2 teaspoons ground mahlepi,
(105 to 115°F)	optional (see page 294)
3 packages active dry yeast	4 cups all-purpose flour
¼ pound (1 stick) unsalted	1 egg yolk beaten with 1 teaspoon
butter, softened	cold water, for brushing on bread
1 cup sugar	2 teaspoons sesame seeds, for
3 eggs, at room temperature	sprinkling on bread

In a small saucepan, heat the milk over low heat just until small bubbles appear around the edge. Set aside to cool until very warm (105 to 115°F). Rinse a small bowl with hot water. Pour the very warm milk and water into the bowl. Sprinkle the yeast over the liquids and set aside for about 5 minutes to soften.

Meanwhile, in the large bowl of an electric mixer, beat the butter and sugar until creamy. Add the eggs, one at a time, beating well after each addition. With the mixer running at low speed, stir in the *ouzo* and *mahlepi*. Stir in the softened yeast mixture. Scrape the batter into a very large bowl. Stir in the flour, ½ cup at a time, scraping the side of the bowl frequently with a rubber spatula, until the flour is completely incorporated into the batter. (The dough will not look like a traditional bread dough, but more like an extremely thick and sticky batter.) Cover the bowl tightly with plastic wrap. Let rise in a warm place for 3 hours. The dough will not rise very much. Punch the dough down, cover and let rise for 3 hours longer. Punch the dough down again, cover and let rise for 3 hours longer.

Cover a large baking sheet with foil. Punch the dough down and cut it into 3 equal parts. (See Note for alternate corkscrew shape.) With buttered hands, work one piece of dough at a time in midair, gently pulling and stretching it into a rope about 14 to 15 inches long. (Since the dough is very sticky, re-butter the palms of your hands during this procedure, but do not flour them.) Lay the dough rope on the baking sheet as shown. Repeat with the remaining 2 pieces of dough, placing them on the baking sheet as shown. Braid

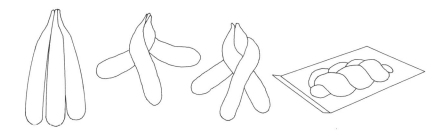

the 3 pieces of dough right on the baking sheet. (Because the dough is soft, it's impossible to get a tight, neat-looking braid; 2 or 3 complete braid turns are sufficient.) Tuck the ends of the braid under the bread. Cover the bread lightly with a piece of oiled plastic wrap and set aside to rise for 1 hour.

Preheat the oven to 375°F. Uncover the bread and brush the top with the beaten egg yolk mixture. Sprinkle with the sesame seeds. Bake for 50 minutes, or until the top turns a rich, deep brown. (Because the loaf will be very dark, do not be tempted to remove it from the oven too soon. In determining whether or not the loaf is fully baked, examine the crevices around the braids, which should split, and the bread should spring back when lightly pressed.)

N O T E : An alternate method—and possibly an easier one—for shaping the bread is to make two loaves that have been twisted into corkscrews. To do this, cut the dough in half. With buttered hands, work one piece of dough at a time in midair, gently pulling and stretching it into a rope about 12 inches long. Holding the rope in the middle with one hand, the two ends hanging free, with the other hand twist the two ends a couple of times and place on the baking sheet. Repeat with the remaining half of the dough.

The braided dough can also be made into two smaller loaves. Baking time for the smaller loaves should be reduced by 5 or 10 minutes.

Olive and Garlic Bread

$\mathcal{T}$he origin of this bread is probably Crete, where olives are used liberally in both cooking and baking. It is rich and flavorful, and may be one of the best of its kind. The recipe makes two loaves, one to eat the minute it has cooled enough to slice and the second one to freeze after it has cooled completely. This glorious-looking bread is particularly compatible with a salad or other light meal, or as a meal by itself with a hunk of cheese and a good bottle of wine.

---

1 package active dry yeast

¾ cup very warm water
  (105 to 115°F)

½ cup (1 stick) salted or unsalted
  butter, softened

2 tablespoons sugar

½ teaspoon salt

4 eggs

5½ cups all-purpose flour

2 tablespoons extra-virgin olive oil

¼ teaspoon minced garlic

1 cup pitted Kalamata olives, very
  coarsely chopped (see page 296)

Regular olive oil, for brushing on
  bread

In the large bowl of an electric mixer, stir the yeast into the warm water until it is completely dissolved. Add the butter, sugar, salt, eggs, and 2½ cups of the flour. Beat at low speed until combined. Stir in 2½ more cups of the flour until well blended. Turn out onto a floured surface and knead for about 15 minutes, adding as much of the remaining ½ cup flour as necessary to make a smooth, springy dough. Place the dough in an oiled bowl, turning to grease the top of the dough. Cover with oiled plastic wrap and set aside in a warm place until doubled in size, about 2 hours.

Heat the extra-virgin olive oil in a small skillet. Add the garlic and cook over medium-low heat, stirring, until the garlic has softened, about 30 seconds. Remove from the heat and set aside. Pat the chopped olives dry on paper towels and set aside.

Preheat the oven to 375°F. Turn the dough out onto a lightly floured surface and cut it in half. Working with one half at a time, roll or pat the dough into a rectangle measuring about 14 by 10 inches. Brush with half the olive oil and garlic mixture. Scatter ½ cup of the olives evenly over the dough, pressing them in slightly and leaving a 1-inch border all around. Starting at a narrow end, roll dough to enclose the olives. Let rest 5 minutes. Gently pat the loaf down until it is about 1½ inches thick. With a single-edged razor blade or the tip of a very sharp knife, make 3 shallow slits in the top of the loaf. Brush the surface of the loaf with regular olive oil. Repeat with the remaining dough. Bake for 25 to 35 minutes, or until golden brown. Transfer the loaves to a rack to cool. Serve warm or at room temperature.

Herb-Filled Olive Oil Bread

YIELD: 1 LOAF

Although not as rich, this moist and extremely fragrant loaf is similar to Olive and Garlic Bread and can be served the same way.

1 tablespoon cornmeal
½ cup milk
5 tablespoons extra-virgin olive oil
1 tablespoon sugar
1¼ teaspoons salt
1 package active dry yeast
½ cup very warm water
  (105 to 115°F)
2½ to 3 cups all-purpose flour
10 to 12 scallions, finely chopped,
  including some of the green tops
  (about 1 cup)

½ cup finely chopped
  flat-leaf parsley
½ cup finely chopped fresh dill
1 clove garlic, put through a
  garlic press
⅛ teaspoon freshly ground
  black pepper
1 egg, lightly beaten
Regular (not extra-virgin) olive oil,
  for brushing on bread

Sprinkle a baking sheet with the cornmeal and set aside. In a small saucepan, heat the milk over low heat until bubbles form around the edge. Remove from the heat and stir in 2 tablespoons of the extra-virgin olive oil, the sugar, and 1 teaspoon of the salt. Set aside to cool to lukewarm.

In a large bowl, stir the yeast into the warm water until completely dissolved. Stir in the lukewarm mixture. Gradually add 2 cups of the flour, beating until well blended. Add enough of the remaining flour to form a stiff dough. Let rest for 10 minutes. Turn the dough out onto a lightly floured surface and knead for 10 to 15 minutes, or until the dough is smooth and springy. Place the dough in a large, oiled bowl, turning to grease the top of the dough. Cover with oiled plastic wrap and let rise in a warm place until doubled in size, about 1 hour.

While the dough is rising, prepare the filling. Heat the remaining 3 tablespoons of extra-virgin olive oil in a large skillet. Add the scallions, parsley, dill, and garlic. Cook over medium-high heat, stirring until the mixture has given off most of its moisture and is reduced by about half. Stir in the remaining ¼ teaspoon salt and the pepper and set aside to cool.

Punch the dough down and let it rest for 10 minutes. Turn the dough out onto a lightly floured surface. Roll or pat the dough into a rectangle measuring about 15 by 9 inches. Brush the surface with some of the beaten egg. Stir the remaining egg into the cooled herb mixture until well blended. Spread the filling over the dough, leaving a 1-inch border all around. Roll up from a narrow end to enclose the filling. Place the roll seam side down on the prepared baking sheet, tucking the ends of the roll under the loaf. Cover with a kitchen towel and let rise for 1 hour.

Preheat the oven to 375°F. With a single-edged razor blade or the tip of a very sharp knife, make 3 shallow slits in the top of the loaf. Brush the surface of the loaf with the regular olive oil. Bake for about 35 minutes, or until the loaf sounds hollow when the sides are tapped. Transfer to a wire rack to cool. Serve warm or at room temperature.

Paximadi

Paximadi looks and tastes very much like zwieback (which can actually be used as a very good substitute for it), but this particular dry bread is nearly as old as breadmaking itself, and the Greeks love it, even though modern baking techniques could easily have rendered it obsolete by now. Visitors to Greece fall in love with it, too, once they have eaten it slathered with honey along with their morning coffee. The twice-baked bread was supposedly invented by a baker named Paxamos, and it was a real boon to the ancients, mostly seamen and soldiers, who otherwise might not have tasted bread for months. The bread was restored, so to speak, by drenching it in olive oil, vinegar, wine, or just plain water.

Paximadi is often used as an ingredient in recipes that call for bread crumbs. There are two kinds: lightly sweetened and unsweetened, which you will probably have no trouble finding, packaged, in Greek grocery stores. But with the right kind of bread, it's rather easy to make *paximadi* yourself. Either Festive Bread or Steve's Sister's Everyday Bread works reasonably well.

Preheat the oven to 225°F. Cut the bread into 1-inch slices and spread them out on an ungreased baking sheet. Bake for about 45 minutes, turning once, until the slices are very dry. Cool the slices on a wire rack and store in a plastic bag or other airtight container to use as needed.

For a change of pace, add a few slices of *paximadi* to the bread basket on the table. The lightly sweetened toast also makes a good snack, spread with honey, butter, or fruit jam. Salads can be spooned over unsweetened toast to soften it a bit. Good choices would be Tomato and Onion Salad or Radishes with Scallions and *Feta*. Or do as the ancients did and simply drizzle the toast with olive oil and vinegar and dust it with crumbled oregano.

Grilled Flat Bread

*A*lthough very good when baked on an oven rack, these chewy bread rounds are infinitely better when a charcoal fire is the source of heat. It's also fun to watch them puff up as they bake, taking on the charcoal-grill marks, while the aroma drives you out of your mind. As you can imagine, these are the ideal accompaniment for any grilled vegetable or meat, but they are simply ambrosial when torn into small pieces and dipped into *Taramosalata* or *Skordalia*.

---

1 package active dry yeast
2⅓ cups very warm
  (105 to 115°F) water
1⅔ cups whole-wheat flour
1 teaspoon salt
3 tablespoons regular (not
  extra-virgin) olive oil

4½ to 5 cups all-purpose flour
¾ cup extra-virgin olive oil
2 tablespoons dried oregano
  leaves, crumbled
¾ cup minced flat-leaf parsley
Coarse (kosher) salt

In the large bowl of an electric mixer, soften the yeast in 1⅔ cups of the warm water for about 5 minutes. With a spoon, stir in the whole-wheat flour, the remaining ⅔ cup of water, salt, and the regular olive oil. Add 1½ cups all-purpose flour and beat on low speed until the ingredients are moistened. Beat on high speed for about 2 minutes, or until the dough pulls away from the side of the bowl. With a spoon, stir in 3 cups of the remaining all-purpose flour. Turn out onto a floured surface and knead for about 10 minutes, or until the dough is smooth, adding a little more flour, if necessary, to keep the dough from sticking. Place the dough in a greased bowl, turning to grease the top of the dough. Cover the bowl tightly with oiled plastic wrap and let stand in a warm place until doubled in size, about 1 hour. Turn the dough out onto a lightly floured surface and knead it briefly. Cut the dough into 6

Paximadi

Paximadi looks and tastes very much like zwieback (which can actually be used as a very good substitute for it), but this particular dry bread is nearly as old as breadmaking itself, and the Greeks love it, even though modern baking techniques could easily have rendered it obsolete by now. Visitors to Greece fall in love with it, too, once they have eaten it slathered with honey along with their morning coffee. The twice-baked bread was supposedly invented by a baker named Paxamos, and it was a real boon to the ancients, mostly seamen and soldiers, who otherwise might not have tasted bread for months. The bread was restored, so to speak, by drenching it in olive oil, vinegar, wine, or just plain water.

Paximadi is often used as an ingredient in recipes that call for bread crumbs. There are two kinds: lightly sweetened and unsweetened, which you will probably have no trouble finding, packaged, in Greek grocery stores. But with the right kind of bread, it's rather easy to make *paximadi* yourself. Either Festive Bread or Steve's Sister's Everyday Bread works reasonably well.

Preheat the oven to 225°F. Cut the bread into 1-inch slices and spread them out on an ungreased baking sheet. Bake for about 45 minutes, turning once, until the slices are very dry. Cool the slices on a wire rack and store in a plastic bag or other airtight container to use as needed.

For a change of pace, add a few slices of *paximadi* to the bread basket on the table. The lightly sweetened toast also makes a good snack, spread with honey, butter, or fruit jam. Salads can be spooned over unsweetened toast to soften it a bit. Good choices would be Tomato and Onion Salad or Radishes with Scallions and *Feta*. Or do as the ancients did and simply drizzle the toast with olive oil and vinegar and dust it with crumbled oregano.

Grilled Flat Bread

*A*lthough very good when baked on an oven rack, these chewy bread rounds are infinitely better when a charcoal fire is the source of heat. It's also fun to watch them puff up as they bake, taking on the charcoal-grill marks, while the aroma drives you out of your mind. As you can imagine, these are the ideal accompaniment for any grilled vegetable or meat, but they are simply ambrosial when torn into small pieces and dipped into *Taramosalata* or *Skordalia*.

---

1 package active dry yeast
2⅓ cups very warm
 (105 to 115°F) water
1⅔ cups whole-wheat flour
1 teaspoon salt
3 tablespoons regular (not
 extra-virgin) olive oil

4½ to 5 cups all-purpose flour
¾ cup extra-virgin olive oil
2 tablespoons dried oregano
 leaves, crumbled
¾ cup minced flat-leaf parsley
Coarse (kosher) salt

In the large bowl of an electric mixer, soften the yeast in 1⅔ cups of the warm water for about 5 minutes. With a spoon, stir in the whole-wheat flour, the remaining ⅔ cup of water, salt, and the regular olive oil. Add 1½ cups all-purpose flour and beat on low speed until the ingredients are moistened. Beat on high speed for about 2 minutes, or until the dough pulls away from the side of the bowl. With a spoon, stir in 3 cups of the remaining all-purpose flour. Turn out onto a floured surface and knead for about 10 minutes, or until the dough is smooth, adding a little more flour, if necessary, to keep the dough from sticking. Place the dough in a greased bowl, turning to grease the top of the dough. Cover the bowl tightly with oiled plastic wrap and let stand in a warm place until doubled in size, about 1 hour. Turn the dough out onto a lightly floured surface and knead it briefly. Cut the dough into 6

Steve's Sister's
New Year's Bread
VASSILOPITA

YIELD: 1 LOAF

*T*hough not as light as the traditional *tsoureki,* this bread, baked in honor of Saint Basil, whose feast day is celebrated on January 1, is quite similar. However, the dough is easier to handle, and it's certainly quicker to make. (Eleteria says the dough for this bread can be substituted for the Festive Bread dough and shaped the same way.)

A gold coin (these days a coin wrapped in foil) is buried in the dough before the bread is baked. When served, the bread is cut into wedges and, as each wedge is cut, it is designated for one of those assembled, with the first piece for Saint Basil and the second piece for Christ. The person whose piece contains the coin is assured of good luck throughout the year. If the coin is in the first two pieces, the money goes to the church. (However, by some motherly magic, finding the good-luck coin is not necessarily a matter of pure chance!) Sliced almonds can be used to form the numbers of the new year on the top of the bread before it's baked.

---

1 cup milk
2 packages active dry yeast
1/2 cup (1 stick) unsalted butter, at room temperature
1 tablespoon solid white vegetable shortening
3/4 cup sugar
3 eggs, at room temperature

1/4 cup orange juice
2 tablespoons grated orange peel
1/4 teaspoon ground mahlepi *(see page 294)*
5 cups all-purpose flour
1 egg yolk beaten with 1 teaspoon cold water for brushing on bread
Sliced almonds, for decorating bread

In a small saucepan, heat the milk over low heat just until small bubbles appear around the edge. Set aside to cool until very warm

(105 to 115°F). Sprinkle the yeast over the warm milk and set aside for about 5 minutes to soften.

Meanwhile, in the large bowl of an electric mixer, beat the butter, shortening, and sugar until creamy. Add the eggs, one at a time, beating well after each addition. Beat in the orange juice, orange peel, and *mahlepi*. The mixture will look curdled. Stir in 4½ cups of the flour. Turn the dough out into a lightly floured surface. Knead in the remaining ½ cup flour. Place the dough in a greased bowl, turning to grease the top of the dough, and cover with oiled plastic wrap. Let rise until doubled in size, about 2 hours. Generously grease a 9-inch round layer-cake pan. Form the dough into a round loaf and place in the cake pan. Cover with oiled plastic wrap and let rise for about 45 minutes. The dough will rise well above the rim of the pan.

Preheat the oven to 350°F. Uncover the bread and brush the top with the beaten egg yolk mixture. Decorate with almonds. Bake for 1 hour or until the loaf is a rich, deep brown. (Because the loaf will be very dark, do not be tempted to remove it from the oven too soon. In determining whether or not the loaf is fully baked, remove it from the oven and, with protected hands, gently attempt to remove the bread from the pan. If it comes out easily, the bread is fully baked. If not, return to the oven for another 5 minutes and try the same procedure again. After the bread is removed from the pan, cool it completely on a wire rack.

equal pieces. Work with one piece of dough at a time, keeping the remaining pieces tightly covered. On a floured surface, roll each piece of dough into a ball and then roll the ball into a 10-inch circle with a rolling pin. Brush one side with about 1 tablespoon of the extra-virgin olive oil, then sprinkle with ½ teaspoon of the oregano, 1 tablespoon of the parsley, and coarse salt to taste, lightly pressing the seasonings into dough. Turn the dough over onto a piece of aluminum foil and repeat brushing with olive oil and seasoning on the other side. Place the dough round, foil side down, on a baking sheet. Repeat the rolling and seasoning with the remaining dough pieces, stacking the rounds on top of one another, separated by the foil. If not grilling immediately, cover and refrigerate for up to 3 hours.

Preheat a charcoal grill. When the coals are covered with gray ash, spread them into an even layer. Set the grid about 3 to 4 inches above the coals for medium-high heat. Using the foil to assist, flip one round of bread onto the grid and peel off the foil. Grill for about 2 to 3 minutes per side, turning once with a spatula, until the bread is lightly flecked with brown on both sides. Take a peek under the bread after it has cooled for a minute or so to be sure that it is not browning too quickly. If it is, raise the grid an inch or so. Repeat with the remaining rounds. The bread is best served warm, but can be served at room temperature.

To grill in the oven, preheat the oven to 450°F. Set the oven rack at the lowest position. Flip 2 bread rounds onto the hot rack and bake for 5 minutes; turn and bake 3 minutes longer. Repeat with the remaining rounds.

NOTE: Baked flat bread can be tightly wrapped and frozen. To reheat, loosen the wrap and place in a 350°F oven for about 10 minutes.

Fried Bread Dough

YIELD: 6 BREADS; 6 SERVINGS

Often a portion of bread dough is set aside on baking day and fried in olive oil. While still warm, the flat breads can be split and stuffed with salad or *souvlaki* and eaten on the spot, or they can be made ahead and reheated, or frozen for 2 or 3 months.

---

2 cups all-purpose flour
1 tablespoon baking powder
1 teaspoon salt
2 tablespoons extra-virgin olive oil

¾ cup milk
Regular (not extra-virgin) olive oil or
    vegetable oil, for frying

In a large bowl, mix the flour, baking powder, and salt until well blended. Sprinkle the extra-virgin olive oil over the dry mixture and mix with your fingertips until coarse crumbs form. Add the milk and stir with a fork just until dough particles cling together. Turn the dough out onto a lightly floured surface and knead briefly until smooth, about 3 minutes. Form the dough into a ball and cut into 6 equal pieces. Work with one piece of dough at a time, keeping the remaining pieces lightly covered. Shape each piece of dough into a ball, then flatten with a rolling pin to make a 6-inch round. Repeat with the remaining portions, stacking them on top of one another, separated with waxed paper.

Pour enough regular olive oil into a medium-size skillet to measure about ¾ inch deep. Heat the oil until it registers 375°F on a deep-fry thermometer. Add one round of dough and cook until puffed and golden brown, about 30 seconds per side. Be careful not to overcook. Lift from the skillet with tongs and set aside to drain on paper towels. Repeat with the remaining rounds, making sure to keep the oil temperature even during frying.

NOTE: Fried Bread can be made ahead, cooled, and stored tightly wrapped. Unwrap and reheat on baking sheets in a 375°F oven.

Sauces and Dressings

For the culinary scholar, learning about Greek sauces and dressings is a comparatively quick study, since there are relatively few of them and they are not very complex, although variations of each one can be endless.

With the exception of tomato sauce and other frequently used sauces that are not uniquely Greek, for instance, mayonnaise and béchamel, the sauces of Greece are hardly contrived, and are most easily understood if viewed as the Greeks view them: as the end result of something else, the ubiquitous *avgolemono* being the best example. Dressings, too, are usually just a more formal combination of things that are always served together anyway, like lemon juice and olive oil, the humble origin for all vinaigrette sauces.

Besides these sauces, many others are given with individual recipes throughout the book, most of which are good examples of "end results," when natural juices and pan liquids are slightly enriched and reduced to a more saucelike flavor and consistency.

Skordalia, which is often thought of as a sauce, and for which three versions are given here, is not really a sauce at all, but a dip. However, it is commonly used as a sauce, especially in this country, and in this book, where it frequently ends up on the plate mainly to enhance something else.

Periyali's Almond Skordalia

*T*his is a luxury *skordalia,* since it is made with almonds, an ingredient that most Greeks can't afford for every day.

---

5 ounces (about 5 slices) firm
  homemade-style bread
½ cup whole blanched almonds,
  coarsely chopped
2 or 3 large garlic cloves, put through
  a garlic press (about 1 teaspoon
  garlic puree)
1 small (about 3 ounces) all-purpose
  potato, peeled, boiled until soft, and
  drained

3 tablespoons lemon juice
3 tablespoons white-wine vinegar
2 tablespoons extra-virgin olive oil
¾ teaspoon salt
½ teaspoon sugar

Trim the crusts from the bread and spread the slices out on a tray to dry for about 24 hours.

In the container of a food processor, place the almonds, garlic, and cooled potato. Process until smooth.

Mix the lemon juice, vinegar, olive oil, salt, and sugar in a small bowl and set aside. Fill a large bowl with cool water. Drop the dried bread into the water, 1 slice at a time. When it is soaked, squeeze about half the water from the bread between the palms of your hands. Add the bread to the ingredients in the processor, alternating with the lemon-juice mixture, and process until smooth. Since the *skordalia* has a tendency to stiffen and become pasty as it chills, the mixture should be quite loose at this point. Taste and adjust the seasoning. Scrape the mixture into a bowl. Cover and refrigerate for several hours to allow the flavors to mellow and blend. If the mixture seems too stiff, beat in a little water before serving.

Nicola's Mother's Zakinthos-Style Skordalia

*H*ere is a very robust *skordalia,* sometimes called "the fisher-man's *skordalia,"* since it is often eaten with fish, especially fried dried cod. It's also an excellent dip for bread. It is important not to peel the potatoes before they are cooked. Otherwise, the *skordalia* will not have the right consistency.

---

6 all-purpose potatoes of similar size (1¼ pounds)	2 teaspoons coarse (kosher) salt
6 large garlic cloves, cut into quarters	½ cup extra-virgin olive oil
	¼ cup lemon juice

Cook the whole, unpeeled potatoes in boiling water until fork-tender. While the potatoes are cooking, mash the garlic and salt in a mortar with a pestle (or in a small ceramic bowl with the back of a wooden spoon) until pasty and set aside. Remove the potatoes from the heat, but do not drain them. Take the potatoes from the hot water, one by one, and peel while still hot. (The easiest way to do this is to place the potatoes on a paper towel and pull the skin off with a small knife and your fingers while steadying the potato with a kitchen fork. Wearing a rubber glove on the hand you use to peel the potato helps, too.) As each potato is peeled, place it in a large bowl and beat by hand or with an electric mixer until it is virtually lump-free. (It is important that the potatoes be mashed while they are still hot.) When all of the potatoes have been mashed, immediately beat in the garlic mixture until well combined. Gradually beat in the olive oil until the mixture is thick and pasty. Beat in the lemon juice. Scrape the mixture into a serving bowl.

Cover and refrigerate for several hours to allow flavors to mellow and blend. Bring to room temperature and drizzle a little more extra-virgin olive oil into the potato swirls just before serving.

Bread-Crumb Skordalia

This is good for dipping artichoke leaves or with any raw or steamed vegetable. It is sometimes called "the poor man's *skordalia*," since it doesn't call for nuts, rather pricey ingredients, considering how much of the sauce can be consumed at one sitting.

---

1 loaf White Bakery Bread (see page 213) or 1 loaf (about 12 ounces) purchased French bread
8 garlic cloves, put through a garlic press
²/₃ cup regular olive oil

²/₃ cup extra-virgin olive oil
¹/₃ cup red-wine vinegar
Salt, to taste
Kalamata olives (see page 296), for garnish

Trim the crust from bread and discard. Break the bread into pieces and place in a blender or food processor. Process until finely crumbled. Spread the crumbs out on a piece of waxed paper and allow to dry for several hours, stirring occasionally. When they are dry, place the crumbs in a large bowl and gradually add as much water as they will readily absorb. Press handfuls of the wet crumbs between the palms of your hands to remove as much moisture as possible. Measure out 2 cups of the damp crumbs and set aside. Place the garlic in a large bowl. Slowly add the damp crumbs, mashing with a wooden spoon until the mixture becomes very pasty. Add a mixture of both kinds of olive oil in a thin stream, beating and mashing the mixture against the side of the bowl until it is very thick and pasty. Stir in the vinegar and salt until well blended. Scrape into a bowl and refrigerate for several hours before serving to allow the flavors to develop. Serve garnished with olives.

Olive Oil and Lemon Dressing

YIELD: ½ CUP

This very simple recipe is excellent drizzled over salad greens, vegetables, and fish.

---

2 tablespoons lemon juice	*6 tablespoons extra-virgin olive oil*
¼ teaspoon salt, or to taste	*1 tablespoon chopped flat-leaf parsley*
Freshly ground black pepper, to taste	*(optional)*

In a small bowl, mix the lemon juice, salt, and pepper. Add the olive oil, drop by drop, and then in a thin, steady stream, beating constantly with a whisk until thick. Stir in the parsley until blended.

Variation For Olive Oil and Red-Wine Vinegar Dressing, substitute red-wine vinegar for the lemon juice.

Thick Lemon Sauce for Fish and Shellfish
LADOLEMONO

YIELD: ABOUT ¾ CUP

Ladolemono is a good substitute for butter with plain broiled or steamed lobster and other shellfish.

½ cup extra-virgin olive oil	1 tablespoon chopped flat-leaf parsley
¼ cup lemon juice	⅛ teaspoon salt
1 small garlic clove, put through a garlic press (optional)	About 5 turns of a pepper mill

Place all of the ingredients in a small jar with a tight-fitting lid. Shake hard until the mixture forms a thick emulsion.

Red-Wine Vinegar and Garlic Sauce
SKORDOSTOUMBI

YIELD: 1 CUP

A few drops of this tangy sauce can liven up soups (especially *patsas*) and plainly cooked or grilled vegetables. Just put it on the table and see what happens.

1 cup red-wine vinegar	1 tablespoon coarsely chopped garlic

Mix the vinegar and garlic in a jar or bottle with a tight-fitting lid. Set aside for a day before using, shaking occasionally. Store in the refrigerator.

Hot Lemon Sauce for Vegetables
AVGOLEMONO

YIELD: ABOUT 2½ CUPS

Cooked vegetables, especially stuffed grape leaves, really respond to lemon juice. We particularly enjoy this thick sauce with steamed asparagus and other green vegetables. Do not make the sauce too far ahead of serving.

2 egg yolks
1 tablespoon butter
1 tablespoon all-purpose flour
1 cup hot Chicken Broth (see
 page 5) or the cooking liquid
 from the recipe for which the sauce
 is being prepared

2 tablespoons lemon juice
1 teaspoon finely chopped flat-leaf
 parsley

Beat the egg yolks in a small bowl and set aside. Melt the butter in the top of a double boiler over barely simmering water. Stir in the flour until smooth. Add the broth and cook, stirring constantly, until the mixture thickens. Reduce the heat under the double boiler until the water stops simmering. Beat a couple of tablespoonfuls of the hot broth mixture into the yolks to temper them, then slowly add the egg yolk mixture to the broth, stirring constantly with a whisk. Add the lemon juice and continue to cook, stirring, until hot. Stir in the parsley until blended. If not using immediately, remove from the heat and set aside, still over the hot water. Press a piece of plastic wrap directly on the surface to prevent a skin from forming. Even if the sauce has cooled slightly when it is served, the heat from the food over which it is served will provide enough warmth to reheat it. Or reheat over hot (not simmering) water, stirring almost constantly.

Demi-glace for Lamb Chops

$\mathcal{A}$lthough this sauce is simple enough to make, it does take about 6 hours from start to finish. It's also a good idea to order the lamb bones in advance, since many butchers don't keep them on hand. Any kind of lamb bones will do, just as long as they are cut into pieces. This recipe can also be used to make a *demi-glace* for beef using Beef Brown Stock.

---

*1 recipe for Lamb Brown Stock
  (see page 4)
Salt and freshly ground black pepper,
  to taste*

1 teaspoon minced parsley

After the bones and vegetables have been removed from the stock, return the pot to medium heat and continue to simmer, stirring occasionally, until the stock is very syrupy. This will not take as long as you might imagine, so watch carefully.

Strain the reduced stock through a fine sieve into a small bowl. Do not press down on the solids in the sieve, which would give the sauce a muddy appearance. Instead, tap the side of the sieve with your hand, or use two sieves, transferring the mixture back and forth between the two and rinsing the sieves between strainings.

For all of this work, you will have about ½ cup sauce, but it will be worth it. Refrigerate the sauce for several hours, or until the fat rises to the surface and solidifies.

Just before serving, remove the congealed fat from the surface. Heat the sauce (which will have jelled) in a small saucepan. Season to taste with salt and pepper and stir in the minced parsley. Spoon the sauce over the lamb chops, dividing evenly.

Desserts and Sweet Treats

Greece is a nation of sugar fanatics, but to see most Greeks smile, one would suppose that most have never indulged in a refined carbohydrate in their entire lives. (Maybe that's because of all the calcium in the yogurt and cheese they also adore.)

Although some of the restaurants in Greece have long since capitulated to the Western dessert custom and generally offer one or two of the more distinguished Hellenic confectionery creations, this is yet another meal course that exists, if it exists at all, solely for foreigners. Most Greeks prefer a finale of fresh fruit and sweet wine or brandy, and those needing real sugar fix generally repair to a nearby sweet shop to choose from a dizzying display of Greek treats, as well as more than a few French, Austrian, Bavarian, and Italian specialties.

Like so many other Greek recipes, certain sweets have been known to exist for nearly two thousand years. Deipnosophistae wrote about cheesecake in A.D. 200, and the ancient forerunner to *baklava* is believed by scholars to have been two pieces of dough stuffed with nuts and sesame seeds and covered with honey and cider syrup.

Whether by design or good fortune, many of the sweets in the Greek repertoire lean heavily on nuts, honey, and dried fruit, with relatively minimal reliance for flavor and richness on dairy fat and other ingredients that we tend to be wary of these days. Curiously, chocolate has yet to make inroads into the Greek culinary culture,

although it is not unusual to see young Greeks popping chocolate candies and wolfing down chocolate cake in the sweet shops, so we wonder how long *that* can last. (Of all the things we are asked to bring to Greece, M&M's are high on the list.)

The splendid desserts on view near the front of the dining room at Periyali never fail to prompt long sighs, and a surprising number of diners who promise themselves they're going to order this or that for dessert actually do.

One of the most requested desserts is Rice Pudding. The secret to Periyali's creamy pudding is stir, stir, stir.

Rice Pudding
R I Z O G A L O

YIELD: 3½ TO 4 CUPS; 6 TO 8 SERVINGS

Making perfect rice pudding seems to come as naturally to the Greeks as breathing, yet the technique remains frustratingly elusive for many others. Cold, creamy rice pudding, liberally sprinkled with aromatic ground cinnamon, is a much-loved summertime treat in Greece. It is eaten as a snack in sweet shops and cafés and off street carts, where little cups of it are embedded in chopped ice. If you like a few raisins in your pudding, stir them in (about ½ cup) when you add the cream, which gives them just enough time to plump up a little.

---

4 cups milk
1 thick strip lemon peel
½ cup regular long-grain raw rice
  (see Note)
1 egg yolk

¾ cup sugar
½ cup heavy cream
½ teaspoon vanilla extract
Ground cinnamon, for dusting
  pudding

Place the milk, lemon peel, and rice in a heavy 4-quart saucepan. Cook, uncovered, for about 1 hour, or until the rice is soft to the bite, but still retains its shape. (While it cooks, it's important to stir the mixture almost constantly to prevent the rice from clumping and to keep a skin from forming on the surface.)

In a small bowl, mix the egg yolk with the sugar until crumbly. Remove the rice from the heat. Rapidly stir a spoonful of the hot rice mixture into the yolk mixture to temper the yolk, then stir the yolk mixture into the rice, mixing steadily to prevent the yolk from cooking too quickly and forming solid particles. Return to low heat and continue to cook, stirring almost constantly, for several minutes. Add the cream and cook, stirring, until the mixture is steaming. Remove from the heat and stir in the vanilla. Continue to stir the pudding until it has cooled slightly, then press a piece of plastic wrap directly onto the surface to prevent a skin from forming.

Although it is traditional to serve rice pudding chilled, it can also be served warm or at room temperature. Dust servings liberally with ground cinnamon.

NOTE: Periyali uses Carolina brand rice.

Summer Plum Pudding

YIELD: 6 SERVINGS

To make this incredibly delicate pudding, Greek women almost always use tender, sweet plums, usually tiny yellow ones that grow on trees that are as close as their own backyards. Although you can substitute the larger commercial purple plums, we think you'll be happier with the results if you take the time to scout out small, locally grown plums. In any case, taste before you buy. A little tartness is desirable, as long as the fruit has a distinct "plummy" flavor. If the plums are too tart, they can always be tossed with a little sugar to add the sweetness that Mother Nature forgot. This is a dessert that should be eaten soon after it's baked, so plan ahead.

---

1 pound small sweet plums
2 tablespoons brandy (optional)
1/2 cup plus 1 to 2 tablespoons sugar
1/8 teaspoon salt
4 eggs

1/2 cup all-purpose flour
1 cup milk
1/2 teaspoon vanilla extract
Confectioners' sugar, for sprinkling on
  pudding

Rinse and dry the plums. Cut into lengthwise halves or quarters and remove the pits. (Larger plums should be cut into eighths.) You should have about 2 cups. Place the plums in a small bowl and stir in the brandy. If, despite your best efforts to find sweet plums, the ones you use are a little tart, also stir in a tablespoon or so of the sugar. Set aside to macerate for 30 minutes to an hour, stirring occasionally.

Preheat the oven to 375°F. Generously butter a 6- to 8-cup gratin or oval baking dish and set aside. In a large bowl, beat ½ cup of the sugar, the salt, and the eggs together with a whisk until well blended and smooth. Sprinkle the flour over the egg mixture, a tablespoon or so at a time, stirring after each addition with a wire whisk until the flour is completely incorporated and the batter is smooth. Beat in the milk and vanilla. Drain off any juices that have accumulated with the plums. Stir the drained plums into the batter, which will be very thin. Spoon the batter into the prepared baking dish. Bake on the middle oven rack for 25 to 30 minutes, or until the pudding is risen and starting to pull away from the side of the dish and a wooden pick inserted in the center comes out clean. Remove from the oven and immediately sprinkle with the remaining tablespoon of sugar. Set the pudding on a wire rack to cool until it is barely warm, 20 to 30 minutes. The pudding will fall as it cools. Serve directly from the baking dish in shallow bowls, sprinkled with confectioners' sugar.

Powder Cookies

KOURAMBIETHES

Depending on whose cookies you eat, these can be round, triangular, or crescent-shaped. They are popular all through the year, especially at family celebrations and weddings, where they are offered as tokens of good luck. At Christmas, a clove is stuck in the center to symbolize the spices brought to Bethlehem by the Three Wise Men. Considering the Greeks' nearly insatiable sweet tooth, it's surprising that these crumbly cookies contain so little sugar. But never fear, for they are rolled in confectioners' sugar—and lots of it—just before serving. By the way, don't even *think* about substituting margarine or some kind of butter blend for the butter in this recipe.

---

1 cup (2 sticks) unsalted butter at
  room temperature
1/4 cup confectioners' sugar
1 egg yolk
1/4 cup brandy
1/2 teaspoon vanilla extract
2 1/2 cups all-purpose flour
1/2 teaspoon baking powder

2 tablespoons granulated sugar
1/3 cup sliced or slivered blanched
  almonds, toasted (see Note) and
  very finely chopped, but not
  pulverized
1/4 cup rosewater (see page 300)
Confectioners' sugar, for sprinkling on
  cookies

Preheat the oven to 250°F. Beat the butter with an electric mixer at high speed until pale and fluffy. Add the confectioners' sugar and egg yolk and continue beating until creamy. Beat in the brandy and vanilla. The mixture will look curdled.

Mix the flour and baking powder together with a whisk in a medium-size bowl until well blended. With the mixer running at low speed, gradually add the flour mixture to the butter mixture. The dough will be soft and will leave the side of the bowl. Mix in the granulated sugar and almonds until well blended.

Using a heaping measuring tablespoonful of dough for each cookie, roll the dough into a ball between the palms of your hands and then flatten to make a ½-inch-thick disk that measures about 1½ inches in diameter. Place on an ungreased baking sheet. With your thumb, make a fairly deep indentation in the center of each cookie.

Form and bake the cookies, one batch at a time (leave the remaining dough in the bowl, covered lightly with waxed paper) in the lower half of the oven for about 30 minutes, or until the cookies have formed a crust and are just beginning to color. They will still feel slightly soft. If you have doubts, break a cookie in half. If it looks unbaked in the center, bake for 5 minutes more. Remove the cookies from the baking sheet to a wire rack to cool completely. While the cookies are still warm, place one drop of rosewater on top of each.

Store the cooled cookies in a tightly covered container, where they will keep nicely for several weeks. Before serving, roll the cookies in confectioners' sugar and stack on a serving platter, sprinkling more confectioners' sugar between the layers.

NOTE: Place the almonds in a small, cold skillet. Cover over medium heat, stirring constantly, until they have a toasty aroma. Remove from the heat and continue to stir until cooled. Chop after toasting.

Name Days

Names in Greece are not just names that are in vogue at the time you're born, and it's difficult for most Greeks to understand why many Westerners give their children whimsical or fashionable names.

A Greek child is named after one of 365 saints, and the day on which your saint is celebrated becomes your name day. And it's even more complicated than that. For instance, depending on whether a family lives on the mainland or an Aegean island, the first boy may be named after his father's father and the first girl after her father's mother. There are fairly strict rules governing this naming business, but Greek names are taken very seriously and they link us with our blood ancestors and our heritage, and with the whole Greek Orthodox community.

Since everyone knows your name day, just by virtue of knowing your name, there's no getting away from the passing of another year, even if it isn't your birthday! My name day is December 6, and if I'm in Greece I can expect many visitors throughout the day. They will probably bring me a little gift of sweets or wine, but the custom is that on my name day *I* am expected to entertain *them*.

Loukoumathes and *tighanites* are two of the things my mother always made to serve on our name days, and on many other days, too, since my sisters and I could, and still can, eat them by the dozen!

—Nicola

Nicola's Mother's Traditional Honey Puffs

LOUKOUMATHES

ઌૐઌૐઌૐઌૐ

YIELD: ABOUT 36

*I*t takes a little practice to learn Nicola's mother's technique for shaping the dough for these little puffs so that they come out in neat rounds. But even if they don't at first, they'll be just as delicious.

Place a big spoonful of the dough in the palm of your left hand —assuming you're right-handed—and make a fist. Tighten your fist, squeezing a little "bubble" of dough, about the size of a walnut, up next to your thumb. Have a serving teaspoon in your right hand and cut the bubble off with the edge of the spoon and carefully lower it into the oil. You can usually get two or three "bubbles" out of each handful of dough. When the spoon begins to get sticky, dip it into some water about every third puff, but be careful not to let any drops of water fall into the hot oil or it will splatter.

3½ to 4 cups all-purpose flour
1 teaspoon sugar
1 teaspoon salt
1 package active dry yeast
1 cup very warm water
 (105 to 115°F)
1 cup warm water

Regular (not extra-virgin) olive oil or
 vegetable oil, for frying
Honey (see page 293), for drizzling
 over puffs
Ground cinnamon, for sprinkling
 on puffs

In a medium-size bowl, mix 1½ cups of the flour, sugar, and salt with a whisk until well blended; set aside. In a large bowl that has been rinsed with hot water, sprinkle the yeast over the cup of very warm water and stir until dissolved. Gradually add the flour mixture to the dissolved yeast, stirring until smooth. Cover with oiled plastic wrap and set aside in a warm place, away from drafts, until doubled in size. Stir in the warm water and enough flour to make a thick batter. Cover again and let rise until the mixture begins to bubble, about 1½ hours. The dough, which is more like a batter, will be thick and sticky.

Line a shallow pan with several thicknesses of paper towels and set aside. Pour enough oil into a wide, deep pan to measure about 4 inches. Set over high heat until the oil registers about 365°F on a deep-fry thermometer. Make the puffs as described above and drop them into the hot oil, about 6 at a time, and fry until golden. Remove with a slotted spoon to the paper-lined pan. Repeat with the remaining dough. (The fried puffs can be kept warm in a 200°F oven until the remainder are fried.) When all the puffs are fried, stack them on a plate and drizzle with honey. Sprinkle with cinnamon and serve very warm.

N O T E : Like all fried breads, *loukoumathes* are best eaten right after they are fried and are still warm. However, they can be made ahead, cooled, and then frozen in a plastic bag or tightly wrapped in aluminum foil. Unwrap and place the frozen puffs on a baking sheet. Reheat at 300°F for 10 to 12 minutes, or until very warm. Drizzle with plenty of honey, sprinkle with cinnamon, and serve immediately.

Nicola's Mother's Quick Fritters

TIGHANITES

Since there's no yeast in this batter, the whole mixing and frying procedure goes very quickly. We like them as much as, or more than, the *loukoumathes*—which is actually just a more traditional version of the *tighanites*—especially when they're reheated in honey the next day.

1½ cups all-purpose flour
3 tablespoons sugar
2 teaspoons baking powder
2 eggs
½ cup milk
Regular (not extra-virgin) olive oil or
  vegetable oil, for frying

Honey (see page 293), for drizzling
  over fritters
Ground cinnamon, for sprinkling on
  fritters
Sesame seeds, for sprinkling on fritters

In a large bowl, mix the flour, sugar, and baking powder with a whisk until well blended. In a small bowl, beat the eggs with the milk. Stir into the flour mixture to make a thick batter.

Line a shallow pan with several thicknesses of paper towels and set aside. Pour enough oil into a wide, deep pan to measure about 4 inches. Set over high heat until the oil registers about 365°F on a deep-fry thermometer. Make the puffs as described for the *loukoumathes*. Drop them into the hot oil, about 6 at a time, and fry until golden. Remove with a slotted spoon to the paper-lined pan. Repeat with the remaining dough. (The fried puffs can be kept warm in a 200°F oven until the remainder are fried.) When all the puffs are fried, stack them on a plate and drizzle with plenty of honey. Sprinkle with cinnamon and sesame seeds and serve very warm.

NOTE: To rewarm, place the fritters in a skillet with a little more honey and a few drops of water. Cook over low heat, stirring frequently, until the fritters are very warm.

Honey-Walnut Cookies

For a dramatic presentation, pile the cookies into a pyramid on a large, round plate and drizzle them with even *more* honey just before serving, so that the cookies absolutely shine! Some cooks also like to sprinkle the pyramid with a few chopped walnuts.

---

1 cup (2 sticks) unsalted
  butter, softened
2/3 cup sugar
2 teaspoons vanilla extract

2 1/2 cups all-purpose flour
1 1/2 cups chopped walnuts
1/2 cup light cream
1/2 cup honey (see page 293)

Line 2 baking sheets with aluminum foil. Butter the foil and set the baking sheets aside.

Combine the butter, sugar, and vanilla in the large bowl of an electric mixer and beat until creamy. Add the flour all at once. With a pastry blender or 2 knives, combine the mixture until well blended and crumbly. Stir in the walnuts. Drizzle the cream over the flour mixture. Mix with your fingertips until well blended. Turn the dough onto a lightly floured surface and knead briefly. Wrap the dough in waxed paper or plastic wrap and refrigerate for about an hour, or until cold.

Preheat the oven to 350°F. Form the dough into 1½-inch balls between the palms of your hands. As they are made, set the balls on a prepared baking sheet and flatten each one slightly with tines of a dinner fork. Brush the tops with honey. Bake for about 15 minutes, or until pale golden. Remove from the baking sheets with a wide spatula and cool on wire racks. Brush with more honey just before serving.

Almond Biscuits from Mykonos
AMYGDALOTA

Even when kept tightly covered, these biscuitlike cookies won't stay soft and chewy for more than two or three days, but given their meltingly delicate flavor and texture, chances are they'll be gone way before that.

---

18 ounces (exactly) blanched whole,
  slivered, or chopped almonds
1½ cups confectioners' sugar

3 large egg whites, at
  room temperature
½ teaspoon cream of tartar

Cover two 17-by-14-inch baking sheets with aluminum foil. Grease the foil very lightly or coat it with nonstick vegetable spray.

Place half of the almonds in a food processor with ¼ cup of the sugar. Process with the steel blade until the almonds are *very finely* ground, stopping the processor once or twice and giving the ingredients a good stir from the bottom. (Processing the almonds with the sugar will help to prevent the nuts from becoming pasty.) Place the pulverized nuts in a small bowl and set aside. Repeat with remaining nuts and another ¼ cup sugar.

Preheat the oven to 325°F. In the large bowl of an electric mixer, beat the egg whites and cream of tartar at medium speed until frothy; beat at high speed until soft, curving peaks form when the beaters are lifted. Gradually beat in the remaining cup of sugar. Continue to beat until the mixture has become a thick meringue. By hand, stir in the ground almonds until very well blended. The batter will be thick and sticky.

With your hands, form the batter into 1-inch balls about the size of a walnut. (Rinsing and drying your hands between every few balls will help to make this process a little less messy.) Place the balls about 2 inches apart on the prepared baking sheets, flattening each one slightly so that it measures about 1½ inches in diameter.

As soon as the first baking sheet is filled, place it on the middle oven rack. Bake for 13 to 14 minutes, or until the cookies are barely colored. Bake the cookies one sheet at a time. Cool completely on the baking sheets set on wire racks. Remove the cooled cookies from the baking sheets with a wide spatula. Store in a tightly covered container or plastic bag. The cookies will stay soft and chewy for 2 or 3 days, but can be frozen for longer storage.

Honey-Glazed Almond Tart

YIELD: 8 TO 12 SERVINGS

*G*reek baking is not without certain refinements. This delicate tart, which stands up well under the most discriminating culinary scrutiny, also happens to be easy to make (no crust) and keeps well for two or three days, not that we've ever known one to actually last that long.

1 cup blanched, slivered, or sliced almonds, toasted (see Note)
¾ cup sugar
¾ cup (1½ sticks) unsalted butter, softened

2 eggs
½ teaspoon vanilla extract
¾ cup all-purpose flour
¼ cup warm honey (see page 293)

Preheat the oven to 350°F. Butter an 8- or 9-inch tart pan or layer-cake pan and set aside.

Place ¾ cup of the toasted almonds in a food processor with ¼ cup of the sugar. Reserve the remaining almonds for sprinkling on top of the baked tart. Process with the steel blade until the almonds are very finely ground. (Processing the almonds with the sugar will help to prevent the nuts from becoming pasty.)

In the large bowl of an electric mixer, beat the butter and the remaining ½ cup sugar at high speed until creamy. Add the eggs, one at a time, beating well after each addition. Beat in the vanilla. With the mixer running at the lowest speed, add the flour and ground almonds until well blended. The batter will be stiff. Turn into the prepared tart pan, smoothing the top with a wide spatula. Bake for 25 to 30 minutes, or until the center springs back when lightly pressed, and a wooden toothpick inserted in the center comes out clean. Remove from the oven to a wire rack. Immediately brush the top of the tart with the warm honey. Sprinkle with the reserved almonds. Serve slightly warm or cool, cut into wedges.

NOTE: Place the almonds in a medium-size cold skillet. Stir over medium heat just until the nuts begin to smell toasty. Remove from the heat and continue to stir for a minute or so until the nuts have cooled.

Preserved-Cherry Cake

YIELD: 8 TO 12 SERVINGS

Assuming that you do not eat all of the Cherry Spoon Sweets you made last summer at one or two sittings, you can finish them up in this dense, moist pound cake. Most of the cherries will sink to the bottom of the cake, no matter what you do, giving you a sort of upside-down-cake effect that's very tasty, so don't worry about it. The Greeks don't. By the way, the cake is still very good without the cherries, and store-bought cherry spoon sweets can always be substituted for homemade.

2 cups plus 2 tablespoons
  all-purpose flour
1 teaspoon baking powder
1 cup drained cherries from Sour or
  Sweet Cherry Spoon Sweets (see
  page 274), cut in half
1/2 pound (2 sticks) unsalted butter,
  softened

1 1/2 cups sugar
4 eggs
1 teaspoon vanilla extract
3/4 cup milk
Confectioners' sugar, for sprinkling
  on cake

Preheat the oven to 300°F (325°F, if using a metal loaf pan). Generously grease with shortening a 9-by-5-by-3-inch glass or metal loaf pan and set aside.

In a medium-size bowl, mix 2 cups of the flour and the baking powder together with a whisk until well blended. Toss the cherries with the remaining 2 tablespoons of flour in a small bowl and set aside.

In the large bowl of an electric mixer, beat the butter and sugar until creamy. Add the eggs, one at a time, beating well after each addition. Beat in the vanilla. With the mixer at the lowest speed, alternately beat in the flour mixture and milk, beginning and ending with the flour. By hand, fold the cherries into the batter until well distributed. Turn the batter into the prepared pan. Bake for about 1½ hours, or until a knife blade inserted in the center comes out clean. Cool the cake in the pan on a wire rack. Run a knife around the sides of the cake. Turn the cake out of the pan onto a serving plate. To serve, cut into slices and dust with confectioners' sugar.

Almond-Fig Cake

*F*igs, which were nearly as important to the ancients as olives, have been growing around the Mediterranean for millennia. The best way to eat figs, of course, and the way the Greeks prefer them, is freshly pulled from the tree, still warm from the sun, soft and sweet. In the winter, figs that have been dried on a screen in the sun are eaten out of hand and are nearly as popular as fresh, often finding their way into desserts and other confections, such as this wholesome, rich-tasting cake that also calls for olive oil instead of butter or other shortening.

---

10 dried figs
2½ cups plus 2 tablespoons
  all-purpose flour
½ cup blanched almonds, ground
1½ teaspoons baking powder
½ teaspoon ground cinnamon
½ teaspoon salt
2 eggs

½ cup regular (not extra-virgin)
  olive oil
1¼ cups plus 1 tablespoon sugar
½ cup orange juice
Grated peel of 1 orange
⅓ cup sliced natural or blanched
  almonds, for garnish

Preheat the oven to 350°F. Grease an 8-inch tube pan with olive oil and set aside. Remove the stems and cut the figs into eighths. In a small bowl, toss the fig pieces with 2 tablespoons of the flour and set aside. In a medium-size bowl, mix the remaining 2½ cups flour, the almonds, baking powder, cinnamon, and salt with a whisk until well blended; set aside.

In the large bowl of an electric mixer, beat the eggs with the olive oil and 1¼ cups of the sugar until thick and creamy. Alternately add the flour mixture and the orange juice, beating until well blended after each addition. By hand, stir in the orange peel and figs until evenly distributed throughout the batter. Turn the batter into the prepared pan and sprinkle with the sliced almonds and the remaining tablespoon of sugar. Bake for 55 minutes to 1 hour, or until the top is lightly browned and a wooden pick inserted in the center comes out clean. Cool completely on a wire rack before turning out of the pan.

Semolina Cake

REVANI

YIELD: ABOUT 12 SERVINGS

*I*t's not the custom to frost cakes in Greece. Instead, cakes are frequently doused with sugar syrup after they're baked, as much as they can possibly absorb. A cake treated this way will last for days if the pan is tightly covered and stored at room temperature. One thing is certain: the cake will never be dry! Americans are sometimes tempted to add a dollop of whipped cream when the cake is served. If you must, at least make it unsweetened whipped cream, or even yogurt, which we think is a better choice.

2 cups all-purpose flour
3½ teaspoons baking powder
¼ teaspoon salt
6 eggs, separated
1 cup sugar
1½ cups (3 sticks) unsalted butter, softened
Grated peel of 1 orange

1 cup orange juice
1 cup fine semolina (see page 300) or regular farina
⅓ cup blanched, slivered almonds
SYRUP
1½ cups sugar
1 cup water
2 tablespoons brandy

Preheat the oven to 325°F. Grease with solid shortening and flour a 13-by-9-by-2-inch glass baking dish; set aside.

In a large bowl, mix together the flour, baking powder, and salt with a whisk until well combined; set aside.

In the large bowl of an electric mixer, beat the egg whites at low speed until frothy. Increase the speed to high and beat until soft peaks form when the beaters are lifted. Gradually beat in ½ cup of the sugar. Continue to beat until stiff and glossy. Turn the beaten egg whites into another bowl and set aside. In the same mixing bowl (no need to wash) beat the egg yolks, the remaining ½ cup sugar, the butter, and the orange peel until creamy. On low speed, alternately beat in the flour mixture with the orange juice and semolina. By hand, stir in about one-fourth of the meringue until well blended. Fold in the remaining meringue until no white streaks remain. Turn the batter into the prepared baking dish, smoothing the top. Sprinkle with the almonds. Bake in the center of the oven for 25 to 30 minutes, or until the top springs back when lightly pressed and a wooden pick inserted in the center comes out clean. Remove to a wire rack to cool completely.

While the cake is cooling, make the syrup. Stir the sugar into the water in a medium-size saucepan. Bring to a slow boil, stirring constantly with a wooden spoon until the sugar is dissolved. Boil slowly for 10 minutes. Remove from the heat and stir in the brandy. Set aside to cool to lukewarm. Pour the syrup over the cooled cake. After the syrup has been completely absorbed, cut the cake in diamonds or squares to serve.

Walnut Cake

KARITHOPITA

YIELD: ABOUT 12 SERVINGS

This is a very basic cake that Greek grandmothers frequently make for the children, and usually the first choice when a good, reliable dessert is needed. Blanched almonds can be used instead of walnuts for a whiter cake, or a half-and-half mixture of the two. Since this cake is a fairly large one, it's helpful to know that it can be frozen, tightly wrapped, *after* it has been cooled and cut.

2 cups all-purpose flour
1 teaspoon baking powder
1 teaspoon baking soda
1/2 teaspoon ground nutmeg
1/2 teaspoon ground cinnamon
1/2 teaspoon ground cloves
2 cups sugar
1 cup (2 sticks) butter, softened
6 eggs

1 cup sour cream
1 tablespoon brandy
1 cup finely chopped walnuts
SYRUP
1 1/2 cups sugar
1 cup water
1 thick strip lemon peel
1 2-inch cinnamon stick

Preheat the oven to 325°F. Grease with solid shortening and flour a 13-by-9-by-2-inch glass baking dish; set aside.

In a large bowl, mix together the flour, baking powder, baking soda, and ground spices with a whisk until well combined; set aside.

In the large bowl of an electric mixer, beat the sugar and butter until creamy. Add the eggs, one at a time, beating well after each addition. Beat in the sour cream and brandy until well blended.

Gradually add the flour mixture to the butter mixture, beating well after each addition. By hand, stir in the walnuts until evenly distributed throughout the batter. Turn the batter into the prepared baking dish, spreading evenly and smoothing the top. Bake for 35 to 40 minutes, or until the top springs back when lightly pressed and a wooden pick inserted in the center comes out clean. Remove to a wire rack to cool completely.

While the cake is cooling, make the syrup by combining the sugar, water, lemon peel, and cinnamon stick in a medium-size saucepan. Bring to a boil, stirring constantly with a wooden spoon until the sugar is dissolved. Boil slowly for 10 minutes. Remove from the heat and set aside to cool to lukewarm. Remove the lemon peel and cinnamon stick and pour the syrup over the cooled cake. After the syrup has been completely absorbed, cut the cake into diamonds or squares to serve.

Nicola's Mother's Yogurt Cake

YAOURTOPITA

We suggest serving this light, tender cake as Nicola's mother sometimes does, with a dollop of thick yogurt and sliced fruit or berries.

---

3 cups all-purpose flour
2 teaspoons baking powder
3/4 teaspoon baking soda
1/8 teaspoon salt
1 1/2 cups sugar
3/4 cup (1 1/2 sticks) unsalted butter,
  softened

3 eggs
1 3/4 cups sheep's milk or other
  whole-milk yogurt (see page 303)
SYRUP
2/3 cup sugar
2/3 cup water
1 thick strip lemon peel

Preheat the oven to 350°F. Grease with solid shortening and flour a 13-by-9-by-2-inch glass baking dish; set aside.

In a medium-size bowl, mix the flour, baking powder, baking soda, and salt with a whisk until well blended; set aside.

In a large bowl of an electric mixer, beat the sugar and butter until creamy. Add the eggs, one at a time, beating well after each addition. Gradually beat in the flour mixture until well blended. (The batter will be very thick.) With the mixer running at the lowest speed, beat in the yogurt just until blended; do not overmix. Scoop the batter into the prepared baking dish, spreading evenly and smoothing the top. Bake for about 35 minutes, or until the top is lightly colored, the cake springs back when lightly pressed, and a wooden pick inserted in the center comes out clean. Remove to a wire rack to cool to lukewarm.

While the cake is baking, make the syrup by combining the sugar, water, and lemon peel in a small saucepan. Bring to a boil, stirring constantly with a wooden spoon until the sugar is dissolved. Boil slowly for 5 minutes. Remove from the heat and set

aside to cool. Remove the lemon peel and pour the syrup over the lukewarm cake. After the syrup has been absorbed, cut the cake into diamonds or squares to serve.

Kadaifi

Kadaifi, a Middle Eastern dough that gives its name to this luscious pastry, not only looks like, but *is* disconcertingly similar to shredded wheat. Making *kadaifi* dough is not something you'd want to tackle at home. Even in Greece it is left to the *kadaifi* baker, who spins out vermicelli-like threads of the batterlike dough onto a hot copper plate, from which it is immediately removed before it has a chance to brown. *Kadaifi* is packaged like *phyllo,* and can usually be purchased at the same places. After thawing, the threads of dough are pulled apart before they're used.

---

1 cup (2 sticks) butter, melted
1 package (16 ounces) kadaifi
 (see page 293)
1 cup shelled pistachio nuts or
 natural almonds, finely chopped
1 tablespoon grated lemon peel

¹/₂ teaspoon ground cinnamon
SYRUP
1¹/₂ cups sugar
1¹/₂ cups water
1 cup honey (see page 293)
1 tablespoon lemon juice

Preheat the oven to 400°F. Pour ½ cup of the melted butter into a 13-by-9-inch glass baking dish. Separate the *kadaifi* into shreds. Sprinkle half the shreds over the butter in the baking dish pressing it down lightly with the palm of your hand. In a small bowl, combine the pistachios, lemon peel, and cinnamon. Sprinkle evenly

over the *kadaifi*. Sprinkle the remaining *kadaifi* over the nut mixture pressing down as before. Drizzle with the remaining ½ cup butter. Bake for 25 to 35 minutes, or until golden.

While the *kadaifi* is baking, in a small saucepan over high heat, combine the sugar, water, honey, and lemon juice and bring to a boil, stirring constantly with a wooden spoon until the sugar is dissolved. Boil for 5 minutes. Set aside to cool slightly.

Remove the *kadaifi* from the oven and set aside to cool on a wire rack for about 10 minutes. Pour the very warm syrup over the *kadaifi*. Cut into squares or rectangles to serve.

Baklava

YIELD: 16 SERVINGS

Baklava, a pastry that consists of crisp layers of *phyllo* and nuts oozing with syrup, needs no introduction. It is without question one of the most splendid and justifiably famous desserts in the world, and, when turned out by the hands of a caring baker, it is angel food. Granted, making your first *baklava* might seem like an intimidating endeavor, but it is not nearly as difficult as it appears. In fact, once you get the hang of working with the *phyllo,* it's quite simple. There's probably no need to mention that *baklava* is very rich and sweet, but since it keeps for days (tightly covered in the baking dish at room temperature) there's no need to eat it up quickly, so you can keep the servings small.

1¹/₃ cups walnut pieces, toasted
  (see Note)
1¹/₃ cups sliced blanched almonds,
  toasted (see Note)
¹/₃ cup dry unflavored bread crumbs
2 teaspoons ground cinnamon
1 box (1 pound) ultra-thin phyllo,
  thawed as package directs
1 cup (2 sticks) Clarified Melted
  Butter (see page 8)

16 whole cloves
SYRUP
2 cups sugar
1¹/₂ cups water
1 3-inch cinnamon stick
3 whole cloves
¹/₂ cup honey (see page 293)
1 tablespoon brandy

Before starting to make the *baklava*, please read "How to Work with *Phyllo*" on page 12.

Place about half of the toasted nuts in a food processor. Pulse several times to chop the nuts finely, being careful not to pulverize them. Turn the nuts into a large bowl. Repeat with the remaining nuts. Add the crumbs and ground cinnamon to the chopped nuts and toss until the mixture is very well blended.

Preheat the oven to 350°F. Butter the bottom and sides of a 13-by-9-inch glass baking dish. Remove the *phyllo* from the package to a work surface and smooth out the stack of sheets. With a pizza cutter or a long, sharp knife, cut the *phyllo* in half to make two stacks of 12-by-8¹/₂-inch sheets. Place 1 piece of *phyllo* in the bottom of the pan. Brush with the melted butter. (Since the *phyllo* is not quite long enough to reach both ends of the pan, as you make the layers of *phyllo*, alternate the sheets so that every other one, more or less, reaches the opposite ends of the pan.) Repeat this procedure to make 21 layers of *phyllo*, but leave the final sheet dry. Sprinkle evenly with about ¾ cup of the nut mixture. Add 4 more sheets of *phyllo*, brushing each with butter before adding another, except for the top sheet, which should be left dry. Sprinkle with an additional ¾ cup of the nut mixture. Repeat this procedure three more times, ending with a layer of nuts. Add the remaining sheets of *phyllo*, brushing each with butter before adding another. Brush the top generously with butter.

With a long, sharp knife, cut the layers into lengthwise thirds. Then cut into diamond shapes, as shown, ending these cuts just short of the lengthwise cuts and the sides of the pan. (This prevents the *phyllo* from curling up as it bakes.) With a short spatula, go around all four sides of the pan, tucking the layers of dough down so that the edges are reasonably smooth. Stick a clove into the center of each diamond shape. Bake for about 1 hour, or until golden brown. Remove the *baklava* from the oven and set on a wire rack to cool completely.

While the *baklava* is cooling, make the syrup by combining the sugar, water, cinnamon stick, and cloves in a 3-quart saucepan.

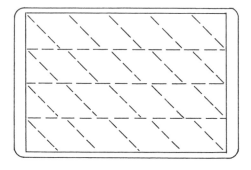

Bring to a boil, stirring constantly with a wooden spoon until the sugar is dissolved. Boil slowly for about 5 minutes. Add the honey and continue to boil slowly for 5 minutes longer. Remove from the heat and stir in the brandy. Set aside to cool to lukewarm. Pour the lukewarm syrup over the cooled *baklava*. Cover lightly and set aside at room temperature for several hours or overnight. Finish cutting the *baklava* into diamonds before serving.

NOTE: Spread the nuts in a single layer in a shallow pan and place in a cold oven. Set the oven temperature at 350°F. Toast the nuts for 9 to 11 minutes, stirring occasionally, or until they smell toasty. Remove from the oven and continue to stir for a minute or two until the nuts are cool.

Bougatsa

*I*n certain Greek towns (Ioannina in northwest Greece being the most famous) you can merely follow your nose to the *bougatsa* places, where they will cut you a piece of this round cream pastry with a strange-looking little curved implement. Once you've eaten it, the memory of *bougatsa* can haunt you forever. Fortunately, it's easy to make, and you can occasionally find it in Greek bakeries in the United States. *Bougatsa* absolutely *must* be eaten warm (rewarmed is okay), sprinkled with lots of ground cinnamon and confectioners' sugar.

---

2 cups milk
1/2 cup plus 2 tablespoons sugar
2 eggs, lightly beaten
1/2 cup fine semolina or regular farina
(see page 300)
3/4 cup (1 1/2 sticks) Clarified Melted
Butter (see page 8)

1/2 pound phyllo
Ground cinnamon, to taste, for
sprinkling on bougatsa
Confectioners' sugar, to taste, for
sprinkling on bougatsa

Before starting to make the *bougatsa,* please read "How to Work with *Phyllo,*" on page 12.

Preheat the oven to 350°F. In the top of a double boiler over simmering water, combine the milk, sugar, eggs, and semolina. Cook, stirring constantly, until the mixture bubbles and thickens. Remove the top of the double boiler from the heat and set aside to cool.

Brush a 15-inch pizza pan with a little of the melted butter. Remove about half of the *phyllo* from a one-pound package and set it aside, covered with waxed paper and a damp cloth. Tightly rewrap the remaining *phyllo* and refrigerate or freeze. On a large work surface, butter half of the *phyllo* sheets, arranging each one in the pan as you go, overlapping the sheets so that they completely cover the bottom of the pan with about half of each sheet hanging over the side. Spread the semolina mixture (it will thicken some as it cools) in the bottom of the pan over the *phyllo*. Butter the remaining sheets of *phyllo,* laying them over the filling, but do not allow these to hang over the side of the pan. Generously butter the top layer of *phyllo*. Bring the bottom overhang over the top to seal. Brush with the remaining butter. Prick the top in many places with the tines of a fork. Bake for 30 to 35 minutes, or until golden brown. Remove from the oven and sprinkle generously with cinnamon. Set aside to cool for about 10 minutes. Sprinkle heavily with confectioners' sugar just before cutting and serving. (A pizza wheel works very well for cutting *bougatsa*.)

NOTE: Leftovers can be covered and chilled. Reheat at 300° for about 10 minutes.

Honey Pastries
DIPLES

YIELD: ABOUT 48 KNOTS

One of the more eye-catching creations on the dessert table at Periyali is a platter heaped with loosely rolled, fried pastries, gleaming with a thick coating of honey. These are invariably a must-try for newcomers. Making these large rolls is tricky, but we assure you that the pastries are just as traditional in a variety of shapes, some simpler than others, although maybe not quite as spectacular. The knots given here are every bit as tasty as the big rolls, and a whole lot easier to make. However, if you have your heart set on recreating Periyali's version, directions for these are given, too.

PASTRY DOUGH
3 eggs
1/4 cup regular (not extra-virgin) olive oil
1 tablespoon cold water
1 tablespoon brandy
1 teaspoon salt
1¾ to 2 cups all-purpose flour

Regular (not extra-virgin) olive oil or vegetable oil, for frying
Ground cinnamon, for sprinkling on pastries
SYRUP
⅔ cup sugar
⅔ cup water
⅔ cup honey (see page 293)

In the large bowl of an electric mixer, beat the eggs, olive oil, water, brandy, and salt until frothy. By hand or with a dough hook, gradually add 1¾ cups of the flour, beating well after each addition, and adding a little more flour, if necessary, until the dough leaves the side of the bowl. The dough should be very pliable and should not stick to your hands. Form the dough into a ball and cut it into quarters. Wrap each quarter in plastic wrap and refrigerate for a few hours or overnight.

Line two large baking sheets with several thicknesses of paper towels and set aside.

Work with one portion of the dough at a time, leaving the remainder in the refrigerator. Roll the dough out on a lightly floured surface with a lightly floured rolling pin into an 8-by-12-inch rectangle. With a fluted pastry wheel or the tip of a sharp knife, cut the dough into twelve 8-inch strips. Loosely tie each strip once at the center and set aside, covered with a barely damp kitchen towel. Repeat with the remaining quarters of dough.

Pour enough oil into a 3-quart saucepan to measure about 3 inches. Set the pan over high heat. When the oil reaches about 375°F on a deep-fry thermometer, drop in the knots, a few at a time, turning once, until golden brown, about 45 seconds on each side. Transfer the fried knots to the prepared baking sheets to drain. Repeat with the remaining knots, making sure to keep the oil up to temperature throughout the frying. Set the knots aside at room temperature, uncovered, until ready to dip into the honey syrup, shortly before serving.

HOLLY GARRISON

To make the syrup, combine the sugar, water, and honey in a 3-quart saucepan. Bring to a boil, stirring constantly with a wooden spoon until the sugar is dissolved. Boil slowly for about 10 minutes. Remove from the heat and cool to lukewarm. Using tongs, dip each knot into the lukewarm syrup. Arrange on a serving platter and sprinkle with cinnamon. Confectioners' sugar can also be sprinkled on the knots just before serving.

Bow Ties: Cut each 8-inch strip into 3 more or less equal pieces. Pinch each piece at the center to form a bow. Fry and serve as directed above.

Periyali's Rolls: Making these rolls requires a pasta machine, since it is almost impossible to roll the dough thin and even enough by hand. Cut each chilled dough quarter into 4 pieces. Run each piece through a pasta machine until it measures about 12 by 3½ to 4 inches. Dust lightly with flour. Cover with a barely damp towel and set aside until ready to fry.

Fill a 3-quart saucepan about three-fourths full of oil. Place over medium-high heat until the oil reaches about 375°F on a deep-fry thermometer. Using a two-pronged cooking fork, place one end of the dough between the tines, giving the fork one turn to secure the dough. Holding the other end of the dough, lower the dough on the fork into the hot oil. Working rather quickly, start rolling the dough counterclockwise onto the fork in the hot oil. The dough will start to cook immediately and hold its shape. In order to keep the roll loose, rotate the fork in the opposite direction a couple of times. As soon as the pastry has turned a light golden color, set it on paper towels to drain. Repeat with the remaining strips of dough, making sure to keep the temperature of the oil constant throughout the frying procedure. Set the rolls aside at room temperature, uncovered, until ready to dip into the honey syrup, shortly before serving.

Oranges with Honey, Nuts, and Mint

YIELD: 4 TO 6 SERVINGS

There's something about this combination that never fails to remind us of *baklava*. Although it's certainly light and refreshing, the nuts and honey contribute just enough richness and sweetness to the oranges to please the most ardent dessert lover.

4 to 6 large navel oranges
1 to 2 tablespoons finely chopped
  fresh mint leaves
¼ to ½ cup honey (see page 293)

¼ cup finely chopped pistachio nuts
Orange-blossom water
  (see page 298)
Mint leaves, for garnish

Remove the orange peels and bitter white pith just beneath with a small, sharp knife or a vegetable peeler. Cut the oranges into ¼-inch slices. Arrange the slices in layers in a shallow serving bowl, sprinkling each layer with the chopped mint, honey, nuts, and a *few drops* of orange-blossom water (don't go overboard; this is powerful stuff), ending with a layer of mint, honey, and nuts. Cover and refrigerate until serving time. Spoon into shallow dessert bowls and garnish with mint leaves.

Manouri with Honey and Pistachios

YIELD: 4 SERVINGS

*I*f you have access to a Greek grocery store, you'll more than likely be able to find this creamy cheese, which is simply Greek ricotta cheese. Ricotta can be substituted, but do make an effort to find the real thing, since it has an interesting and unusual flavor.

8 ounces manouri *cheese*
½ cup honey *(see page 293)*

¼ cup lightly toasted pistachio nuts, almonds, or walnuts, coarsely chopped (see Note)

Crumble the cheese into a medium-size bowl. Press some of the cheese into a ¼-cup dry measure or ice cream scoop and unmold into a shallow dessert bowl. Repeat with the remaining cheese. Drizzle 2 tablespoons of honey over each serving. Sprinkle with nuts, dividing evenly. Serve with fresh fruit.

NOTE: Place the pistachios in a small, dry skillet. Cook over medium heat, stirring constantly, just until the nuts begin to smell toasty. Remove from the heat and continue to stir for a few moments until the nuts are cool.

Poached Quinces

YIELD: 8 SERVINGS

A dessert that mimics Quince Spoon Sweets but is easier to prepare. Sour quince is the perfect fruit for poaching in a sweet sauce, and because it's rock-hard when it's raw, it keeps its shape and doesn't become mushy when it's cooked. At Periyali, the quince is served with a little whipped cream, but yogurt, or even vanilla ice cream, would be good, too.

4 quinces
¾ cup sugar
1½ cups orange juice
1 cup dry red wine

1 cup Coca-Cola
2 cinnamon sticks, broken in half
12 whole cloves

Preheat the oven to 400°F. If there is a fuzzy coating on the quinces, rub it off. Rinse the quinces and cut each one in half through the stem. Trim the stem and blossom ends, then scoop out the cores with a melon-ball cutter. Arrange the quinces core side down in a 13-by-9-inch baking dish.

In a medium-size saucepan, combine the sugar, orange juice, wine, Coca-Cola, cinnamon sticks, and cloves. Bring to a boil over high heat, stirring until the sugar is dissolved. With a large spoon, skim off the foam from the surface of the syrup; pour the syrup over the quinces. Bake for about 1 hour and 45 minutes, occasionally spooning the sauce in the pan over the quinces until they are tender and the sauce has thickened. Watch carefully toward the end of baking time, when the syrup can quickly thicken too much and burn. Serve the quinces warm, at room temperature, or chilled, with some of the syrup spooned over each serving.

Stuffed Apples Baked with Honey

✺✺✺✺

YIELD: 4 SERVINGS

Since many parts of Greece are almost devoid of fresh produce during the winter, it becomes quite a challenge to make do with what little is available. This recipe is an imaginative example of what a good cook can do with ingredients that are likely to be found in the root cellar and kitchen cupboard.

<table>
<tr><td>

1/2 cup sugar
1 thick strip lemon peel
1/2 cup water
1/4 cup honey (see page 293)
1/2 cup finely chopped walnuts
1/2 cup raisins
1 teaspoon ground cinnamon

</td><td>

1 tablespoon brandy
4 large (about 8 ounces each) Golden
  Delicious, Rome Beauty, or other
  baking apples
Thickened Yogurt (see page 303), for
  garnish

</td></tr>
</table>

Add ¼ cup of the sugar and lemon peel to the water in a small saucepan. Bring to a boil, stirring constantly with a wooden spoon until the sugar is dissolved. Boil slowly for 5 minutes. Remove from the heat and stir in the honey; set aside.

Preheat the oven to 350°F. In a small bowl, mix the walnuts, raisins, remaining ¼ cup of sugar, cinnamon, and brandy.

Core the apples through the stem end, leaving about ½ inch of flesh at the bottoms. Enlarge the openings slightly with a small knife. Stuff the apples with the walnut mixture, mounding it slightly. (There may be some stuffing left over.) Arrange the stuffed apples in a shallow baking pan just large enough to hold them comfortably with some room to spare. Sprinkle any leftover stuffing in the bottom of the pan. Spoon some of the syrup over each apple, then pour the remainder into the bottom of the pan. Bake for about 40 minutes, basting frequently with the syrup, until the apples are soft. Remove from the oven and cool. Serve luke-warm or at room temperature in a shallow bowl with some of the pan syrup spooned over and around the apples, and a spoonful of Thickened Yogurt, if you like.

A Sweet for Children

Greek children are rarely given candy. Instead, their mothers make more natural treats for them, like this one. There's no actual recipe for this. When you get tired of spooning out the seeds from pomegranates (two or three is usually anybody's limit), mix the seeds with an equal amount, or slightly less, of raisins or dried currants. Add a little honey or sugar and a few drops of lemon juice, if you think it needs it, and stir until well blended. Serve a small amount of the sweet in a bowl to be eaten with a spoon.

Sesame Seed Bars

PASTELLI

This is the Hershey bar of Greece, and a good example of how clever the Greeks are at combining healthful ingredients and turning out something delectable enough to satisfy the most intense craving for sweets. However, if you value your teeth, the best way to eat this chewy stuff is to pop a whole piece into your mouth and let the honey melt.

---

1 cup sesame seeds (see page 301)   *1 cup honey (see page 293)*

Preheat the oven to 350°F. Butter an 8-inch-square baking pan and set aside.

Spread the sesame seeds in one layer in a shallow baking pan. Place the seeds in the oven for about 10 minutes, watching carefully until they begin to smell toasty. Remove from the oven and set aside.

In a small saucepan, bring the honey to a boil over medium heat. Stir in the toasted sesame seeds and continue to boil slowly until a candy thermometer registers 280°F. Remove from the heat and immediately pour into the prepared pan, patting the mixture down evenly with a wide spatula. Set the pan on a wire rack to cool. Score into 1-by-2-inch pieces as soon as the candy has started to set. Allow to cool completely before breaking apart. Wrap each piece of candy in plastic wrap or waxed paper and store in a tightly covered container. (We don't know how long the candy can be stored, since it's never been around long enough to find out.)

Stuffed Dates

After they're stuffed, give the dates a few days to mellow and ripen before serving them. Stored in an airtight container, they keep well for at least several weeks. We like them for sweet snacking anytime, but especially at Christmas, when they seem especially appropriate.

½ pound pitted dates
¼ cup honey (see page 293)
¼ cup finely chopped toasted
 almonds (see Note)
¼ cup finely chopped toasted walnuts
 (see Note)

¼ cup grated orange peel
1 teaspoon brandy (optional)
Granulated sugar, for sprinkling
 on dates

With a small knife, cut a slit in one side of each date. In a small bowl, mix the honey, nuts, grated orange peel, and brandy. With a demitasse spoon, stuff each date with the nut mixture through the slit, then roll the date in sugar which has been sprinkled on a sheet of waxed paper. Pack the dates in an airtight container, separating the layers with waxed paper. Store at room temperature, and sprinkle with more granulated sugar just before serving.

NOTE: Sprinkle the nuts in a small, dry skillet. Cook over medium heat, stirring constantly, just until they begin to smell toasty. Remove from the heat and continue to stir for a few moments until the nuts are cool.

A Poor Man's Sweet

Here is one of the simplest Greek sweets, and one of the easiest. In a bowl, mix toasted or untoasted walnut halves or large pieces with just enough honey to coat them lightly. Serve in a communal bowl with little spoons. Delicious served by itself accompanied by an after-dinner brandy, or with a platter of cut fruit and grapes.

Spoon Sweets
(GLYKA TOU KOUTALYOU)

"Spoon sweets" are fruits (almost every kind imaginable), vegetables (usually lilliputian eggplants or cherry tomatoes), nuts, or even flower petals preserved in a sweet, thick syrup. Offering this little confection to guests (sweets to the sweet, so to speak), is a custom as old as Greek hospitality itself.

Serving spoon sweets involves a simple ceremony that rarely varies. After visitors are seated and a short time has been spent in polite small talk, the hostess brings forth her spoon sweets. They are presented on a tray in a small bowl that has slots around the edge for spoons. The server can be quite plain or highly ornate, sometimes made out of silver, depending on the financial circumstances of the hosts. A small amount of the sweet is dished onto a flat plate and eaten with a spoon, accompanied by a tall glass of cold water.

This is a charming practice, to be sure, but one that is not likely to catch on in the United States any time soon. However, that shouldn't stop you from trying your hand at a batch or two. Spoon sweets are just as good served as a dessert topping or a relish, in place of fruit preserves, or, best of all, stirred into thick, creamy yogurt.

Quince Spoon Sweets

KYDONI GLYKO

YIELD: ABOUT 4 CUPS

---

*3 pounds (about 4) slightly underripe
quinces (skins should be light green
with traces of yellow)*

*3 cups water
3 cups sugar
1 tablespoon brandy or lemon juice*

Cut each quince into quarters through the stem and remove the core. Peel the quarters and cut each one into ½-inch cubes. (To keep the quince cubes from turning brown, have ready a large bowl of cold water that has been acidulated with the juice of a lemon.) As the cubes are cut, place them in the bowl of water. Drain the quince cubes and place them in a large, heavy saucepan or Dutch oven. Add the water and bring to a simmer over medium heat. Cover and simmer slowly until tender, 5 to 10 minutes. Uncover and stir in the sugar. Boil gently, uncovered, until the liquid is the consistency of thin honey, or a candy thermometer reaches 220°F. Remove from the heat and stir in the brandy. Ladle the sweets into small, dishwasher-clean jars, dividing the fruit and syrup evenly. Cool slightly, then cover tightly and store in the refrigerator. The spoon sweets will keep well for several months.

Sour Cherry Spoon Sweets

KERASSI GLYKO

2¹/2 pounds sour cherries
4 cups sugar
2 cups water

¹/4 cup lemon juice
¹/4 cup toasted, slivered almonds
(optional; see Note)

Pick over the cherries and remove the stems. Discard any cherries that are not smooth, firm, and blemish-free. Place in a large bowl and rinse several times in cold water. Drain in a colander. Use a cherry pitter or a clean, common-nail head to push the pits out of the cherries, working from the stem end and being careful to keep the cherries whole.

Place the cherries and the sugar in layers in a large, heavy saucepan or Dutch oven, starting and ending with a layer of sugar. Pour the water over the cherry mixture and set the pan over medium heat, stirring once or twice, until the sugar has dissolved. Increase the heat to medium-high and boil gently for about 25 minutes, stirring often, and skimming off all of the froth with a large spoon as it rises to the surface. Remove from the heat, cover, and leave at room temperature for 12 hours or overnight.

The next day, return the pan to the heat and boil gently, uncovered, for about 25 minutes until the liquid is the consistency of thin honey, or a candy thermometer registers 220°F. Remove from the heat and stir in the lemon juice and almonds. Ladle into small, dishwasher-clean jars, dividing the cherries, syrup, and almonds evenly. Cool slightly, then cover tightly and store in the refrigerator. The spoon sweets will keep well for several months.

Variation: For Sweet Cherry Spoon Sweets, follow the recipe for Sour Cherry Spoon Sweets, using Bing cherries and decreasing the sugar to 3 cups and the water to 1½ cups.

NOTE: To toast the almonds, place them in a dry skillet. Cook over medium heat, stirring constantly until they start to turn a pale brown and have a toasty aroma. Remove from the heat and continue to stir until cooled.

Cherry Drink
VISSINATHA

"Waste not, want not" is a very real motto in Greece, especially when it comes to anything sweet. With the syrup left in the container after the Cherry Spoon Sweets have been devoured, the Greeks make a very thirst-quenching summer beverage by stirring a spoonful or two of this sweet stuff into an ice-cold glass of water. Sometimes the cook even contrives to make sure that there will be plenty of syrup left for *vissinatha* by cooking the fruit in more sugar and water than is actually needed.

Wine, Spirits, and Beverages

Wine is wonderfully wholesome for man in sickness and in health, provided that it is taken at the right time and in the right quantity to suit individual needs.

—HIPPOCRATES

For Greeks, wine is an element as old as Mount Olympus, as intrinsic a part of the culture as temples built to glorify the gods, blue sky over indigo water, and sun-washed islands. Perhaps that's why the Greek attitude about wine is so natural and unaffected. In Greece, there are few pretensions regarding wine and wine-drinking. Greek vintners make wine to be drunk with food. They have little of the compulsive tendency of other wine-producing cultures to intellectualize the subject. They don't make wines to win medals or to be ceaselessly analyzed. Wine drinking remains a simple and natural pleasure, an enduring element of the eternal trilogy of grapes, olives, and wheat.

Needless to say, Greek wines marry well with Greek food and are worth seeking out to accompany the recipes in this book.

The Classifications of Greek Wines

Greek wines fall into three general classifications: "own label" wines, frequently blends of different varietals from different areas, which are produced and bottled by leading commercial wine companies; "country" or "barrel" wines, which are locally produced and rarely seen outside of Greece; and "typical" or "controlled appellation" wines (there are currently twenty-eight of these), made with indigenous grape varieties from a delimited region conforming to government regulations and quality levels. Generally speaking, the highest-quality wines come from this last group.

In addition to these main categories, there are Greek rosé wines and, of course, *retsina,* the pine-flavored wine that's in a class of its own. A three-thousand-year-old tradition, *retsina* is unique to Greece and an appellation protected by law, so that no other country is allowed to produce it. The uninitiated might ask why anyone else would *want* to produce this strange-tasting wine flavored with the resin of the Aleppo pine, a tree that flourishes in the heart of mainland Greece. For the non-Greek palate, the harsh and even jarring combination of pine and wine is not necessarily a pleasing one. But the Greeks seem to have been born with a taste for it, and even its severest critics concede that icy-cold *retsina* is a good foil for sometimes oily, zesty Greek food. Most commonly a white wine (although a rosé variety does exist), *retsina* accounts for more than 50 percent of Greek wine production. Its origins date to the days when wine was transported in clay jugs sealed with a mixture of plaster and pine resin. The ancient Greeks believed that it was the resin, and not the seal, that preserved the wine, and so they continued to resinate the wine even when the amphora gave way to more modern receptacles. By then, the national palate had become so collectively accustomed to this unusual flavor that *retsina* eventually became known as "the wine of Greece." And, although it remains the best-known and most widely consumed Greek wine, it confers—according to some modern wine makers—something of a stigma, too, often preventing even sophisticated wine-drinkers from further exploration of Greek wines.

A Brief Tour of the Wine-Producing Regions of Greece

PELOPONNESE PENINSULA: This region extends like a giant paw off the southern coast of the mainland, and is the largest grape-growing area in the country. One-third of Greece's vineyards are here, although many of them are devoted to producing table grapes and raisins. Three main subregions give their names to the wines they produce: Patras, Nemea, and Mandinia. Patras is best known for its sweet, red wine, Mavrodaphne de Patras, which is as distinctly Greek as *retsina*. Patras also produces two muscats: Muscat de Patras and Muscat de Rio Patras, as well as light, dry wines known simply as Patras. Nemea is a dry, full-bodied red wine, so dark and rich that it has been dubbed the Blood of Hercules. It ranks among Greece's best dry red wines. Finally, there is Mandinia, a light, fruity wine from the center of the region.

CENTRAL GREECE: Ranking second in Greek wine production, this region encompasses the broad Attica plain, as well as Boeotia and the island of Euboea. Although the majority of the crop goes to the production of wines intended for local consumption—much of it resinated—some very drinkable, supple dry whites are also produced here, notably Kantza, one of the country's controlled-appellation wines.

MACEDONIA AND THRACE: These northernmost wine-producing regions profit from a cool climate, a generous annual rainfall, and soil that is particularly conducive to the production of good wines. Both areas have been known for their red wines since as long ago as the fourth century B.C., when the wines of the island of Thasos were among the most prized in the ancient world. Although a virulent vine disease devastated the vineyards in the early part of this century, they have since been replanted and enlarged, and now produce some of modern Greece's most promising red wines. The four appellations produced here are Naousa, Amynteon, Goumenissa, and Côtes de Meliton. Two of the country's biggest commercial producers, Boutari and Carras, are closely associated with these regions. Boutari's Naousa Grand Reserve, made from Greece's noble *xynomavro* grape, ranks as one of Greece's best reds. Carras's Côtes de Meliton is also highly regarded.

THESSALY: Wedged between Macedonia to the north and Attica to the south, this central mainland region is divided into four growing areas. The most renowned of these is the Raspani vineyards, planted on the slopes of Mount Olympus, producing a powerful red wine called Raspani that ages extremely well. Sea-level vine-yards along the Pagasitikos Gulf, Kardhitsa, and Tirnavos produce a dry white wine called Anchialos.

EPIRUS: Directly west of Thessaly, this area is characterized by rugged terrain and a rather harsh climate that is less than ideal for producing great wines. Nevertheless, two wines worth noting, Zitsa and Metsovo, come from here. The first is one of Greece's few sparkling wines, produced in the extreme western corner of the region. Metsovo comes from the country's most mountainous vineyards, and is one of the very few Greek reds made with the Cabernet Sauvignon grape, planted here after native varieties were destroyed by vine disease. Metsovo is expensive and highly re-garded.

IONIAN ISLANDS: Some fine wines, particularly whites, come from these islands off the western coast of Greece. Perhaps the most notable among them is the full-bodied, fragrant white Robola wine from Cephalonia, rated by some as one of the country's best whites. Cephalonia is also known for its Muscat and Mavrodaphne. Corfu produces a dry white wine, and from Zakinthos comes a white wine from the verdea or green-grape variety. The intensely dark red wine Santa Mavra is from Lefkada.

EASTERN AEGEAN ISLANDS: These islands dot the Aegean sea to the east of mainland Greece and produce some notable appellations, including Samos, one of Greece's most celebrated wines. The pale, golden Samos, named for the island where it's made, is a sweet wine made from the muscat grape. Limnos produces a red wine, Limnio, as well as good muscat wines. The island of Chios is the source of Mastiha, a liqueur fermented from mastic, a resinous gum extracted from a shrub native to this island.

CRETE: One of the most fruitful of the wine-producing islands, Crete is famous for its full-bodied reds and boasts four appella-tions: Dafnes, Sitia, Archanes, and Peza. The most prized of the four are Archanes and Peza, both from the region of Heraklion, both rich and complex reds. Peza also gives its name to a fruity white wine. Crete is also the source of a legendary dessert wine, Malvasia. Myth has it that the formula for this sweet, topaz-colored wine was the Oracle of Delphi's gift to King Minos. Known during medieval times as Malmsey, this wine was said to symbolize wisdom and was much prized throughout Europe.

CYCLADES: Considered the cradle of ancient Greece's viticultural glory, these islands profit from climatic conditions well suited to the cultivation of the vine. Nearly all of the islands in this group produce wines. The most notable among them include Paros, with its own appellation made of a blend of two local varietals, resulting in a notably fine, ruby-hued, oak-barrel-aged red. Also worth noting are the wines of the breathtakingly beautiful Santorini island, including two highly prized appellations, the dry white Santorini and the sweet white Visanto. Another white wine indigenous to the island is the highly alcoholic Nichteri.

DODECANESE: Rhodes is the principal wine producer in this group of twelve southern Greek islands. One of ancient Greece's most important exporters of wines, Rhodes currently produces two appellations, one a dry white wine and the other a dry red. There are also Muscat de Rhodes and Muscat de Trani, both sweet whites.

Matching Greek Food and Wines

The basic guidelines for matching food and wine certainly apply to Greek wines, although, as noted before, the startling contrast of an icy *retsina* is the traditional accompaniment to many Greek foods, *if* you can develop a taste for it. However, Periyali's wine list offers an extremely wide range of other wines, including many of Greece's finest.

Periyali's manager and maître d', Nick Gouras, suggests fruity, full-bodied white Agioritikos from Tsatali, made near the Holy Mountain of Agion Oros, to counterbalance the rustic flavors of *taramosalata, tzatziki,* and *skordalia.* The smoky crispness of Robola also marries well with the specialties found on the *meze* table. For die-hard traditionalists, Nick recommends Kourtakis *retsina.*

Greece's repertoire of white wines offers a multitude of possibilities for matching wine with the ubiquitous grilled fish of the islands. The light, white Santorini, from the limestone island of the same name, is particularly well suited to delicate, sweet-fleshed fish, while oaky Patras or Robola goes very nicely with the oilier varieties, such as grilled swordfish or tuna, and with *plaki*, fish baked in tomato sauce.

Roast lamb and other red meats call for one of Greece's increasingly notable reds. Nick suggests light but tannic Grand Reserve made by Boutari, with its flavors of aging Burgundy, to accompany red meats, or sautéed chicken livers over warm lentils, a favorite first course at Periyali. Another Boutari, Nemea, is rich with plummy fruit and a good match for rabbit *stifado* or other "well-done" meat dishes. With *moussaka* or charcoal-grilled shish kabob of lamb, Nick's choice would be Carras's rich, oak-aged Côtes de Meliton, a relatively recent appellation made with Cabernet Sauvignon grapes.

The traditional Greek finish to a meal is, of course, sweet, heady Samos Muscat wine, a velvety partner for the selections on Periyali's dessert table, or dessert in itself, along with strong Greek coffee.

Although Greek wine production far overshadows the output of distilled spirits, an overview of Greek beverages would not be complete without mention of some of these.

OUZO

Heading the spirits list is *ouzo*, thick, clear, and licorice-flavored. *Ouzo* vies with *retsina* for the title of the Greek national alcoholic beverage. A by-product of wine production, *ouzo* is distilled from the residues of pressed grapes. It originated, according to some accounts, in Tirnavos, a town known for the quality of its liqueurs and its textiles, notably silks, both of which were sold under the name of *uso*.

Some of the best *ouzo* still comes from Tirnavos, and is flavored with anise, mastic, lime, and coriander. The Greeks generally have it straight and at room temperature, with water on the side. However, *ouzo* can be served over ice and lightly diluted with water, which makes it cloudy but doesn't affect the flavor. Like *retsina*, *ouzo* is best appreciated on a hot day, while lounging on a white-washed terrace contemplating an expanse of azure sea.

BRANDY

Like coffee and spoon sweets, brandy is an integral part of Greek hospitality. Home cooks traditionally flavor brandy with fruits and fruit pits, which are allowed to macerate for various periods of time (sometimes under the hot Greek sun), making an interesting home-made liqueur.

Although many non-Greeks consider Metaxas the generic name for all Greek brandy, there are other notable commercial producers, such as Cambas and Botrys.

MASTIHA

In ancient times, this clear aperitif, fermented from mastic, the resinous gum extracted from a shrub native to the island of Chios, was prescribed by Hippocrates as a remedy for colds and coughs. Like *retsina*, *mastiha* is a Greek original and something of an acquired taste. *Mastiha* is slightly sweet and subtly flavored with anise. It should be taken neat at room temperature.

Yogurt Milkshake

YIELD: ABOUT 2 CUPS

This is a refreshing and extremely healthful concoction that is drunk throughout Greece during the summer, a sort of liquid version of honey and fresh fruit stirred into thick yogurt.

1 cup cold skim milk
1/2 cup cold sheep's-milk yogurt or
  other whole-milk yogurt (see page
  303)
2 tablespoons honey (see page 293),
  or to taste

1/2 cup whole raspberries, blackberries,
  or blueberries, or chopped fruit, such
  as strawberries, peaches, or apricots

Process the milk, yogurt, honey, and fruit in a blender, until smooth and frothy. Pour into a tall, cold glass and serve immediately.

Sparkling Lemonade
LEMONATHA

YIELD: 8 SERVINGS

*I*n Greece, requests for lemonade are usually met with a can of Sprite, with one notable exception: a bottled, sparkling lemon- and vanilla-flavored drink that is the perfect elixir for cooling off on a hot day. The same syrup can be used to make a regular lemonade by using still water instead of sparkling water.

1 cup water
1 cup sugar
1 piece of lemon peel, measuring
  about 1 by 1/2 inch
1 teaspoon vanilla extract

1 cup lemon juice
Cold sparkling or still water
Thin lemon slices and mint leaves,
  for garnish

Mix the water with the sugar in a medium-size saucepan. Bring to a boil with the lemon peel over medium heat, stirring with a wooden spoon until the sugar is dissolved. Continue to boil slowly for 5 minutes. Remove from the heat and set aside to cool to room temperature. Stir in the vanilla until well blended. At this point, the syrup can be tightly covered and refrigerated until needed.

To make lemonade, add about 2 tablespoons of the syrup to a tall glass. Stir in about 2 tablespoons of the lemon juice, or to taste, until well blended. Stir in the chilled sparkling water. You can add ice cubes, although the Greeks don't. Garnish with a lemon slice and a sprig of mint, although the Greeks don't do this, either.

Kafé Frapé

Despite its French-sounding name, this drink is a relatively recent Greek invention, often taken instead of hot coffee on warm days. The Greeks refer to all instant coffee as Nescafé, and that's what's always called for when making this refreshing drink. Obviously, any instant coffee will work just fine, even decaffeinated coffee.

---

1 tablespoon instant (not dried granules) coffee
1 tablespoon hot water
½ cup cold water

2 tablespoons milk
1 to 2 tablespoons sugar
3 ice cubes

In a blender or a cocktail shaker, dissolve the coffee in the hot water. Add the remaining ingredients and blend or shake until very frothy. Pour into a cold glass and serve immediately.

The National Beverage: Coffee

There is no such thing as a quick cup of coffee in Greece. A cup of coffee is serious business, something to be contemplated, savored, and lingered over, even when the coffee drinker is alone. Business is done and friendships and love affairs often blossom—and end— over coffee, and the person with whom one takes coffee is almost as important as the coffee itself. It is the Greek national drink, before wine and even *ouzo*. Coffee is rarely served in restaurants, and is drunk all day long. For a coffee, you must go to a café or to a sweet shop.

Greek coffee is hot, thick, and strong, usually served sweet and sometimes very sweet, with a layer of froth on top. Although some Greeks take their coffee plain *(sketo)*, this is rare considering the Hellenic penchant for sweets, and most coffee is drunk medium-sweet *(metrio)* or very sweet *(glyko)*. And there are countless degrees of sweetness in between, many Greeks having their own special coffee-to-sugar ratio for the perfect cup. Coffee is always served with a tall glass of cold water, which is drunk first to clear the palate.

These days, many of the coffee places in Greece use a machine, something like a cappuccino maker, to produce coffee with lots of froth on top. But purists prefer coffee made the old-fashioned way, in a long-handled, cylindrical pot called a *briki,* which can be purchased for very little money in most Greek and Middle Eastern neighborhoods. Lacking one of these, a tall butter-warming pan can be substituted, or even a small saucepan, but it's hard to get the all-important head of froth without using the *briki.* You will also need rich-roasted coffee beans, ground to a powdery consistency, and four-ounce cups. Coffee is served without spoons, since the spent grounds sink to the bottom of the cup like fine mud.

A number of charming customs surround the ritual of coffee drinking. For instance, if the coffee happens to spill onto the saucer as it's being served, it means the drinker will be receiving money, and Greek women often amuse themselves by "reading" the grounds left in the cup. Although it takes a soothsayer to actually decipher these, looking for shapes in the cup that resemble animals and other objects is fun. First, turn the empty cup containing the grounds upside down on the saucer and leave it there for several minutes. Turn the cup right side up and examine the designs left by the grounds on the side of the cup. (Please note that Greek women only do this in each other's company and not in public, where it is frowned upon by their husbands.)

At Periyali, coffee is made using a *briki*, boiling up countless coffees one or two cups at a time, and no one will frown if you make a mess in the saucer by reading the grounds.

Greek Coffee

YIELD: 1 MEDIUM-SWEET COFFEE

---

1 heaping measuring teaspoon finely ground coffee

1 heaping measuring teaspoon sugar
4 ounces cold water

For each cup of coffee, stir the coffee, sugar, and cold water together in a 1- or 2-cup *briki*. Place over medium-high heat and, holding the *briki* by its long handle, stir continuously with a long-handled spoon (an iced-tea spoon works well) until the coffee rises to the rim of the *briki*. Remove from the heat and immediately pour the coffee into a cup and serve. If making more than one cup at a time, be sure to divide the froth evenly between the cups.

A Glossary of Greek Ingredients

The list of ingredients that follows is by no means all-inclusive. It includes only those we thought could use some further clarification for a better understanding of what's needed to prepare the recipes in this book, how to use those ingredients, and, in some cases, where to find them.

Capers

Tiny wild capers, the unopened flower buds of a scrubby bush native to the Mediterranean region, are hand-picked in southern Greece in the early summer and preserved in a vinegar brine to enliven salads and other dishes through the winter months. Capers are particularly tasty with seafood and lamb. Served in a small dish on the *meze* table, they're good eaten with cheese or sprinkled on nearly anything that needs a piquant flavor lift.

Cheese

The Greeks are the world's leading consumers of cheese *(tiri)*. They produce literally hundreds of local varieties that never see the light of day outside Greece, or even in other parts of Greece. Most cheese-making takes place after the spring and autumn rains, while the sheep and goats are nibbling on delicately flavored shoots of wild grasses and herbs. Greek cheese is unaffected and unsophisticated, meant simply to be eaten for nourishment, often with a few olives, tomatoes, and a loaf of bread.

The cheeses listed here, with acceptable substitutions, are all available in the United States, either imported from Greece or made here using Greek techniques.

ANTHOTIRO: A soft or semi-hard white goat's- or sheep's-milk cheese with a lovely, delicate flavor. Although it is not called for in this book, it's worth a taste if you happen to come upon it. The semi-hard version is molded into a cannonball shape. It is good served as a table cheese with fruit, or shredded on pasta.

FETA: The most famous Greek cheese, *feta* is a semisoft, highly salted white cheese, pickled in brine. Originally it was made from goat's milk, later from sheep's milk, and sometimes from a combination of the two. It is best eaten as fresh as possible, while it is still soft and a bit crumbly. The longer *feta* sits, the more moisture evaporates, making it harder and more pungent.

In Greece, *feta* is eaten in hundreds of ways: by itself, cooked, and baked into or crumbled on top of many recipes.

BUYING AND STORING

Feta cheese is easy to get in the United States. In addition to ethnic markets, an ever-increasing number of food stores are stocking a good variety of imported and domestic *fetas*. You might even be fortunate enough to find a local producer of sheep's-milk *feta* (see Hollow Road Farms under Sources) or goat's-milk *feta*.

Finding *feta* that you like is a matter of taste, taste, and taste some more. A lot of this tasting can be done as you stand in front of the cheese counter, but after you've tried two or three, most of them begin to seem pretty much alike. Smell the cheese first. It should have a pungent, pleasing aroma. If it has the least sour or barnyard smell, or a bitter or soapy taste, find another cheese store.

As a rule, sheep's-milk *feta* is less tart and creamier than goat's-milk *feta,* and tends to have a more complex range of flavors. A mixture of the two milks can produce a cheese with the most interesting characteristics of each. Cow's-milk *feta* is milder (too mild for most tastes) and slightly grainy, but it can be a good segue for the uninitiated into the more intensely flavored varieties.

For short-term storage, wrap *feta* tightly in plastic wrap and refrigerate for up to a week or two. For longer storage, up to three or four weeks, place the cheese in a plastic container and immerse in brine. Many stores will give you brine, if you ask for it. Or make your own by mixing 3 tablespoons of salt in 4 cups of water.

CONTROLLING SALTINESS

It's the brine that gives *feta* much of its characteristic flavor and also acts as a preservative, but if the cheese is a little saltier than you like, some salt can be removed by soaking the *feta* in cold water in the refrigerator for two or three hours. Pat the cheese dry, wrap it tightly, and use within a couple of days, for even partially desalted *feta* will not stay fresh for long.

GRAVIERA: The Greek version of Swiss Gruyère, which can be used as a substitute. *Graviera* is semi-hard with small holes, and has a pleasant, nutty flavor, but without the creamy quality of the Swiss product, since Greek milk has a lower fat content (a plus, these days) due to the lack of lush grazing land. *Graviera* is mostly used as table cheese or grated over macaroni dishes.

HALOUMI: A white goat's-milk cheese from Cyprus, similar to salted mozzarella, which can be used in place of it. *Haloumi* is often flavored with a touch of mint. In Greece, it is usually eaten as a table cheese (try small cubes of it in a green salad), but it is also wonderful grilled or fried. *Haloumi* is sold in sealed, dated packages. Unopened, it will keep in the refrigerator for several months, and after it's opened it will keep up to two months, tightly wrapped.

KASSERI: Goat's-milk cheese that has a light, creamy color, mild flavor, and semi-soft texture. *Kasseri* is usually eaten on its own with bread, but sometimes fried and eaten hot *(saganaki)* or shredded over macaroni dishes. *Kasseri* is similar to provolone, which can be used as a substitute.

KEFALOTIRI: A yellow cheese with tiny holes, similar to *kasseri,* but harder and saltier. Literally, "head cheese" (*kefali* means "head"), since it is often sold in head-shaped lumps. It is usually grated over pasta and sometimes fried and eaten hot. Equal portions of grated *kefalotiri* and *kasseri* make the Greek equivalent of Parmesan, and one can usually be substituted for the other.

MANOURI: The Greek version of firm ricotta cheese, but which can be used in place of it. *Manouri* is sometimes mixed with herbs and spread on bread. It also goes well with fruit and honey.

MIZITHRA: Almost, but not always, a fresh, white pot cheese made from the whey of *feta,* salted or unsalted, and similar to Italian soft-curd ricotta, or regular (small-curd) cottage cheese, both of which can be used in place of it. The best comes from the town of Metsovo in northwest Greece, but the only *mizithra* you're likely to find in the United States has been made here, since it is extremely perishable. However, in Athens and some other parts of Greece, *mizithra* is the name of the hard-cheese variety that is used primarily for grating over pasta. The salted soft version is used mainly in cooking (pasta, stuffing, pies, etc.), and the unsalted version, although a little bland, is usually eaten plain.

English Cucumber

The thin-skinned English cucumber, sometimes called "gourmet" or "hothouse" cucumber, is crisper and has fewer seeds and a more delicate flavor than regular, waxy supermarket cucumbers. You can recognize it easily because it's nearly a foot long and almost always comes covered with a tight plastic wrap.

Giant White Beans (Dried)

These look very much like huge dried lima beans, or butter beans, which can be used instead of the giants in a pinch. Nevertheless, try to find "giant white beans" in Greek or Middle Eastern markets or specialty food stores, where they are sometimes marked *"gigandes."* These beans don't fall apart, but hold their shape extremely well during long cooking. For more information about dried beans, see page 26.

Granulated Flour

The secret to a perfectly even, pale golden crust on fried food is the use of granulated flour instead of all-purpose flour for coating. Charles Bowman uses Wondra brand granulated flour, which can be found with other flours at any supermarket.

Grape (Vine) Leaves

You can tell it's spring in Greece by the large piles of fresh grape leaves for sale in the markets. In the United States you will be lucky ever to *see* a fresh grape leaf unless you happen to have access to a grape arbor or live across the road from a vineyard. In that case, go ahead and try the fresh leaves, but use only young ones (the fourth ones down from the tip are about the right size and tenderness) that you are sure have not been treated with toxic chemicals. Otherwise, you will have to settle for leaves that have been preserved in brine and are sold in jars, neatly wrapped into cigar-shaped rolls. Even the Greeks use these most of the year, so you don't have to feel that you're compromising. Both fresh and brined grape leaves need some pre-treatment before they're used, which is explained in Basic Recipes, Ingredients, and Techniques.

Herbs

By comparison with other European cuisines, Greek cooking relies on only a very few herbs to produce traditional flavors, although many more are kept on hand to make tea and medicinal tonics. Fragrant herbs grow wild all over the place in Greece, making a summer walk in the country a heady experience.

The leading Greek herb is, of course, dried oregano *(rigani)*, which the Greeks use with a heavy hand, often just crumbling it over salads and *feta* cheese. Greek oregano (so marked) is more pungent than the Italian variety you may be used to. After oregano, fresh dill (only fresh and never the seeds), fresh mint and flat-leaf parsley, bay leaves (both fresh and dried), and, finally, dried garden thyme (not wild thyme) are the culinary herbs of choice.

Less frequently, Greek cooks use rosemary (although rosemary branches are often tied together and used as a basting brush), allspice, celery leaves, coriander seeds, cilantro (fresh coriander), ground nutmeg, caraway seeds, cumin seeds, anise seeds, fennel seeds, and ground mace. Basil, which is on every windowsill, is cultivated mainly for religious purposes and as a fly repellent! Only a few very progressive cooks use it for flavoring food, and then only in tomato sauce and some breads for holy days. Ground cinnamon and whole cloves are used liberally in desserts.

Honey

We know that honey *(meli)* has been the traditional Greek sweetener, at least since the Greeks started writing down their recipes eons ago. Besides drenching many desserts with it, the Greeks stir honey into yogurt and slather it on bread for a morning snack, and women swear by it as a purifying face mask. Nearly everywhere in Greece you see brightly painted beehives up in the hills and on mountain slopes, where the busy gorge themselves on the nectar of wildflowers and herbs and produce what many believe is the world's purest and most delicious honey. The best Greek honey, presumably, comes from the bees that live on Mount Hymettus near Athens, although the overriding and slightly medicinal flavor of wild thyme in this honey takes some getting used to. Greek food stores always stock a good supply of imported honey. It is darker and a little thinner than our version, with a rich flavor and aroma. American buckwheat, orange blossom, or clover honey is a decent substitute.

Kadaifi

Strands of *phyllo* dough that are used, among other things, to make a famous dessert of the same name. *Kadaifi,* which is a lot like *baklava,* is drenched with syrup and loaded with nuts. *Kadaifi* strands are packed in rolls that look a lot like shredded wheat, and are frozen in one-pound packages. After thawing, the rolls are either used as is or pulled apart. Fragile *kadaifi* dries out almost as quickly as *phyllo* sheets and must be kept damp and handled with care. For more information about *kadaifi,* see the recipe on page 257.

Lemons

Along with olive oil and oregano, lemon juice forms the trio that is most essential to Greek cooking. It takes less than fifteen seconds to squeeze a lemon, so please don't, under any circumstances, use anything but the real thing.

Mahlepi

A ground spice made from the seeds of the Syrian *mahlepi* bush, which produces a wild fruit similar to a cherry. *Mahlepi* can be purchased in small jars in Greek and other Middle Eastern grocery stores. If it is not available, for each 2 teaspoons you can substitute 1 teaspoon ground cinnamon, ¾ teaspoon ground cloves, and ¼ teaspoon ground allspice.

Octopus

Seafood stores in Greek and Latin neighborhoods, or fish stores that specialize in out-of-the-ordinary seafood, are the most logical places to buy octopus. Almost without exception, octopus is frozen, or has been frozen, having been cleaned and mechanically tenderized beforehand, so that all you need do before using is defrost it. Most frozen octopus weighs 2 to 3 pounds. Any much larger than this will undoubtedly be tough. Baby octopus, those weighing about a pound, are also gaining popularity, but their tiny tentacles are too small for grilling and are more suitable for pickling. For more information about octopus, see page 82.

Olives

According to legend, the goddess Athena bestowed two great gifts on the Ancient Greeks: wisdom and olives *(elies)*. Along with wheat and grapes, olives must surely rank as nature's greatest gift to the Greeks. Not just in Greece, but in all of the countries surrounding the Mediterranean, it would be hard to imagine food without olives and the life-sustaining, green-to-gold oil they've provided for thousands of years. Olive trees are an intrinsic part of the Greek landscape. The gnarled, silvery-green trees positively flourish in austere growing conditions and rocky, dry soil, requiring only sunshine and very little in the way of nurturing to produce abundant harvests.

Most olive farms in Greece are less than a dozen acres, mostly family-run operations that have been passed down through successive generations to the point where it is not unusual for one olive tree to have had several owners. Although the trees take quite a long time to get going, they have a life span of literally hundreds and occasionally thousands of years.

Of the billions of olives that are produced in Greece every year, only a select few attain the status of table olives.

Greek olives are named for the region in which they are grown. The harvest takes place in the fall, when both ripe and unripe olives are "milked" by hand or shaken from the branches, making a pleasant rhythmic sound as they plink-plunk down onto the tarp-covered ground. Those that are perfect are set aside for table olives. The rest will be turned into oil. Curing (to remove the bitterness in both mature and unripened olives) takes place in wooden barrels over the winter, and the first of the new crop is ready to eat by early spring.

The best place to buy olives is in Greek or Middle Eastern stores, where they are presented in huge barrels that are nowadays more often plastic than wood. In such a situation, it's expected that you will taste before you buy, and close to the barrels you will probably see a little paper cup for the pits. First, sniff the olives in the barrel. The aroma should be fresh and pleasantly pungent. Olives range in color from bright green to purple to mauvish-brown to jet black, in various sizes and conformations that include tiny ovals, almond shapes, and large rounds. If you can't find a source of barrel olives, a high-quality imported or domestic brand of jarred Greek olives can be quite good.

You may be tempted to refrigerate olives, but it's better to coat them with olive oil and set them aside, covered, in a cool place, where they will keep for several weeks, although the sooner they are eaten the better.

AMFISSA: The classic olive of Greece, round, and often the choice for nibbling or to accompany cheese and bread. Grown on the lower mountain slopes near Delphi, these meaty, dark-brown olives, picked at the moment of ripeness, have an exquisitely nutty flavor and slightly sweet finish.

ATALANTI: Grown near the seaside town of the same name, this large, greenish-purple olive is firm yet fleshy, wonderful eaten straight out of its brine or after having been marinated in flavored olive oil.

CRACKED GREEN: Cracking olives before they are cured intensifies their flavor by allowing the cure to permeate the flesh, imparting a sharp, almost smoky flavor. Cracked green olives are excellent served with a mellow cheese and other appetizers that are not too salty or spicy.

ELITSES: From the island of Crete, where they are used mainly for oil, these olives have only recently become available in the United States. They are jet black, similar to French Niçoise olives, but with a richer, sweeter flavor.

IONIAN GREEN: An olive-lover's olive, large and crunchy, with a bright color and mild flavor. It is excellent as a salad garnish, marinated, or eaten straight from the brine, and is marvelous on a cheese platter.

KALAMATA: The olive that is indigenous and unique to Greece, and some say the finest in the world. This almond-shaped, dark purple olive, with an instantly identifiable flavor, comes only from the Messenia province in a corner of the Peloponnese. Kalamatas have almost unlimited uses, but are usually thought of as the olive in Greek salad, and their presence in any dish instantly marks it as Greek.

THASOS: Black olives, usually dry-cured, from the island of the same name in the northern Aegean Sea. Because much of its natural moisture has been removed, the flavor of this wrinkly little olive is quite intense, but delicious.

Olive Oil

It was the Greeks, of course, who introduced olive trees and olive oil *(eleoladho)* to France, Italy, and Spain, the other main producers and exporters of olive oil. Take away olive oil, and Greek cooking and eating would just about come to a standstill. The whole cuisine is based on the liberal use of olive oil, both for cooking and flavoring.

In simpler times, before a certain amount of mechanization took over, olives were gently crushed between two monstrous, tirelike stones turned by a donkey. These days, steel often replaces stone, and the donkey has long since been retired in favor of electricity, but the process of pressing olives for oil in Greece is essentially unchanged since ancient times. Now, as then, a mass of crushed olives is smeared onto straw mats. These are stacked one on top of another and squeezed with a hydraulic press that first produces extra-virgin olive oil and finally ends with fire fuel, fertilizer, or fodder made from the dried residue after every drop of oil has been extracted.

(When the subject of olive oil comes up, Nicola likes to talk about her father's olive grove on Zakinthos. "When we lived in London, he had his own olive oil sent there. He takes a big spoonful of it every day, which, like a lot of Greeks, he believes is some sort of miracle elixir.")

Until a few years ago, the olive oil imported and consumed in the United States was barely more than a trickle. But thanks to the health benefits attributed to the oil by medical scientists (something Hippocrates knew long ago), and our eagerness to embrace methods of cardio-friendly Mediterranean cooking, it's reasonable to assume that olive oil is here to stay.

When shopping for olive oil, there are only three labels you need to consider:

EXTRA-VIRGIN OLIVE OIL: Obtained from the first pressing of the olives. It is usually, but not absolutely always, pale to dark green (the green is merely chlorophyll), and carries a hint of the flavor and aroma of the fruit (olives are fruits, not vegetables) from which it was pressed. It is the most expensive, and the one to be used for flavoring rather than cooking. More than 80 percent of the olive oil produced in Greece is extra-virgin.

VIRGIN (REGULAR) OLIVE OIL: Consists only of cold-pressed oil, with good flavor and aroma. It usually has a pale- to medium-yellow color. Choose virgin olive oil whenever you want a nearly flavorless oil with good properties, such as for cakes and other desserts. Virgin, or "regular," oil is our choice for frying and deep-frying.

OLIVE OIL/PURE OLIVE OIL: A blend of refined and virgin oils that is also the least expensive. A good, sturdy oil for deep-frying, but not recommended for salads and other dishes where the "character" of the oil is important.

Since the Greek government is extraordinarily picky about the quality of the oils it exports, you would do well to use it for the recipes in this book. On the average, it's less expensive than other imported olive oils, too.

Selecting extra-virgin oil is a lot like selecting wine. A great deal remains unknown until the bottle is opened and the contents are sniffed, tasted, and considered. Pour a few drops into your hand, rub your palms together, and inhale. The oil should have the clean, fresh aroma of olives. Dip a small piece of bread into the oil and chew it slowly. The flavor should be delicately balanced, not too heavy, not too bland, and should linger in your mouth, so that it will mingle with the flavors of the food with which it is used.

A bottle of opened olive oil does not need refrigeration unless it is to be kept for more than a year or so. (In that case, chill the oil. It will coagulate, but returns to its natural state, the flavor unchanged, when it is brought to room temperature.) Otherwise, store olive oil in a cool, dark place. If you like, you can decant the oil into a dark bottle for further protection.

Orange-blossom (Flower) Water

A highly flavored and perfumed water distilled from fresh orange blossoms that is used *sparingly* to flavor desserts, cookies, and sometimes beverages. Orange-blossom water is usually available in small bottles in Middle Eastern grocery stores or pharmacies. It can also be ordered by mail from some specialty stores, such as Sultan's Delight (see Sources). Flower water keeps well when stored in a dark, cool spot, but does lose its strength over time.

Pasta

A lot of the pasta eaten in Greece is in the form of wide egg noodles or ¼-inch squares called *hilopites* that are often homemade. The latter can be purchased in one-pound packages at Greek and other Middle Eastern grocery stores, or other tiny pasta shapes can be used instead. Orzo, a tiny, ricelike pasta, is also very popular. Most other pasta goes under the general name of *makaronia,* and the Greeks stick with just a few basic shapes, such as short cuts of macaroni, and bucatini or perciatelli, long, hollow, spaghetti-shaped pastas. For more information about pasta, see page 197.

Paximadi

Twice-baked bread slices available in Greek grocery stores. Sometimes you will see two kinds: slightly sweetened and unsweetened. For dunking into coffee or spreading with honey, the slightly sweetened variety is quite pleasant, but for savory dishes, use the unsweetened type. *Paximadi* is very much like zwieback, which can be used in place of it. For more information about *paximadi,* see page 225.

Phyllo (Filo or Fillo)

Phyllo (the word means "leaf") is the amazingly thin pastry dough that's essential to many Greek recipes, the most famous being the quintessential cheese pies and, of course, *baklava.* Some Greek women still make their own *phyllo,* a mind-boggling undertaking, to say the least, but these days most cooks purchase it ready-made, even in Greece. In the last few years, *phyllo* has become extremely popular in the United States, so it's easy to find, even in supermarkets, frozen in one-pound packages. The *phyllo* is ready to use after it has been slowly thawed in the refrigerator and then brought to room temperature. Even then, great care must be taken that the leaves don't dry out and crumble, which is explained in Basic Recipes, Ingredients, and Techniques. Purchase *phyllo* where the turnover is rapid. If the sheets in a newly purchased package of *phyllo* look the least bit ragged at the edges, it's past its prime and attempts to work with it will only be frustrating. (We think the packages should carry a sell-by date.)

Quince

An autumn fruit that looks vaguely like a cross between a green apple and a pear, and varies in color from yellow to pale green. Quinces are hard and very bitter, and are used mostly in Greece to make spoon sweets. The flesh is almost white, but keeps its shape and turns a lovely shade of pale pink after it's cooked.

Rosewater

Rosewater is distilled from fresh rose petals. It should not be confused with rose essence, which is much stronger. Rosewater is used the same way as orange-blossom water and can be purchased in the same places.

Sausage

Sausage in Greece is another local product that varies enormously, but most is made with beef or pork, which is highly seasoned and smoked and is similar to many salamis. Garlic, coriander, wine, and orange peel are the most typical flavorings. Most Greek grocery stores usually carry at least two kinds of sausage; otherwise any pungent smoked sausage—very often a salami, if it's not too hard —can be used instead.

Semolina

In Greece, "semolina," which technically means the endosperm of a grain kernel, is a catchall word that describes at least two frequently used Greek ingredients: a granulated flour (similar to Wondra flour) and small, dried pellets made from semolina flour and salted water. You can find both of these products in plastic bags at Greek grocery stores, but it's easier to substitute dry, regular cream of wheat or farina for the granulated flour, and medium-grain couscous for the pellets, since they are nearly identical.

Sesame Seeds

If you buy sesame seeds off the spice shelf in little jars, they will cost a fortune in any quantity. Instead, look for untoasted sesame seeds in plastic bags in Greek or Asian grocery stores, where the price is comparatively—and surprisingly—infinitesimal.

Squash Blossoms

The blossoms that develop on squash vines are not only edible—both cooked and raw—but have an exquisite, delicate flavor. For more information about picking, buying, and preparing squash blossoms, see page 181.

Squid (Calamari)

This little cephalopod is closely related to, and looks something like, an octopus, although it's the squid's body pouch that is valued for eating more than the tiny tentacles. Many fish markets sell cleaned squid pouches and tentacles ready for the pan, but since cleaned squid stays fresh an especially short time, make sure your fish merchant is reliable. Whether they are whole or pan-ready, squid should smell fresh and clean, something like ocean water. If the squid is sold whole, you'll have to separate it into edible segments yourself, an easy job but nevertheless something of a nuisance. The simplest way to master the technique is to watch someone do it. Otherwise, proceed this way:

STEP 1. Pull back the rim of the pouch and feel around until you find the top of the transparent cuttlebone, often referred to as a quill. Gently, but steadily, pull it out and discard it.
STEP 2. Holding the body with one hand and the head with the other, carefully pull the two sections apart. The innards, along with the ink sac, should come along with the head. (Be careful not to

break the ink sac.) If not, what remains inside will have to be scraped out of the pouch. Set aside the head with the attached tentacles. Pull away the membrane that lines the pouch.

STEP 3. The milky white body pouch is covered by mottled skin. Slip a finger between the skin and the pouch, pull it off, and discard it. Carefully pull off the triangular fins at the base of the pouch; skin the fins, then cut them in half.

STEP 4. With a sharp knife, cut the tentacles off at the base of the head just below the eyes. They should come away intact. Just within the rim of flesh that connects the tentacles is a beaklike mouth. Squeeze the beak out and discard it.

STEP 5. Rinse the squid pieces and drain. If they are not to be used immediately, cover and refrigerate, but for no longer than a day.

Tarama

Mullet or cod roe that has been semi-preserved with salt and sometimes oil, sold in small jars in the refrigerated section of all Greek grocery stores and many supermarkets as well. *Tarama* has a pretty coral-pink color, but must be mixed with other ingredients to tone down its pungent flavor—mainly bread crumbs, olive oil, and lemon juice to make *taramosalata,* the most famous Greek dip of them all. You can also buy *taramosalata* ready-made in jars, usually right next to the *tarama,* so don't confuse the two.

Toursi Pickled Peppers

Small, pale green, tapered peppers, similar to pepperoncini. They are nippy without being hot, and can be served like olives. Marinate them if you like, or use to decorate salad plates, or serve in a bowl on the *meze* table.

Vinegar

When cooking Greek, about the only vinegar *(xsithi)* you'll need to bother with is red-wine vinegar. As much care is taken in producing vinegar in Greece as wine, and maybe more. Greek wine vinegar has more body and flavor than most others, and in order to fairly duplicate Greek recipes, you should try to find a good imported Greek red-wine vinegar that appeals to you. A little balsamic vinegar, which resembles many Greek red-wine vinegars, can be used as a flavor and body booster for more insipid reds. An agreeable vinegar, like olive oil, is usually a matter of personal preference.

Yogurt

To eat yogurt *(yaourti)* once in Greece is to crave it for a lifetime, say some who never quite recover from the memory of their first spoonful. There is simply no comparison between thick, creamy Greek yogurt and the thin, low-fat yogurts you may be accustomed to. Most Greek yogurt is made from whole sheep's milk, not as sinful a practice as you might think, since sheep's milk is lower in fat than cow's milk. For Greek cooking, it's worth the effort to try to find sheep's-milk yogurt. Greek and other Middle Eastern stores carry it routinely, and it's possible to order it by mail. (See Hollow Road Farms under Sources.) Goat's-milk yogurt, which is enjoying enormous popularity in the United States these days, is good, although it lacks the creaminess and body of sheep's-milk yogurt and is not as good a substitute for sheep's-milk yogurt as you might think. Whole cow's-milk yogurt would be a better choice.

Sources: Shopping for Greek Groceries

If this book had been written a mere few years ago, the list that follows would undoubtedly have been longer. However, with the sudden surge in popularity of Mediterranean cooking, there is nothing so rare and remarkable about Greek ingredients that most of them—or good substitutes—can't be found in well-stocked supermarkets, and almost always in grocery stores that cater to Greek and Middle Eastern shoppers.

During recipe testing for this book, I had surprisingly little difficulty finding most of the ingredients I needed in ordinary supermarkets, although now and then I made trips to the grocery stores in Astoria, the Greek community in New York City. Most large cities have similar enclaves with a few grocery stores, where, in addition to cheese and other perishables, you can often buy such things as Greek coffeepots, coffee cups, and other pieces of authentic cooking equipment.

There are literally thousands of retail stores, manufacturers, and importers in the United States that carry Greek groceries. These are ones we happen to know and can recommend. Some of the sources that follow offer mail-order service, which is noted.

ANDRONICO'S
Berkeley, California
510/524-2696

A five-store supermarket chain in the Berkeley–San Francisco area that carries a dazzling array of produce and seafood, as well as many Greek ingredients. Unfortunately, Andronico's is not set up to do mail order, but if you live in the area, this is the place to shop for many Greek ingredients. Even if you're just visiting, a trip to one or two of these impressive stores is a memorable experience. Call for store locations.

ATHENA INTERNATIONAL FOODS
77 Legion Parkway
Brockton, Massachusetts 02401
508/588-9731

This store carries a full line of Greek and other Mediterranean products. Except for perishables, these friendly people will send anything anywhere. Write or call for information.

ATHENS FOODS
Customer Relations
13600 Snow Road
Cleveland, Ohio 44142
216/676-8500

The makers of Apollo brand *phyllo* and *kadaifi* dough, which can be found everywhere in the U.S.A. However, if you're having trouble locating Apollo products, or have questions about them, write or call and the Customer Relations Department will gladly help.

BALDUCCI'S
424 Avenue of the Americas
New York, New York 10011
212/673-2600

New York's premier source for impeccable produce, seafood, and delicacies of every kind. Even tour buses make this amazing store a regular stop. Balducci's is well equipped to handle mail and phone orders. To receive a catalog, place an order, or obtain information, call 1-800-BALDUCCI.

C & K IMPORTING
2771 West Pico Boulevard
Los Angeles, California 90005
213/737-2970

Carries most Greek ingredients and will fill mail orders, even cheese, if special arrangements are made. Call or write for information.

HOLLOW ROAD FARMS
R.R. 1, Box 93
Stuyvesant, New York 12173
518/758-7214

Makers and distributors of the best sheep's-milk yogurt (in the authors' opinions; it's the one used at Periyali) outside Greece, as well as young *feta* cheese and other dairy products. Hollow Road Farms products are only for sale in specialty food stores in the New York City area, but they will air-ship to all parts of the continental United States. Call or write for information.

KRINOS FOODS, INC.
47-00 Northern Boulevard
Long Island City, New York 11101

The largest importer and manufacturer of Greek food in North America, with over 400 different products ranging from cheese to vine leaves. They distribute nationally, but if you have trouble locating something, write and they'll be happy to suggest a retailer in your area.

PELOPONNESE
2227 Poplar Street
Oakland, California 94607
415/839-8153

Importer of Greek delicacies, which they distribute nationally under the Peloponnese name. They have an extensive line of Greek foods that keeps growing, from grape leaves, olives, and olive oil to fresh cheese, which can be found in specialty stores and many supermarkets, too. A mail-order division, The Aegean Trader, will ship any and all of their products, even cheese when special arrangements are made. Write or call for information and to place orders.

SULTAN'S DELIGHT
25 Croton Avenue
Staten Island, New York 10301
718/720-1557

A mail-order source for many Greek ingredients and some cooking utensils. Write or call for their fascinating catalog.

TITAN FOODS
25-30 31st Street
Astoria, New York 11102
718/626-7771

Restaurant and retail suppliers of almost any imaginable Greek food, including a particularly large selection of domestic and imported cheese and sausage. Unfortunately, they don't do mail order, but this store is a virtual treasure trove of Greek goodies, and easy to get to by subway from midtown Manhattan. Call and they'll direct you.

TREASURE ISLAND FOODS, INC.
Chicago, Illinois
312/327-4265

Seven stores in downtown Chicago and the northern suburbs, where the specialties are foods of the world, arranged in well-defined sections for easy shopping.

The following importers supply fine Greek wines to Periyali. Those listed below distribute wines nationally, unless noted. Write or call for a wine merchant in your area.

ATTIKI IMPORTERS & DISTRIBUTORS, INC.
515 Peninsula Boulevard
Hempstead, New York 11550
800/966-3520

ITC IMPORTS
206 Westbury Avenue
Carle Place, New York 11514-1605
516/997-9314

Some wines distributed only in New York State; others nationally.

JASON BROOKE IMPORTS
40 Underhill Boulevard
Syosset, New York 11791
516/921-7111

Distributes only in the New York–New Jersey area.

NESTOR IMPORTS, INC.
6-12 North Union Avenue, Suite 2
Cranford, New Jersey 07016
908/272-2060

PEERLESS IMPORTERS, INC.
16 Bridgewater Street
Brooklyn, New York 11222
718/383-5500

Inquiries should be directed to the Wine Department.

Index

Almond
  biscuits from Mykonos, 248
  fig cake, 252–53
  honey-glazed, tart, 249–50
  skordalia, Periyali's, 239
Amygdalota, 248
Appetizers (meze). *See also* Dip(s)
  about, 15–17
  beetroot salad, 41
  black-eyed pea salad, 31
  broiled *haloumi* cheese seasoned with
    lemon and mint, 55
  cheese baked in grape leaves, 54
  cheese pies and spinach-and-cheese
    pies, 49–53
  eggplants in tomato sauce, tiny, 30–31
  fresh yogurt cheese with olive oil and
    herbs, 38–39
  giant white beans with garlic sauce,
    Irene and Victor's, 27
  grilled calamari, 61–62
  marinated artichoke bottoms, 42
  marinated olives, 17–18
  mashed-potato cakes from Pelion,
    little, 57–58
  pickled
    baby octopus (or shrimp), 34–35
    onion rings, 46–47
    vegetables, 36–37
  radishes with scallions and *feta,* 40
  rice-stuffed grape leaves, Irene
    Gouras's, 32–33
  roasted peppers with olive oil and
    vinegar, 37–38
  saganaki, 56
  sausage grilled in grape leaves, fresh,
    58–59
  seasoned toasted bread, 25
  skewered meat, 60
  tomato and onion salad, 44
  tomatoes stuffed with orzo and wild
    mushrooms, 45–46

  tomatoes (or peppers) stuffed with
    rice, 43–44
  zucchini fritters, Irene and Victor's,
    48–49
Arnaki fournou, 190–92
Arnaki me rizi ke yaourti, 127–28
Arni kapama, 128–29
Artichoke(s)
  baby, with potatoes, pearl onions, and
    carrots, 173–74
  baby, with wild mushrooms, 79–80
  grilled Greek, 167
  marinated bottoms, 42
Astakos, 115–17
Avgolemono, 235

Baby artichokes with potatoes, pearl
    onions, and carrots, 173–74
Baby artichokes with wild mushrooms,
    79–80
Baklava, 258–60
Bakaliaros, 102–3
Basics
  beans, giant white, 8
  broth
    chicken, 5
    fish, 7
    freshening canned chicken or beef, 6
  brown stock, lamb or beef, 4
  butter, clarified melted, 8
  grape leaves, how to work with, 14
  phyllo, how to work with, 12
  spinach-and-*feta*-cheese filling (for
    phyllo), 13
  yogurt, homemade, 10
  yogurt, thickened, 11
Beans. *See also* Giant white beans
  about dried, 26
  black-eyed pea salad, 31
  lentil soup, 93
  lentils, sautéed chicken livers served
    over warm, 76–77

Beans *(cont.)*
    split yellow pea puree, 28–29
    stewed in tomato sauce, Nicola's
        mother's, 180
    white, soup, 91–92
Beef
    broth, freshening canned, 6
    brown stock, 4
    macaroni pie, Nicola's mother's, 203–4
    meatballs, Nicola's mother's, 149–50
    sausage, giant white beans with, 153
    skewered meat, 60
Beet(s)
    dip, 24
    platter of, and -greens, 183–84
    -root salad, 40
Beverages
    Greek coffee, 287
    kafe frape, 285
    sparkling lemonade, 284
    yogurt milkshake, 283–84
Black-eyed pea salad, 31
Boneless leg of lamb marinated in
    yogurt, 126
Bougatsa, 261
Bowman, Charles, xv, 19, 50, 65, 76, 91,
    144, 169, 186
    tips for perfect charcoal grilling,
        136
Brandy, 283
Bread
    about, 209–10
    -crumb *skordalia,* 232
    everyday, Steve's sister's, 214–15
    festive, Steve's sister's, 217–19
    fried bread dough, 228
    herb-filled olive oil bread, 221–22
    grilled flat bread, 226–27
    Kalamata olive muffins from Crete,
        216
    New Year's, Steve's sister's, 223–24
    olive and garlic, 220–21
    paximadi, 225
    seasoned toasted, 25
    traditional Easter, Steve's sister's,
        195
    white bakery, 213–14
    whole-wheat country, 210–11
Briam, 162–63
Broiled *haloumi* cheese seasoned with
    lemon and mint, 55
Broiled tomatoes, 164
Butter, clarified melted, 8

Cake(s)
    almond-fig, 252–53
    preserved-cherry, 250–51
    semolina, 253–54
    walnut, 254–55
    yogurt, Nicola's mother's, 256–57
Calamaria tis scharas, 61–62
Calamarakia tiganita, 85–86
Calf's liver with red onion and vinegar
    sauce, sautéed, 141–42
Capers, 288
Caramelized onions, 179
Casserole of eggplant and ground lamb,
    151–52
Cheese. *See also Feta* cheese
    about, 228–91
    fresh yogurt, with olive oil and herbs,
        38–39
    broiled *haloumi* cheese seasoned with
        lemon and mint, 55
    macaroni pie, Nicola's mother's, 203–4
    manouri baked in grape leaves, 54
    manouri with honey and pistachios,
        266–67
    Metsovo-style noodles, 205–6
    pasta with chopped tomatoes and,
        207–8
    pasta with olives and, 208
    pies, 50–52
    saganaki, 56
    short pasta with yogurt and, 206–7
    Sunday and clean Monday, 202
Cherry
    drink, 275
    preserved-, cake, 250–51
    sour, spoon sweets, 274
Chicken
    about, 121
    broth, 5
    broth, freshening canned, 6
    and fennel brochettes, grilled, 70–71
    oven-grilled, 137
    and potatoes baked in phyllo, 147–49
    pot-roasted, and potatoes with vinegar
        sauce, 133–34
    seared and braised breast of, with leeks
        and lemon cream sauce, 131–32
    sautéed breast of, with lemon sauce,
        129–31
    sautéed, livers served over warm
        lentils, 76–77
    stuffed roasted, Nicola's Mother's,
        134–35

Choriatiki, 64–65
Clarified melted butter, 8
Coffee
    about, 286
    kafe frape, 285
    Greek, 287
Cookies
    almond biscuits from Mykonos, 248
    Easter, Steve's sister's, 194–95
    honey-walnut, 247
    powder, 241–42
Couscous (semolina) timbales, 169–70
Crisp calamari served on mixed greens,
        85–86
Crisp snow peas, 162
Cucumber and yogurt salad, 22–23

Demi-glace for lamb chops, 236
Dessert(s). *See also* Cake(s); Cookies;
        Fruit; Honey; Pastry
    about, 237–38
    manouri with honey and pistachios,
        266–67
    quick fritters, Nicola's mother's, 246
    rice pudding, 238–39
    sesame seed bars, 270
    summer plum pudding, 239–40
Dip(s)
    beet, 24
    cucumber yogurt salad, 22–23
    fish roe (*taramosalata*), 19–20
    quicker cucumber salad, 23
    roasted eggplant salad, 21–22
    split yellow pea puree, 28–29
Diples, 262–65
Dolmathakia, 32–33
Duck stew, 144

Easter
    about, 187–90
    bread, Steve's sister's traditional, 195
    cookies, Steve's sister's, 194–95
    menu, 189
    at Periyali, 190
    salad, 196
Egg(s)
    about, 197–98
    Easter salad, 196
    festive bread, Steve's sister's, 217–19
    grilled Greek, 167
    and lemon soup, 89–90
    over spinach-and-*feta*-cheese filling,
        200

peasant omelet, 199
in tomato sauce, 201
tripe soup with, and lemon sauce,
        155–56
Eggplant(s)
    casserole of, and ground lamb, 151–52
    oven-baked mixed vegetables, 162–63
    and semolina, 171–72
    in tomato sauce, tiny, 30–31
    roasted, salad, 21–22
Elafi psyto, 138–39
English cucumbers, 291

Fasianos sto fourno, 145–46
Fassolada, 91–92
Fennel
    grilled chicken and, brochettes, 70–71
    grilled Greek, 167
    pan-seared scallops and, 77–78
Feta cheese
    about, 118, 288–90
    Greek country salad, 64–65
    radishes with scallions and, 40
    red onions and rocket, 80
    salmon wrapped in phyllo with
        spinach-and-, filling, 119–20
    sliced tomatoes with spinach-and-,
        filling, 165
    snails with garlic, spinach, and, 86–87
    spinach-and-, filling, 13
    spinach-and-, pies, 49–53
Festive bread, Steve's sister's, 217–19
Fileto xifia, 107
Fillet of snapper baked with tomato,
        onion, and garlic, 99–100
Fish and seafood. *See also* Octopus
    broth, 7
    filled with fresh herbs, currants, and
        nuts, 104–5
    fillet of snapper baked with tomato,
        onion, and garlic, 99–100
    fillets wrapped in grape leaves, 98–99
    fried salted cod with *skordalia,* 102–3
    grilled
        calamari, 61–62
        lobster with olive oil, lemon, and
            herbs, 115–17
        shrimp with herbs and lemon, 114–
            15
        tuna, 112–13
        tuna or swordfish salad, 110–11
        whole fish, 108–9
    lemon sauce for, thick, 233–34

Tripe soup with egg and lemon sauce, 155–56
Tsoureki, 217–19
Tzatziki, 22–23
Tzolis, Steve. *See* Steve('s) Tzolis

Vassilopita, 223–24
Veal with oregano and olive oil, grilled scallops of, 140
Vegetable(s). *See also* Individual vegetables
  about, 157–58
  greens, great, 175
  grilled Greek, 166–68
  lamb and fresh, soup, 94
  lemon sauce for, hot, 235
  okra or green beans with tomatoes, 172–73
  oven-baked mixed, 162
  snow peas, quick, 162
  skewered marinated swordfish with, 68–69
  zucchini and carrots, 161–62
  wild field greens, 186
Venison marinated with herbs and olive oil, grilled scallops of, 138–39
Victor Gouras('s). *See* Irene and Victor Gouras('s)
Vinegar, 303
Vissinatha, 275

Walnut cake, 254–55
Watermelon with red onions and mint, 81
White bakery bread, 213–14
White bean soup, 91–92

Whole-wheat country bread, 210–11
Wild field greens, 186
Wine, 277–82
"Wondrous curls," 82

Xifias souvlaki, 68–69

Yaourtopita, 256–57
Yemistes domates laderes me rizi, 43–44
Yiahni, 180
Yogurt
  about, 303
  boneless leg of lamb marinated in, 126
  cake, Nicola's mother's, 256–57
  homemade, 10
    fresh cheese with olive oil and herbs, 38–39
  lamb with rice and, Nicola's mother's, 127–28
  leg of lamb in pita bread with, sauce, 192–93
  milkshake, 283–84
  thickened, 11
    beet dip, 24
    salad, cucumber and, 22–23
    short pasta with, and cheese, 206–7

Zanithos-style *skordalia,* Nicola's mother's, 231
Zucchini
  and carrots, 161–62
  Irene and Victor's fritters, 48–49
  lamb and fresh vegetable soup, 94
  oven baked mixed vegetables, 162–63
  pickled baby vegetables, 36–37
  skewered marinated swordfish and vegetables, 68–69

About the Authors

❧❧❧❧

Until recently, Holly Garrison *was the food editor for* Parents *magazine, a position she held for eight years. She was also a contributing chef for* Time-Life's *continuity series,* Great Meals in Minutes, *and is the author of* Comfort Food *and* The Thanksgiving Cookbook. *Ms. Garrison makes her home in a Manhattan loft with her husband, Gery Repp, who is a graphic artist. She collects American antiques and occasionally indulges in her favorite sports endeavor, horseback riding.*

❧❧❧❧

Nicola Kotsoni *was raised in London and on the Greek Ionian island of Zákinthos. She is trained as a classical ballet dancer and was a member of the Stuttgart Ballet before coming to New York in 1976. She lives mainly in Manhattan in a landmarked Federal house that she recently restored.*

❧❧❧❧

Steve Tzolis *was born in Domvraína, a small town in Central Greece. In his youth he was an Olympic bicyclist. In 1967 he came to New York, where he became involved in the restaurant and real estate businesses. He lives mainly in Manhattan, but spends as much time as possible at his home on the island of Mykonos.*

❧❧❧❧

Steve and Nicola opened Periyali in 1987, mainly to address the need for a good Greek restaurant in New York that serves up the sort of home-style cooking they both remember from their childhoods. In addition to Periyali, Nicola and Steve are partners in two other successful Manhattan restaurants: Il Cantinori and Aureole.